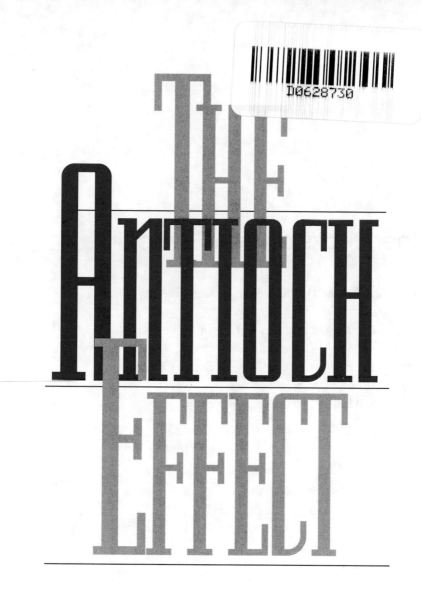

THE ANTIOCH EFFECT

Other Books by Ken Hemphill

*Mirror, Mirror on the Wall: Discovering Your True Self Through
    Spiritual Gifts*
The Official Rule Book for the New Church Game
The Bonsai Theory of Church Growth
Spiritual Gifts: Empowering the New Testament Church
Growing an Evangelistic Sunday School
Life Answers: Making Sense of Your World

8 Characteristics of Highly Effective Churches

THE ANTIOCH EFFECT

KEN HEMPHILL

BROADMAN
& HOLMAN
PUBLISHERS

Nashville, Tennessee

0-8054-2018-5
Dewey Decimal Classification: 262
Subject Heading: CHURCH
Library of Congress Card Catalog Number: 93-40622

Unless otherwise noted, Scripture quotations are from the *New American Standard Bible*, © The Lockman Foundation, 1960, 1962, 1963, 1968, 1971, 1972, 1973, 1975, 1977, used by permission. Scripture quotations marked (NIV) are from the Holy Bible, *New International Version*, copyright © 1973, 1978, 1984 by International Bible Society; and (KJV) from the *King James Version*.

Graphs and charts were provided by the Home Mission Board of the Southern Baptist Convention.

Library of Congress Cataloging-in-Publication Data
Hemphill, Ken S., 1948-
    The Antioch effect: 8 characteristics of highly effective churches / Ken Hemphill.
        p. cm.
    Includes bibliographical references.
    ISBN 0-8054-3016-4 (hc)
    ISBN 0-8054-2018-5 (pb)
    1. Church growth.   2. Christian leadership   I. Title.
BV652.25.H448   1994
254'.5—dc20   93-40622
                    3 4 5 02 01 00   CIP

To my daughter Rachael,
a truly sensitive and caring believer,
on the joyous occasion of your graduation,
with the prayer that you will
continue to grow in belief and commitment.

Table of Contents

Acknowledgments

I cannot remember writing a book in which I had greater sense of divine guidance. I do not want in any way to imply that this book is inspired or infallible in what it says. I want only to say that I have stood in awe of the way God, in His sovereign timing, has arranged the right context for me to hear some truth that proved to be a key understanding for writing about a certain characteristic. These events and persons involved are too numerous to mention. I only want to pray that you will sense God's divine presence as you read this book. I pray that this book will provide you with biblical fundamentals to experience personal growth and thus to be used of God to grow His church.

There are certain individuals to whom I am deeply indebted. During the writing of the first two characteristics, I was privileged to discuss many of my ideas with my colleague Henry Blackaby. I have sought to build upon the foundations of a church that has experienced the living God. I owe a great debt to Jimmy Draper, president of the Sunday School Board, and Larry Lewis, president of the Home Mission Board, for their vision in establishing the Southern Baptist Center for Church Growth and their confidence in me to serve as its first director. My colleagues at both agencies have contributed both directly and indirectly to many of the insights in this book. I have frequently bounced ideas off my good friend Chuck Kelley, the director of the Center for Church Growth at New Orleans

Seminary. My editor, Forrest Jackson, has gone beyond the call of duty in ensuring a readable manuscript.

The material for characteristic 1, "Supernatural Power," was first introduced in the Sizemore Lecture at Midwestern Baptist Theological Seminary. The material for characteristic 2, "Christ-Exalting Worship," was first introduced in the Gurney Lecture at New Orleans Baptist Theological Seminary. I want to thank these schools for inviting me to give these lectures and allowing me to use part of these ideas in this book.

I owe my most profound thanks to my wife Paula and my three girls, Kristina, Rachael, and Katie, for the sacrifices they have made when I have been working under the pressure of deadlines. My wife has been a true helpmate and fellow-laborer. She heard and helped refine many of these ideas while still in their infancy.

I pray the Lord will receive glory through this book as it is used to grow His church.

Prologue

Not Another Church Growth Book

You've got to be kidding! Another book on church growth? I have a library full now. I haven't read most of those I already own. I haven't begun to put into practice all the steps and principles and methods recommended in those books. Why do I need to collect any more books I can't use? Which brings me to another issue that bugs me! How many steps and keys and principles can there be? One author lists three, another seven or ten or twelve *ad nauseam*. I've covered enough steps now to climb the Eiffel Tower, and what do I have to show for it?

It's all a bit confusing. One writer assures me that cells are the wave of the future, another espouses Sunday School, while still another pushes "seeker-friendly" worship. One author pleads the case for biblical and expository preaching while the next opts for topical, need-centered, short sermons.

I'm told by one to organize for visitation while another argues that visitation and confrontational evangelism are fossils of a past generation. One conference leader cites statistics to show that worship is the front door through which most "seekers" first come to church while another argues that the "front door" is closing; people want to enter through the "side door," a needs-related cell group. Truth is, I'm still having a little difficulty finding the door to my office!

This brings me to another pet peeve. Who are these "experts" talking to anyway? Seeker-friendly services with drama, praise singers, and theatrical lighting—they must be kidding! It would be an item worthy of praise if I could find somebody to help type the bulletin! Theatrical lighting and state-of-the-art sound? I would be happy to replace a few of the burned out bulbs and use a microphone that is not a reject from the Ted Mack amateur hour. Speaking of sound systems—a new one wouldn't do me much good as long as Tone-deaf Tommy controls the sound board. He's our chairman of deacons but feels "called" to run the church sound system. I think he just needs some switches to fiddle with while I preach. How often can one mike need to be adjusted? How many varieties of feedback and squeal can one man produce?

Finally, I thought I had found a conference that would really help—"Targeting Boomers." Armed with the conviction that targeting would turn our church around, I went hunting for the Boomers in Lickskillet. Since our population base was only six hundred, I decided to widen my search to the whole county. A four-thousand-population base provided a larger target. Now I could nail those Boomers! First, the demographics. I found 397 Boomers in the whole county, and half of whom live on the northern edge of the county, a thirty-five-minute drive to get here. No problem, I'm a user-friendly, seeker-sensitive, Boomer-targeted, market-driven pastor. I began my phone survey with great enthusiasm. Got that idea from a "phones-for-you" conference. (I was going to use direct mail, but our offset machine smeared the print and the only billboard in the county was already taken by the funeral home.) The Boomers I did manage to contact were attending Big Honcho Church in the county seat near them. How can a little church like mine reach Boomers who want the services of the big church? Maybe we're just destined to remain small. It doesn't really matter. Most of my people say they like Tiny Church just the way it is. It is comforting to know everybody by name.

But I couldn't give up! I was determined to try one more growth conference. The seminar on demographics sounded promising. I wasn't sure what it meant, but the title was impressive. I discovered the reason Tiny Church wasn't growing—a misdirected marketing plan. News to me since we didn't have such a plan. First, I needed to do an environmental study and determine my community and church life-style. Demographics I finally grasped. I learned through trial and error that the Boomer population in my county provided too small a target. But psychograpics, "acorns" and "vals"! What was this guy talking about? I knew that a blind hog could sometimes find an acorn, but otherwise, I was clueless. I guess you have to be a rocket scientist to know how to grow a church today. I wasn't called to be a CEO; I just wanted to be a pastor.

Truthfully, I'm glad I didn't understand what my conference leader was talking about because I couldn't handle much more rejection at the hands of my church. You see, my biggest problem was not finding a method that would work better than the one I don't have now. My problem was that everything I suggested was met with the same refrain. "We tried that before. Didn't work!" Sometimes I hear the second verse. "We don't do it that way here!" I can't figure this out. *If we can't do anything we've tried before and we can't do anything we've never done before, WHAT CAN WE DO?* That's a rhetorical question. I already know the answer. Same thing we did last year and the year before, and the century before, and we'll get the same results. No growth! A church for the twenty-first century? You've got to be kidding! I would be happy to pastor a church that knew it was the twentieth century.

I've been the pastor here for five years now and I really should know better than to suggest any new idea. The bottom line is that my church really doesn't want to grow. The last time that happened, twenty years ago, they had to build a new educational building. Most of my folks haven't recovered from all that extra giving. Besides, it would be hard adjusting to any new people. Some of them would want to be leaders and all the good positions are taken. Starting new teaching units is painful. Splitting classes always offends someone. I just don't want to bruise any tender reeds. Pretty biblical, don't you think?

What's so great about church growth anyway? The only reason pastors get excited about it is their own ego. They want to see their names in the associational bulletin. I'm not that interested in numbers. I'm into quality. I know everybody at my church. If more people were to join, I would have to sacrifice my hands-on-ministry. I visit the sick, bury the dead, and marry the intended. On Fridays I pray at the high school game. I'm well respected in my community.

I don't have enough time to attend any more of those growth conferences anyway.

Does any of this pastor's saga sound vaguely familiar? It echoes a collection of complaints and commentaries I have gathered while leading growth conferences around our nation. The faces change, but the responses are often the same. Many of the participants attending conferences leave more discouraged than when they came. The concepts presented don't seem to fit their situation. The ones that do have been tried in their churches before with little results. A pastor can handle only so much rejection.

Many pastors and churches are tired of new methods that promise so much and deliver so little. They know they need to reach their communities, but really don't think they can, and honestly don't know if they want to try.

Are We Growing?

"Church growth" has become a field of study, a topic of considerable interest and debate, and big business. Growth conferences are sponsored by virtually all evangelical denominations at varying levels from the local churches to the national conventions. Centers for church growth abound, and seminaries and colleges are jumping on the bandwagon. Books, tapes, marketing studies, and models abound. More people are attending more conferences and buying more materials than at any time in the history of the church, and yet few visible results can be detected. Certainly some churches are growing. The megachurch has become the Cinderella story of this decade. New churches are being added to a growing list daily. But is *The Church* really growing, adding people to the kingdom of God through all this activity? That is another question and must be honestly addressed.

We cannot show substantial church growth. The brutal truth

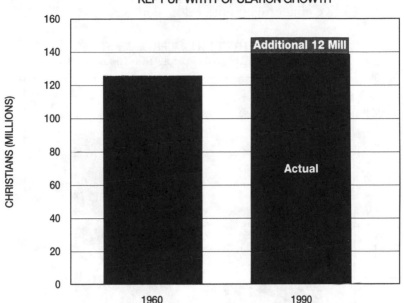

is that church growth is not keeping pace with population increases. Total members in U.S. churches increased by 28 percent from 1960 to 1990 while population increased by 39 percent. If membership had kept pace with population, we would have twelve million more church members today in the United States (see graph above).

Our growth in number of churches has not kept pace with the population increase either. The number of churches in the U.S. increased by 7 percent from 1960 to 1990. If the number of churches had grown at the same percentage as our population, today we would have an additional 96,000 churches (see graph on the next page).[1]

Other church growth authors and statisticians have made the same observation. In an article in *Christianity Today,* Ken Sidey acknowledged that our church growth principles don't seem to be working.[2] Statisticians such as Gallup and Barna have consistently and faithfully documented the woeful results of the evangelical community's attempts to reach unchurched America. Such results have prompted some to conclude the church growth movement is simply not working. While there is some validity to that accusation, we must ask what the state of the church would have been if there had been no conferences or books to give encouragement and new ideas?

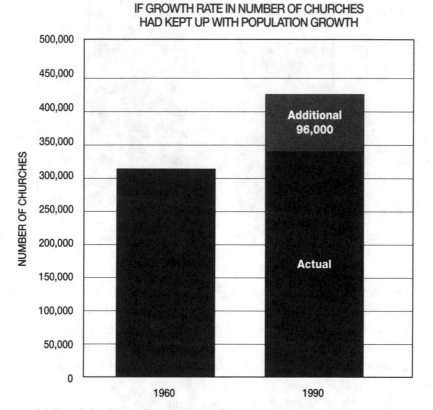

IF GROWTH RATE IN NUMBER OF CHURCHES
HAD KEPT UP WITH POPULATION GROWTH

What Is the Problem?

Where do we place blame? Do the statistical results previously mentioned prove the church growth movement is not working? Consequently, do we now blame the consultants and gurus of church growth? Have they not discovered the right methods to reach and keep a new generation who seemingly do not respond to the methods that reached the last generation?

Should we blame denominational structures and personnel? After all, they are paid to develop programs and materials that will grow churches. Right? If these denominational servants weren't so hopelessly out of date, our churches would be growing. Besides, they are only interested in selling materials and programs, not growing churches. In fact some futurists think denominations are on the way out. Maybe we ought to just bid them a fond farewell since they are at the heart of the church growth dilemma anyway.

We can't let the seminaries off without censure. After all, it is their task to train and equip ministers to grow Great Commission churches. Surely some of the blame for the current lethargy in the church should be borne by those on seminary campuses. Hopelessly out of date, that's what I think. The emphasis is much too academic and theological. Boomers don't want theology anyway. Why don't seminaries just teach us what works?

On a more fundamental level, we could blame the local pastor. He is the only person who can actually motivate and change his church. Today's pastors just aren't committed. They aren't willing to pay the price like those giants of a past generation. They're too sophisticated to get their hands dirty growing the church. They're looking for some new gimmick or gadget that guarantees instant results. They want an easy way out, a church growth plan without work. They've lost their passion for ministry and for evangelism. It's their fault!

While we're passing out blame, why should we leave the people themselves out of this? Most churches in America would be growing if the laity wasn't so unconcerned and uncommitted. They don't want to give, visit, teach, or volunteer for any service. They just don't care. They're more attuned to comfort than evangelism. We ministers announce and promote visitation, but only a few faithful ever show. Personally, I'm tired of begging these people to give and go. Why should I work so hard to reach the community when my people don't welcome them when they come? People today want it all handed to them on a silver platter. They want all the services without any cost or commitment on their part. They just want to be entertained.

We could, of course, blame the world itself. We're not living in the good old days when people were expected to attend church. Back then no self-respecting businessman would think of not showing up for Sunday morning worship. That would be professional suicide. No longer! Today they do business on the golf course on Sunday morning. We're living in a secular society. People just aren't interested in spiritual matters or the church. They are not about to give up their one day for recreation and relaxation to come to church. Who are we kidding anyway? We're living in a post-Christian era, and we might as well get used to it. Things are bad in the church, and they're going to get worse.

Boy, I'm glad I got all that out of my system! It's easy to place the blame, isn't it? Perhaps you found yourself nodding assent to some of the suggestions just put forward. On the other hand, you may have been offended or angered by some others. Let's look over them once more, this time without the intention to blame.

What about the church growth of authors and speakers? Many of them have been used of God to lead their churches to grow. Most are sincere and desire only to help other churches to experience biblical and balanced growth. They do what they do with a sense of calling. Once again we might ask what the state of the church today would be if God had not raised up pastors, professors, and statisticians who search out what is working and then communicate that to others.

Further, it has been my personal experience that most denominational workers are gifted people of great integrity who are serving God in their present position because of their passion to assist the local church. Most attempt to be on the cutting edge of ministry. It is true that denominational structure itself sometimes inhibits change, particularly rapid change, but even that difficulty can assure stability and structure. I do not believe denominationalism is dead. If we were to dismantle denominational structures, our need for cooperation and mutual care, particularly for smaller churches (which make up the vast majority of American churches), would demand that we rebuild denominational ministry structures in a similar form.

We could make the same observation about seminaries and their professors. Most are serving at great personal sacrifice out of a deep sense of call. Many seminaries are working diligently to address practical as well as theological issues at the forefront of church growth concerns.

Pastors certainly receive their share of the blame, especially at the local church level. The focus on church growth, particularly the numerical dimension of church growth, has created inordinate pressure on some pastors to "produce results or hit the road." In some instances the pastor is held solely accountable for the lack of tangible growth. Small wonder that the average tenure of a senior pastor is about four years. Certainly there are some pastors who are apathetic about growing churches and are just collecting a pay check. But for every pastor in this category, there are hundreds who have a passion to see their churches grow and reach the lost. In truth, many of those who are apathetic or less than effective have become so discouraged by the lack of results to their hard work that they have nearly given up on ministry, much less growth. Many of these God-called persons could be restored to zealous ministry if they saw a spark of desire and a glimmer of hope for their churches to grow.

Many discouraged pastors want to blame the laity for the sad state of church growth in America. And, in truth, there are laypersons who fear and resist the changes that growth brings. Unregenerate or carnal persons in leadership may work against the pastor who is committed to the Great Commission. They had rather play church than be church. Even so, my experience is that churches of all sizes include laymen and laywomen who have a deep and abiding passion to see their churches grow and reach their communities. Many have been praying for just such an awakening in their churches for years. This faithful remnant is the kindling awaiting the match of spiritual awakening.

It is true that America is much more secularized today than in the past. Going to church is no longer the thing to do, but this may be more a blessing than a curse. Lost, "cultural Christians" are much more difficult to reach than secular persons. Cultural Christians think they are Christians because they were raised in a Christian environment or culture. The secularist makes no pretense to being a Christian. The church entering the twenty-first century could be facing a greater opportunity for evangelistic outreach and results than we have seen in this century. To seize such an opportunity, the church of necessity must change. How must it change and how can it change?

Are We Treating Symptoms?

With the focus in church growth on methods, models, and marketing strategies, we only treat the symptoms of the illness robbing the church of its vitality. We're not looking at the true source of the illness. *As long as we continue to talk only about symptoms, we will persist in thinking we can heal the sickness with another new program, method, or model.* These too, whether they be traditional or non-traditional, will only provide surface relief to problems that are bone deep. *If we want to cure the problems keeping church growth from taking place, we must go much deeper.* It is not so much that our programs, methods, and marketing strategies are out of date. Our primary problem in churches is a spiritual one, not a methodological one.

Church growth is not produced by a program, plan, or marketing strategy. Your church's greatest need is not a clearer understanding of its demographics, but a clearer understanding of its God. Church growth is not something we do or produce in the church. Church growth is not the result of any program or plan. *Church growth is the by-product of a right relationship with the Lord of the church.* Church growth is by definition a supernatural activity and thus is accomplished through the church by the Lord Himself. When Jesus founded the church He promised that He Himself would build the church (see Matt. 16:18). Paul, recounting his ministry in Corinth, declared: "I planted, Apollos watered, but God was causing the growth" (1 Cor. 3:6).

What Is the Solution?

The solution will not be found in methods, models, or marketing strategies. These are not unimportant issues; they simply are not the primary issue. The church growth movement may have inadvertently produced a subtle sense of carnality in the church causing some to conclude a method or program could produce church growth. Such thinking is both wrong and carnal. "IT," whatever cherished program, model, method, or marketing strategy "IT" may be, cannot cause your church to grow. Scripture is clear and insistent that God alone can grow

His church. The attempt to produce church growth results through a certain method is an attempt to do supernatural work through natural power. This has led to great confusion in many congregations where model after model and method after method have been espoused as the solutions to the stagnancy in the church. It has in many cases heaped failure upon failure, so much so that many churches recoil at the very mention of the term *church growth.*

Lest you overreact or think I am overreacting, I am not arguing against methods, models, marketing strategies, or programs. God is not a God of confusion. He works through human beings and uses strategy and organization. The Scripture is full of illustrations where God worked supernaturally through persons with clear strategies. I am simply suggesting that the program is not the first or most crucial issue in prompting church growth. The vast variety of methods and programs being employed successfully across our nation bear powerful testimony to this truth. *The critical issue is the supernatural empowering of the church which occurs when the church dwells in right relationship with its Head, Jesus Christ.*

Thus, this book is a foundational book to other books on church growth methodology. It addresses the primary question, "What is the character of the church that God has chosen to work through?" We have long recognized and taught that it is the character of an individual that ultimately determines the actions and fruitfulness of that person. *I think it is equally true that the character of a church will ultimately determine the ability of that church to grow.*

What Do We Mean by "Church Growth"?

How do we know if a church is growing? Immediately, many of us would respond by pointing to enlarged conversion statistics or increased Sunday School or worship attendance. In other words, we would point to numerical evidence that our church is growing.

We certainly do not need to apologize for an emphasis on numerical growth. Luke, writing the Book of Acts, frequently chronicled the continual, spectacular, numerical growth of the early church. In recounting the events at Pentecost, Luke told of three thousand baptisms, and then concluded that account by noting: "The Lord was adding to their number day by day those who were being saved" (Acts 2:47). Luke later wrote: "And all the more believers in the Lord, multitudes of men and women, were constantly added to their number" (Acts 5:14). Creation of the ministry of deacons was caused by the growth in the number of disciples in Jerusalem (see Acts 6:1–6). Three times in the account of the church at Antioch, we are told that large numbers of people were being reached (see Acts 11:21, 24, 26). If we are not interested in numerical growth, we are not interested in fulfilling the Great Commission, and we are not in harmony with the Word of God.

But is numerical growth the full measure of church growth? What about issues of maturational growth such as the discipling of believers, the deepening of relationships, and the transformation of culture. Surely those must be considered. Luke wrote that the early church was devoted to doctrinal teaching, fellowship, worship, and prayer (see Acts 2:42). The early believers were so committed to one another that they willingly sold their property and shared with those in need (see Acts 2:45). The church in Antioch joyfully participated in a famine relief offering for Jerusalem and inaugurated the first church planting mission strategy (see Acts 11:29–30; 13:1–3). The early church also had a profound impact on its society. Paul and Silas liberated the fortune-telling woman from her exploitative masters (see Acts 16:16–18). They stood up against the corrupt magistrates who wanted to sweep their improper imprisonment under the rug (see Acts 16:35–40). Yes, church growth is more than numerical growth.

How then do we develop a simple definition and an understanding of church growth which will encompass both numerical and maturational concepts? I think we must develop both our definition and understanding from the Bible itself. When Jesus founded the church, as recorded in Matthew 16:13–19, He promised He would build His church. Thus church growth is not something we accomplish for God, but it is a divine activity in which God calls and gifts His children to join Him. We must first recognize that church growth is not something we do; it is the by-product of a right relationship with Jesus, the Lord of the church.

In that light our definition of church growth must clearly reflect His design for the church. At the end of Matthew's Gospel we find the marching orders of the church given by her resurrected and exalted Head: "All authority has been given to Me in heaven and on earth. Go therefore and make disciples of all the nations, baptizing them in the name of the Father and the Son and the Holy Spirit, teaching them to observe all that I commanded you; and lo, I am with you always, even to the end of the age (Matt. 28:18–20).

Here then is my working definition of church growth: *Church growth occurs when the local church supernaturally and faithfully fulfills the Great Commission in its unique context and with a vision for the world.*

Where Can We Find a Model Church?

This book derives its title, outline, and much of its content from studying the church at Antioch, the church that was at the center of much of the mission activity recorded in the Book of Acts. Several unique statements are made concerning this church. First, the hand of the Lord was on the church, and as a consequence great numbers of people were being saved (see Acts 11:21). Second, when Barnabas arrived from Jerusalem to strengthen the church, Luke noted that Barnabas saw the grace of God (see Acts 11:23). How does one see the grace of God in the church? Barnabas saw Jews and Gentiles enjoying fellowship together. Who would have believed that would have been possible in the first century? Third, note that the disciples were first called Christians in Antioch (see Acts 11:26). This attested to their witness before the pagan community.

What can we learn from this first-century church that will empower churches for fruitful ministry into the twenty-first century? Hopefully a great deal. We will learn about eight characteristics of the church that God used in the past and continues to use in the present.

Characteristic 1:

Supernatural Power

W e have experienced so little church growth we seem to be obsessed with getting the latest church growth gadget. We run from conference to conference looking for a new idea or program to grow our church. Our desperation stems from the fact we have had so little response to the programs and plans we are now using that we have come to believe success will be found in some new method.

Sometimes we fall into the trap of attempting to copy the method that worked for a successful, polished pastor who led a session on "How to Make Your Church Sizzle." We came home, plugged in the "surefire, microwaveable guaranteed-to-grow-your-church" strategy only to stare helplessly as our people balked and the program fizzled rather than sizzled. The model worked for him, so we are led to conclude that something must be wrong with us. Thus many pastors have discovered growth conferences to be depressing events that lead to discouragement and guilt. Untold numbers resign themselves to another year of no growth and make a mental note not to attend the next church growth conference.

Or perhaps your experience has been sitting in the conference listening to the news about guaranteed marketing strategies for the church, the newest technology and methodology for making your worship come alive, or a new organizational plan guaranteed to improve attendance by 20 percent the very first week. These guaranteed growth plans remind me of the ads in golf magazines for equipment guaranteed to make you putt like Ben Crenshaw and drive like John Daly. If all those gadgets, balls, and clubs could deliver as promised, there wouldn't be room on the pro tour for all us weekend professionals. The implement never seems to work as well in my hands. Even while listening to the guarantees of church growth, you realize you have neither the budget, the staff, the gifts, nor the opportunity to utilize many of these new ideas. Thus you leave the conference more defeated than when you arrived, convinced that church growth is an unattainable goal.

We seem to have overlooked the fact that models and methods have certain inherent limitations. *First, you can't transfer context.* What works on the west coast in a large metropolitan community has little relevance for rural Kentucky. When we plop a seemingly successful model down in a different context, it may prove to be nothing more than a highly visible failure. *Second, you can't transfer gifts and personality.* What works well for one gifted leader may not work well for you with your unique mix of gifts. That doesn't mean you are any less gifted or important to the kingdom. You're just different. If you attempt to impersonate the leadership style and methods of another, you will generally come across like an Elvis impersonator. He may be entertaining for a song or two, but a little of this guy goes a long way. *Third, you can't transfer spirituality.* Your attempt to copy a working model can easily neglect both your spiritual character and the spiritual development of your church.[1] *Fourth, we can't transfer the unique gift mix of a particular congregation.* Not only is the pastor of this model church uniquely gifted, but so are the members of his church. *Fifth, we can't transfer time and maturation.* It may have taken the model church years of diligent seeking, personal experimentation, and program development to arrive at the dynamics of ministry we see today. To think we can duplicate that ministry overnight is utter foolishness.

Yet we have not really come to the crux of the issue. Why are the church growth methods and models not working for a vast majority of our churches? Why aren't *they* producing church growth? Simply because church growth methods and models cannot grow the church. We have made secondary issues primary ones. We have focused on methods rather than on the supernatural promises of God. We have forgotten that Jesus promised He would build the church. We cannot substitute methods, models, and marketing strategies for the supernatural empowering of God. Such a strategy would be equivalent to building a house by erecting the rafters first, a clearly impossible task. We must start with foundational issues. *We must first build the character of the church.*

If we depend upon methods to grow our church, we run the risk of making an idol of church growth methodology by suggesting that "IT" can grow the church. In some arenas church growth has degenerated into our feeble attempts to do in a mechanical fashion what God desires to do in a supernatural fashion. The sin of carnality is nothing more than the attempt to do supernatural work through human ability. Jeff Jernigan echoes the same sentiment when he writes: "If programs and formulas were able to generate growth then we would depend on them and move toward self-sufficiency rather than active dependence—faith—on the sovereignty of God."[2]

The Bible is replete with examples where men attempted to help God do His work. Abraham, for example, attempted to help God fulfill His supernatural promise to produce an heir through him by first adopting his slave and then by having a child through Hagar, Sarah's handmaiden (see Gen. 15–16). The results were predictably disastrous. On two occasions the people of Israel were numbered. The first instance, recorded in chapter 1 of Numbers, was at God's command and intended for the care and protection of the people. The second instance was David's idea and grew out of his pride for the military strength of Israel (see 1 Chron. 12). On this occasion the numbering of Israel was condemned because it showed their reliance on military might to deliver them from their enemies. God wanted Israel to know that He alone was responsible for their victory.

When church growth comes through the supernatural work of the Holy Spirit, then the glory will always go to Christ, not to the person or the method. We must be careful in the field of church growth that we do not come to believe we can grow the church through our methods devoid of supernatural power.

Hear me carefully. I am not suggesting we do not need to

study and learn effective growth principles and methods which God has blessed in growing churches. God is not a God of confusion; He often chooses to work through structure and organization. I am not proposing an end to growth conferences. I am, however, arguing that church growth is by its very definition a supernatural event and therefore must begin with a supernatural encounter with Holy God. The first priority of the pastor and the church must be to develop a deep relationship with Him. *Church growth is not something we do to the church; rather, it is the by-product of a proper relationship with Christ, the Head of the church. Thus growth is not an end in and of itself; it is the result of supernatural empowering.*

When a church falls deeply in love with Jesus, most issues of church growth resolve themselves. It is out of this deep love relationship that the desire to win the lost, serve the saints, and share graciously our material possessions emerges. However, any time we attempt to force growth methods upon people who are spiritually unprepared, the results will be chaotic carnality. Many pastors and excited laypersons have returned from a growth conference or spiritual retreat with an exciting vision for their churches only to be met with casual indifference or downright hostility. Why? Because in most instances the churches were not in proper relationship with their Head so as to experience change for the sake of growth.

Before the Lord commissioned Peter to tend His sheep, Jesus asked him three times if he truly loved Him (see John 21:15–19). "Simon, son of John, do you love Me more than these?" Bible teachers have had a running debate about what Jesus meant by the phrase "more than these." Was Jesus asking Peter to compare his love with the love of the other apostles, or was He asking him whether he loved Him more than he loved all these things around him, including his fishing business, friends, and family? Could Jesus be asking us whether we truly love Him more than all the methods we so treasure or the accolades we accumulate for growing the church? It is possible to become more enamored with growing the church than living in a growing relationship with Holy God. God doesn't want you to be a successful church growth practitioner; He wants you to be deeply in love with Him so that He can grow His church through you.

This chapter considers the scriptural basis of supernatural empowering for church growth—first, the promise of the Lord of the church in Matthew 16; second, a look at our model church in Antioch; third, a look at the personal experience of Paul; fourth, a quick scan of the pattern of Scripture; fifth, a look at Paul's prayer for the empowering of the church; and finally, the practical implications of our study.

The Promise of the Lord

It would be odd to attempt to talk about church growth without first giving attention to the founding of the church by the Lord Himself. In Matthew 16 we are thrust into a critical moment in the ministry of our Lord. If we glance at the preceding chapters and note the context of this passage, we find Jesus had been on an extended preaching mission in which He accomplished many miracles. Some of the onlookers had begun to speculate about His identity. Shouts of messianic titles such as "Lord, Son of David" must have been commonplace (see Matt. 15:22). Thus, in verse one of chapter sixteen we read that the Pharisees and Sadducees had come to Jesus testing Him and seeking a sign from heaven. In other words, they were asking Him to prove He truly was the Messiah. Jesus refused to give any sign other than the sign of Jonah, His death, and His resurrection.

Matthew then took an insightful look at the disciples who were still struggling to believe in Jesus' ability to meet their daily needs (see 16:5–12). They had taken His saying about the leaven of the Pharisees in a literal fashion because of their physical hunger, and thus had missed its spiritual impact. Their spiritual prowess and maturity was not all that impressive at that point in time.

For that reason, the confession of Peter and the ensuing revelation of Jesus' strategy for reaching the world are startling. Jesus first inquired about the current speculation concerning His identity. The disciples replied that some believed Him to be John the Baptist raised from the dead, others Elijah, still others Jeremiah or one of the other prophets (see 16:13–14). An impressive list of prophetic luminaries, yet far short of the truth. Jesus was and is the Messiah, the Son of the living God. Peter, as spokesman for the twelve dared to vocalize such an audacious idea: "Thou art the Christ, the Son of the living God" (Matt. 16:16).

We may have grown indifferent to the radical nature of the confession uttered by Peter. Remember, a few short years later many of these men would die for this confession. This confession was not just radical; to many it was scandalous heresy. Peter was saying that Jesus was God's anointed Messiah, the fulfillment of all the prophetic promises, the One to bring redemption to the world. Yet more, He was the Son of the living God, not a mere human king, but God in the flesh. If you have come to believe this, then it must forever control your thinking about the nature of the church.

Jesus immediately affirmed this attestation by declaring Peter had been the recipient of divine revelation. What a moment in history! God's redemptive plan fulfilled in human flesh. But there was more to follow: "And I also say to you that you are Peter, and upon this rock I will build My church" (Matt. 16:18).

Peter's apostolic confession—that Jesus is the Christ—is the rock, the sure foundation on which the church is built. A popular song captures well this powerful truth when it says: "Upon the rock of revelation, I will build a strong and mighty nation."

God's redemption of the world necessitated the sending of His Son, the Messiah, to die upon the cross to pay the penalty of human sin. Yet there was more to His mission. He came to build a community, a messianic community to which He would give the keys of the kingdom, a community in which the decisions made would be of such momentous and cosmic significance that the binding and loosing which occurred in that community would last throughout eternity. Jesus came to establish and build the church—a called-out people who would be His body, His building, His bride—a chosen race, a royal priesthood, a holy nation, a people whom God Himself would possess (see 1 Pet. 2:9).

This understanding alone of the church gives us reason to talk about church growth. Jesus came to found the church; He promised that He Himself would build the church; He died to redeem the church; He triumphed over all the authorities and powers and dominions so He might fill the church to become the full expression of Him who fills all in all (see Eph. 1:22–23); and one day He will return for His church.

Until Jesus returns for His church, it is our privilege and responsibility to live in holiness and obedience so that we are vessels through which His power flows for the building of His church. Authentic church growth emanates from a proper theological understanding of the church, its nature, and its mission. In a recent study conducted by the Lutheran Church-Missouri Synod, researchers found that a key factor in church growth is the understanding that the church has a mission beyond their current membership.[3] Church growth is mandated by the origin, nature, and purpose of the church, and the great need of the world.

Authentic church growth is a promised divine activity for the church rightly related to Christ. The first step to all church growth is supernatural empowering.

We should note church growth is at once supernatural and at the same moment natural. God designed His church to grow, He desires that it grow, and He has empowered it to grow. For those reasons church growth is natural. It is supernatural because only God can cause it. Thus when we do see church growth, He receives the glory. When we are privileged to join Him in this activity, it is the result of His grace alone. We cannot engineer true growth; it is God's sovereign activity.

The Church at Antioch

What do we discover about supernatural empowering from the church at Antioch? In Acts 11:21 we are told the hand of the Lord was with them. This phrase clearly points to supernatural empowering and the results indicate such: "and a large number who believed turned to the Lord" (v. 21). It would be a worthwhile study for any pastor or layleader to look up the Old and New Testaments' references to the hand of the Lord. When the hand of the Lord is on or with someone, the activity is supernaturally empowered and successful. When the Lord removes His hand or places His hand against someone, the results are always disastrous. A case in point is King Saul. When God removed His hand of anointing and empowering, the results were immediate and catastrophic.

Do you sense God's hand on your church and your ministry? What evidence leads you to that conclusion? Without the supernatural anointing of the Lord, nothing of lasting significance can be accomplished.

The church at Antioch was founded by laypersons who were scattered by the persecution that arose in connection with Stephen (see Acts 8). Not one apostle was among them. These laypeople, uprooted from their homeland and worldly security, began preaching the Lord Jesus to the Greeks. Because they were in proper and obedient relationship to their Head, He supernaturally empowered their witness, and large numbers turned to Christ. The church at Antioch was founded by laypeople whose first priority was to walk in obedience to Christ. Out of that obedience came church-building witnessing.

The second significant phrase is found in 11:23, "Then when he (Barnabas) had come and witnessed the grace of God." How does one see or witness the grace of God? We often think about experiencing or feeling the grace of God, but have you ever thought about *seeing* the grace of God? What did Barnabas *see* that convinced Him He was witnessing nothing less than the activity of God's grace? Several things come to mind immediately from the text. Barnabas saw great numbers of people turning to the Lord (see 11:24). Conversion is always a sign of God's activity. He saw serious prayer and fasting (see 13:1–3). When God's people truly encounter Him, they develop an insatiable appetite for regular communication with Him. Barnabas witnessed sacrificial and spontaneous giving. According to 11:27–30 this church immediately responded to the message of the prophet Agabus about the great famine that would affect the brethren living in Judea. Barnabas saw a church with a vision for the world. The church at Antioch began what we now call Paul's missionary journeys.

Perhaps the most visible witness to the grace of God was the fellowship established in the church at Antioch between Jew and Gentile. In the letter to the Galatians, Paul related how the Jews and Gentiles were accustomed to eating together in Antioch (see Gal. 2:11–12). Apparently they were taking the Lord's Supper together. This may not impress us as significant, but Jews and Gentiles eating together was unheard of in the first century. The barriers that divided them were not only racial but also religious and cultural. Seemingly insurmountable barriers were obliterated in a moment by the grace of God. When a church is touched by the grace of God, you will see healing of relationships and supernatural kingdom living. When the God of the universe indwells a people, you will always see evidence of the grace of God. If we see no such evidence, we must first ask, "Are we fully surrendered to the Lord?"

The final noteworthy phrase is found in Acts 11:26: "And the disciples were first called Christians in Antioch." The word "Christian" was probably a term of derision given to the disciples at Antioch by the secular community around them. Perhaps they were accusing the disciples of attempting to be "little Christs," that is, imitators of Christ. We should pray that the secular world at the doorsteps of our churches would accuse us also of being imitators of Christ.

The Experience of Paul

The apostle Paul would have to be classified as one of the greatest church planters and church growth experts of all times. The Pauline letters have proven to be helpful guides to church leaders in every generation who sought to develop biblical patterns for church growth. Let's look at two passages which synthesize the thinking of Paul about church growth. One we will consider here; the second I will use to conclude this chapter since it is a prayer for the church.

The Corinthian church presented Paul with a lifetime of pastoral problems. The Corinthian believers were particularly impressed with powerful men and their powerful methods and messages. The focus on men had created dissension in the church. Some Corinthians were saying: "'I am of Paul,' and 'I of Apollos,' and 'I of Cephas,' and 'I of Christ'" (1 Cor. 1:12). This passionate desire to identify with a certain leader appeared to center around the Corinthians' quest for wise teaching and their penchant for the spectacular gifts of the Spirit.

Paul found it necessary to deflate their spiritual bubble. He declared that he could not speak to them as to spiritual persons because they were behaving carnally; their strife and jealously clearly proved this (see 1 Cor. 3:3–3). Their claims of attachment to spiritual leaders indicated their carnal thinking. They were behaving as if these men had themselves been responsible for building the church.

Listen to Paul's response. "What then is Apollos? And what is Paul? Servants through whom you believed, even as the Lord gave opportunity to each one. I planted, Apollos watered, but God was causing the growth. So then neither the one who plants nor the one who waters is anything, but God who causes the growth" (1 Cor. 3:5–7). Twice in one short paragraph Paul underlined the truth that church growth is caused by God. He uses human vessels, yes, but He alone can give the growth (compare Gal. 2:8–9).

For eleven years I was privileged to pastor First Baptist Church of Norfolk, Virginia. We saw explosive and supernatural growth during those years. I was acutely aware of the hand of the Lord on the church. I constantly reminded our people that former pastors and laypersons had played a significant role in the planting and watering of the seed that we were privileged to harvest, but that God Himself was causing the increase. I left Norfolk in June of 1992 to become the director of the newly established Southern Baptist Center for Church Growth. During that interim period, a local religion reporter came to see "how things were going" at First Norfolk. She asked a layman what the church would do without Dr. Hemphill. He responded simply but profoundly: "The same thing we did when he was here. We'll keep visiting the lost and nurturing the saved. Besides," he added, "this church wasn't built on Ken, it was built on Christ." Amen! It was a joy to watch First Norfolk continue to grow even during an interim period and now with a new pastor, Dr. Bob Reccord.

Church growth is a supernatural activity in which God has graciously called and empowered us to join Him. Our responsibility is to be responsive to God, prepared to join Him, and willing to utilize the opportunities God gives us. You do not have to build a megachurch to be successful in church growth, but you do have to be a growth steward in the context where

God has placed you. You do need to be available and submitted so that God can use you as He builds His church. It is a humbling experience to realize that God is working supernaturally in and through us.

The Pattern of Scripture

The pattern of God's activity is consistent throughout Scripture. God is always at work. He desires a people through whom He can work. When people join God in His supernatural activity, the plan and work of God are accomplished by His power; therefore, He receives the glory. When human beings, however noble their motives, attempt to do God's work in human strength and strategy, the results are carnal failure. Let me warn you, even numerical success can be a spiritual failure if accomplished in human might.

Let's look first at two familiar Old Testament stories. God desired to free His people from Egyptian bondage. We are told in Exodus 3:7 that God had seen their affliction and given heed to their cries. Note the connection between divine activity and the concerted prayer of God's people. Verse 8 declares: "So I have come down to deliver them from the power of the Egyptians." How, you ask? God called Moses to be that instrument through which His divine activity could be focused. "Therefore, come now, and I will send you to Pharaoh, so that you may bring My people, the sons of Israel, out of Egypt" (Ex. 3:10). Moses asked two questions, the first of which was irrelevant. First he asked: "Who am I, that I should go to Pharaoh?" (3:11). Not only was the question irrelevant, it was irreverent. Who are human beings to question the call of God? The second question is more to the point. He asked who he should tell them had sent him. In response, God said to Moses: "I AM WHO I AM" (3:14). I am the uncaused cause, the sovereign God of the universe who has been active throughout history; I am sending you—this was the message of God's name.

The results are predictable once you know God. The people, when they knew God had seen their affliction, bowed low and worshiped (see Ex. 4:31). The confrontation with Pharaoh that Moses feared was to be a supernatural one, and Moses was but a mere instrument in the hand of God. Look at Exodus 6:6–8. Underline the phrases that denote supernatural activity. "I am the Lord"; "I will bring you out"; "I will deliver you"; "I will also redeem you"; "I will take you for My people"; "I will be your God"; and "I will bring you to the land which I swore to give to Abraham, Isaac, and Jacob, and I will give it to you for a possession." This entire passage is punctuated by the reminder, "I am the Lord." You know the rest of the story of the supernatural encounter with the Pharaoh and the parting of the Red Sea. God's work is always supernaturally accomplished.

To effectively grow the church, we must learn more about God. We desperately need a renewal of theological thinking. For some today, theology is seen as irrelevant, and by others a barrier to growth. Our zeal for getting something practical, something that works, reveals the shallowness of our understanding of the nature of God.

The greatest danger of the over-emphasis on methods and marketing is not that some may not work in a certain situation. We may well add numbers of people to our attendance roles through clever marketing strategies or novel methods. The great danger is that such apparent success might cause us to think our human efforts have grown the church. In this way, we may subtly take the glory from Him alone who can enable the church to grow.

On the other hand we are sometimes tempted to look at our apparent lack of resources and to think our church can never grow. When you are tempted to think your church can't grow, when you doubt your ability as a leader, remember it was Paul's weakness that became the forum for the display of God's strength (2 Cor. 9–10). God has made a career from making something great out of seemingly insignificant things. When God uses what appears to be *nothing* to achieve *something,* it is certain He will receive the glory. Don't be paralyzed by the fear that your church can't grow. Such fear casts doubt at the One who declares that He is the Lord. The sovereign Lord has promised that He will build His church.

In Joshua 6 we read about the supernatural defeat of the walled city of Jericho. The plan may have appeared foolish in human thinking; but God's ways are higher than ours. God required Israel's obedience to His plan. The people marched around the city, and God destroyed the walls and gave them victory. The unorthodox, but supernatural victory at Jericho was followed by the shattering and humiliating defeat at Ai. What went wrong? Simply this—the taking of Ai was a human effort borne out of human arrogance (see Josh. 7:3). The spies argued that they needed to send only a few men because Ai was so weak. Yet the warriors at Ai repelled them and "the hearts of the people melted and became as water" (7:5). The source of the problem was the people's relationship with their God—it was distorted by sinful pride. The Lord told Joshua: "Israel has sinned, and they have also transgressed My covenant which I commanded them" (7:11). Because of sin the people of Israel could not stand before their enemies. The solution? "Rise up! Consecrate the people and say, 'Consecrate yourselves.'" (7:13). Before any church can truly experience supernatural growth, it must have a clear understanding of who God is in His holiness and sovereignty; this in turn will bring a profound sense of brokenness and repentance for sin which will lead to revival and supernatural empowering. God is looking for a cleansed vessel through which He can demonstrate His glorious power. Our methods and programs will fail until there is a supernatural encounter with Holy God.

The New Testament pattern is the same. Let's take a brief look at the Book of Acts. If your heart's desire is to understand church growth, you need to immerse yourself in the Book of Acts. I can only suggest a pattern and leave you to do the rest. Note that in Acts 1:8 the disciples were waiting to receive the empowering of the Holy Spirit before they began any church growth activity. How did they prepare themselves for the supernatural anointing? Look at 1:14: "These all with one mind were continually devoting themselves to prayer, along with the women, and Mary the mother of Jesus, and with His brothers." Church growth is inaugurated in a supernatural encounter with the living Lord, and this occurs only in the context of concerted and united prayer. If you want to see your church grow, *teach your church to pray.*

Pentecost marks the beginning and the empowering of the New Testament church. It marks a unique transformation in the lives of the members of the early church. After Pentecost we see high-voltage Christianity. If we ourselves and our churches do not have a Pentecost experience, we will never be bold witnesses and never know supernatural church growth.

The results of Pentecost are multifaceted. There was a baptismal service for about three thousand new believers. The disciples committed themselves to apostolic teaching and community ministry which led to a sacrificial sharing of possessions and property with anyone in need. Look at the spontaneous joy of the church members as they went from house to house, taking their meals together with gladness and sincerity of heart. They were praising God and having favor with all the people. Notice, too, that as the people of God authentically praised the Lord, *"the Lord was adding to their number day by day those who were being saved"* (Acts 2:47, author's italics).

Allow me an aside if you would. In our passion to market our worship service to the lost by making it seeker-targeted, we may actually sacrifice some of the supernatural mystery and power of God drawing people to Himself as His people praise Him. We forget that Jesus frequently told His disciples that no one could come to the Father except the Father draw him (see John 12:32; 6:44). If we remove the distinctively biblical aspects of worship, we may be trading a deep well for a broken cistern. We will look at worship in greater detail in a later characteristic.

As we follow the story of Acts, we find Peter and John before the Sanhedrin (see Acts 4). What amazed the Sanhedrin was not the methodology of the early apostles, rather "as they observed the confidence of Peter and John, and understood that they were uneducated and untrained men, they were marveling, and began to recognize them as having been with Jesus" (Acts 4:13). The presence and power of the resurrected Lord enabled them to share with confidence. When they were threatened, they did not petition Caesar, complaining that their first amendment rights had been violated; they petitioned the King of Kings. "And when they had prayed, the place where they had gathered together was shaken, and they were all filled with the Holy Spirit, and began to speak the word of God with boldness" (4:31).

The rapid growth of the church created unique opportunities

for the early apostles to seek direction from the Lord. In Acts 6 the church momentarily plateaued because it was difficult to continue to assimilate new members and, at the same time, care for the needs of the congregation as a whole. The Hellenistic widows felt their needs were being ignored. The diaconate ministry was thus born to meet the needs of the growing church. Notice the confirmation: "And the word of God kept on spreading; and the number of the disciples continued to increase greatly in Jerusalem." (Acts 6:7).

Our look at the church in Antioch continues the pattern of Acts. Notice that the emphasis throughout Acts is on the activity of God in adding disciples to the church. God was sovereignly at work growing His church through yielded human instruments, and it is my conviction that the immutable God desires to give supernatural growth to His church in our generation.

Paul's Prayer for Your Church

The letter to the Ephesians is probably my favorite letter in all the Bible. It was written as a companion letter to Colossians by Paul from prison. Epaphras, the leader of the Colossian church, had visited Paul in prison. During their time together, he had shared with Paul his concern for the heretical teaching which the church was encountering in the whole of proconsular Asia. This heretical teaching may have sown the seeds of gnosticism, but at this time it was not that well developed. The false teachers had created a great deal of excitement about experiencing the "fullness" of God. They may have seen Jesus as *a way* among many ways to experience that fullness, but they discounted His unique status as *the way*. The heresy confronting that early church was not unlike current day New Age thinking. Satan has no new ideas; he simply repackages old heresies.

In the Colossian letter Paul countered false teaching directly. "See to it that no one takes you captive through philosophy and empty deception, according to the tradition of men, according to the elementary principles of the world, rather than according to Christ. For in Him all the fullness of Deity dwells in bodily form" (Col. 2:8–9). Christ contains the full sufficiency for victorious Christian living.

Yet Paul was concerned for all the churches of Asia Minor, and so he took this opportunity to write the more general letter of Ephesians to be shared among them. In this letter Paul attacked the heresy in a different manner by exalting the church. You see, our view of Christ and our view of the church are inextricably bound together. When we correctly conclude that Jesus is Messiah, the only means of redemption, then His earthly body, the church, takes on great and eternal significance.

The Ephesian letter is aimed at calling Christians to be fully empowered so that the church can truly be the church as God intended it to be. For example, in the first chapter, Paul prayed believers would have a spirit of wisdom and revelation so that they would know the hope of His calling, the riches of the glory of His inheritance in the saints, and the surpassing greatness of His power made available to those who believe (see vv. 15–19). These promises are assured by the working of God's strength with which He raised Jesus from the dead. But notice the conclusion: "And He put all things in subjection under His feet, and gave Him as head over all things to the church, which is His body, the fullness of Him who fills all in all" (vv. 22–23). Remember in Colossians 1:19 Paul noted that in Jesus was found the fullness of God. In Ephesians Paul declared that the church was now empowered to express the fullness of God. Do you believe that the exalted Christ wants to and will express His fullness through your church?

In chapter two Paul began by discussing the wonderful gift of God's grace—our salvation. Yet in the second half of this chapter Paul moved quickly to underline the corporate implications of our salvation. Those who have been saved by grace are His workmanship. That workmanship is expressed in the church, made up of Jew and Gentile alike, made anew into one new person. The Ephesians were now fellow citizens with the saints, members of God's household, built upon the foundation of the apostles and prophets, growing into a holy temple which God Himself will indwell.

In the first half of the third chapter Paul confessed his sense of awe at being given a stewardship of grace to preach to the Gentiles about the unfathomable riches of Christ. Beyond that, he had been chosen to reveal a mystery which had been hidden since before creation—the church made up of Jew and Gentile alike and now the centerpiece of God's creative activity. "And to bring to light what is the administration of the mystery which for ages has been hidden in God, who created all things; in order that the manifold wisdom of God might now be made known through the church to the rulers and the authorities in the heavenly places. This was in accordance with the eternal purpose which He carried out in Christ Jesus our Lord" (3:9–11). The church is the centerpiece of God's creation, designed to manifest His glory and wisdom. Does yours?

Because of the great calling of the church Paul offered a passionate prayer for the church which is recorded in Ephesians 3:14–19. He prayed *first* that they would know supernatural strengthening, for theirs was a supernatural task.

Second, he prayed that they would experience the indwelling of Christ through faith. The Lord must be Lord of the church. Is He truly Lord of your planning to reach your community? Do you think according to His power, or yours? Is He Lord of your business sessions? Is He Lord of your budget planning process?

Third, he prayed that they would know the love of Christ which surpasses knowing. While at first it may appear to be contradictory to pray that they would know that which by definition surpasses knowing, the paradox is solved with the phrase, "with all the saints" (v. 18). We can only know the fullness of God's love in the context of family. Each of us alone can know by experience some aspects of the love of God, but all of us together can begin to see the magnificence of His love.

Fourth, Paul prayed that they would be filled up to all the fullness of God. There is that word *fullness* again. As Christ expressed the fullness of God (see Col. 1:19), God has now empowered the church to express that fullness. Paul prayed that they would become all Christ died to make them to be.

Paul ended his prayer with a moving and challenging benediction. Listen! "Now to Him who is able to do exceeding abundantly beyond all that we ask or think, according to the power that works within us, to Him be the glory in the church and in Christ Jesus to all generations forever and ever. Amen" (Eph. 3:20–21).

God is able to do more than you can dream or ask, and He desires to in order that He might grow His church. Note that it is this power that works within us. Church growth is a divine human encounter. When supernatural church growth occurs, the glory will go to the risen Christ. Onlookers will know that it is beyond human achievement. When God grows His church, there will always be a sense of the mysterious. It is not that we are guilty of attempting too much in the church; if anything, we have been unwilling to expect the supernatural. Henry Blackaby has noted: "We've become satisfied today to live without the manifest presence of God."[4]

One author has argued that the primary reason for the lack of church growth lies in marketing. "My contention, based on careful study of the activities of American churches, is that the major problem plaguing the Church is its failure to embrace a marketing orientation in what has become a marketing-driven environment."[5] Your church might improve its image through marketing, but that is by no means its greatest problem. The greatest issue of church growth in our day will not be resolved by debates over traditional or non-traditional methods; it will not be solved by new programs or marketing strategies; and, it will not be settled by developing different models for pastoral leadership. Our greatest problem is an anti-supernatural bias, and that will only be resolved as we have a fresh encounter with the living God.

We don't have any problem believing in a supernatural God of the past—that's history. We also have the confidence to believe He will one day return supernaturally powerful in glory for His church—that's our assured hope. We struggle, however, to believe that He can actually grow our church today—that's an issue of faith and obedience.

I know what you're thinking. "But you don't know my circumstances." "You don't know the apathy of my people." Or perhaps, "You don't know the weaknesses of our preacher." Maybe you don't know *the power of Almighty God*. The problem is not our circumstances or lack of resources; the problem is our lack of supernatural empowering.

In one of my early pastorates I ran into such carnal human thinking. I had only been the pastor for about six months when budget preparation time rolled around—always a spiritual highlight in most churches. I had proposed several new ideas which required additional funding. Someone gently reminded me that inflation was only about 4 percent that year and wondered out loud from where I thought the additional money to fund such an increase in the budget was coming. First, I suggested somewhat humorously that I didn't realize that God, who owned the cattle on a thousand hills, was so affected by inflation. Noticing that no one caught my joke, I pressed on. I suggested we might reach some new families who would give, and perhaps God would change the hearts of some of our people who were robbing from God by keeping His tithe. My inquisitor looked at me with one of those "we'll-forgive-you-because-you're-only-a-preacher" looks and said; "Pastor, you just don't know these people like I do. They're not going to change." I responded instinctively, but honestly: "Perhaps, you don't know my God like I do. If God is not still in the business of changing lives and attitudes, we had better close up shop and quit playing church."

We do struggle with the supernatural power of God in the present to grow His church. Have you nearly given up on your church? Have you tried every method and model on the market with no visible results? Why not try God's way? Stop right now and confess your sin of unbelief and apathy, and ask God to begin His supernatural work with you.

The "greater works" promised by our Lord in John 14:12 were made possible by His death, resurrection, and ascension. The exalted Lord, the Head of the church, wants to do through us only that which God can do. You can't make it happen, but He can—through you. The "and" of John 14:13 may be one of the most important linking words in the New Testament: "And whatever you ask in My name, that will I do, that the Father may be glorified in the Son." God is not concerned about your ability to grow the church, but in your availability.

What Are the Implications?

1. Your church can grow. God Himself promised it, and He desires to work through His people to grow His church.

2. A supernatural encounter with the resurrected Lord must precede the implementation of methodology. A supernatural awakening will be evidenced by your awareness of human sinfulness and God's holiness, and thus will lead to deep repentance and cleansing.

3. There will be visible evidence of spiritual awakening. First, it will create a renewed hunger for serious prayer. Second, it will be seen in a renewed passion to reach lost people. You cannot encounter Holy God without sharing His burden for the lost. Third, it will result in the healing of relationships among God's people. Fourth, it will create an atmosphere of spontaneous generosity essential to all church growth. Fifth, it will lead to the development of a personalized methodology to accomplish the work to which God has called you.

4. Sound methodology comes from God and enables us to participate in His supernatural work. Once the supernatural encounter has occurred, God's people will begin to inquire about methods to do God's work more effectively. It is at this point that the church is receptive to make the changes church growth will require. If, however, you attempt to introduce new methods to an unrevived church, you will face only carnal confusion.

5. Since church growth is supernatural, prayer is the substance of all authentic church growth.

6. The preachers or laypersons who desire to see their churches grow and reach their communities must first be persons of God and persons of prayer.

When the people of God fall deeply in love with Him, He will empower them, enabling them to participate as He grows His church.

Characteristic 2:

Christ-Exalting Worship

Vance Havner, well-known North Carolina evangelist of a past generation, used to remark that we wouldn't need to schedule so many "revivals" if our church remained in a state of "vival." I'm confident "vival" is not a word, but his Carolina quip communicated volumes. Why do we tend to lose the glow, the anointing, the revival spirit so easily?

We've all experienced the phenomenon! Our church is touched by the hand of God during a special "revival" meeting, conference, or prayer meeting. We have true confession and repentance, holiness is restored, relationships are healed, vision and vitality are once again evidenced in the church, and supernatural results are experienced. We bask in the moving of God's Spirit and think that nothing could ever deter us from remaining in this empowered state of supernatural living. Yet we watch as conditions change and everything returns to "normal." We sigh impotently and muse, "I knew it was too good to last."

Is it too good to last? Must we experience the inevitable rollercoaster of spiritual highs and lows in the church, living more on the plains of human empowering than in the heights of supernatural experience? Are we simply expecting too much to think we can have the empowering hand of the Lord continually upon us?

I think we are expecting too little rather than too much. We have grown so accustomed to living the Christian life and conducting the work of the church in human empowering that we view the moments of supernatural empowering as abnormal, as deviations from the norm. The norm for your life and your church should be supernaturally empowered living: "Now to Him who is able to do exceeding abundantly beyond all that we ask or think, according to the power that works within us, to Him be the glory in the church and in Christ Jesus to all generations forever and ever. Amen" (Eph. 3:20–21). This promise of God's Word is not only true, it applies to your church.

In the last characteristic we discussed the necessity of supernatural anointing for church growth. In the next two characteristics we will look at prayer and praise as the two key elements for maintaining the empowered life.

A Look at Antioch

Look once again at our model church. Acts 13:2–3 provides a profound insight into the continual empowering of the church at Antioch. "And while they were ministering to the Lord and fasting, the Holy Spirit said, 'Set apart for Me Barnabas and Saul for the work to which I have called them.' Then, when they had fasted and prayed and laid their hands on them, they sent them away."

Notice that Luke emphasized, by repetition, the role of prayer and fasting in the life of the church at Antioch. Fasting is mentioned in both the Old and New Testaments. In Matthew 6 we find a detailed discussion of prayer and personal piety given to the disciples by the Lord Himself. Note the parallel phrases in verses 2, 5, and 16: "When therefore you give alms"; "And when you pray"; and "And whenever you fast." We have virtually ignored that the Lord Himself gave directions for fasting and prayer.

Some Bible interpreters even read this passage as negative instruction on fasting because it mentions the gloomy face of the hypocrites. Such is not the case. With careful reading you will note Jesus criticized the manner of giving alms and praying as well as the manner of fasting. In each case the hypocrites were abusing legitimate expressions of religious commitment. Jesus first corrected the abuse and then issued positive directions for giving alms, praying, and fasting. In the case of fasting, Jesus taught: "But you, when you fast, anoint your head, and wash your face so that you may not be seen fasting by men, but by your Father who is in secret; and your Father who sees in secret will repay you" (Matt. 6:17–18).

Matthew 17:14–21 is a second critical passage on fasting. The disciples had failed in their attempts to deliver a demon-possessed child. After Jesus delivered the boy, the disciples inquired about their inability to cast the demon from the lad. Jesus told them it was due to their little faith. Then He instructed them: "But this kind does not go out except by prayer and fasting" (v. 21). Fasting aids concerted and focused prayer.

Fasting is often linked with abstinence from food or drink for a period of time for the specific reason of focused prayer. Fasting may be planned or spontaneous. At times we are so driven by a specific burden that bodily needs such as food and drink are simply ignored. At other times we may establish a particular period of time to fast and pray for a specific need. The abstinence required by fasting provides additional time and gives greater focus to our prayer.

On one occasion at First Norfolk we had several days of planned prayer and fasting related to specific growth needs of the church. We provided prayer times at the church during meal times for those who could come and pray together, and challenged others to use that meal time for prayer at the home or office. The results were immediate and electric. For some, the physical hunger pangs created spiritual hunger pangs. One senior adult confessed this was the first time in his Christian life he had fasted for prayer. He couldn't come to the church but went into his camper parked beside his house for prayer. The physical hunger provided a constant reminder of his need for prayer. He was not only revived in his spiritual walk, but God used him to help meet the growth needs of our church. His story could be multiplied many times over. Skipping a meal or two is not a gimmick to get God's attention, but simply frees up time and helps us to focus in our prayer life.

Focused supernatural prayer was at the heart of the empowering of the church at Antioch. Notice that God gave this church a vision for sending Paul and Barnabas on a church planting mission beyond Antioch during worship as a direct result of their prayer and fasting. We've read the accounts of the Pauline missionary journeys so often they have become commonplace to us.

Think about it for a minute! Antioch was a newly established fellowship. Christianity itself was in its infancy. Mission trips were a novel idea to say the least. Travel was difficult and dangerous. How could one church have the audacity to believe they could be an instrument for spreading the gospel to the then-known world? Yet that is precisely what the Antioch church believed. This church was at the heart of the Pauline missionary journeys. Why? and how? Simply because they were willing to listen to and obey God. The vision to reach the world came from God and was received by the believers in Antioch. They were receptive because they were listening to God in prayer. I wonder how many churches miss out on the moving of the Spirit of God in their community simply because they are not listening in prayer?

Notice, too, they were ministering to the Lord (see Acts 13:2). The Greek word which is translated "ministering" is *leitergeo*, from which we get the English word *liturgy*. This church was not only praying and fasting, they were worshiping God. If we are going to see authentic and lasting growth, we must restore worship to its rightful place in the church. Worship, by its very design, causes us to focus our attention on God who alone is worthy of praise and worship. This focused attention keeps the church plugged into the power source for victorious Christian living and church growth. Prayer and praise are essential to church growth because God alone can grow His church.

The Biblical Pattern

The Bible is replete with examples where powerful prayer and praise form an indispensable channel for the empowering of God to flow through His people.

One clear example is the rebuilding of the wall of Jerusalem under the leadership of Nehemiah. The Babylonian captivity was a crushing blow to the national pride of Israel. The chosen people of God had been dragged from their homeland as their beloved temple was reduced to rubble. They found it difficult to worship their God in a strange land and longed for the day they could return and rebuild the temple and the city of Jerusalem. After seventy years, the captives were granted freedom by Cyrus, king of Persia, to return to the holy land and rebuild the temple. The Old Testament book of Ezra recounts the story of the rebuilding of the temple.

Yet, the opening paragraph of the Book of Nehemiah tells us that the remnant who returned to Jerusalem were in great distress and reproach because the wall of Jerusalem was little more than a rubble heap (1:3). Nehemiah had not returned to Jerusalem but had remained in Susa, the capital of Babylon, as a cupbearer to the king. Nehemiah's comfort zone was shattered when he heard the news that the wall of Jerusalem was broken down and the people were distressed.

Nehemiah's reaction to this news and the subsequent events of this book provide a model for the supernatural flow of God's power through His people. Nehemiah's first response was to pray: "Now it came about when I heard these words, I sat down and wept and mourned for days; and I was fasting and praying before the God of heaven" (1:4). The spontaneous prayer of Nehemiah was not a "one-time, back-against-the-wall" reaction. As you read the Book of Nehemiah, you find constant references to prayer.

For example, in Nehemiah 2:4–5 Nehemiah had come before King Artaxerxes. The king noticed his sad countenance and inquired about his distress. After hearing about the conditions of Jerusalem the king asked Nehemiah: "What would you request?" Notice the response, particularly its order: "So I prayed to the God of heaven. And I said to the king." Even before Nehemiah asked a favor of the king, he consulted with the God of heaven. Later when the work of rebuilding was ridiculed and opposition arose, how did Nehemiah respond? "But we prayed to our God, and because of them we set up a guard against them day and night" (4:9). When the enemy tried to discourage and frighten Nehemiah and his workers, he whispered a prayer: "O God, strengthen my hands" (6:9).

Prayer must precede and produce activity if our activity is to be productive. Too often in the church we plan our strategy and programs with little thought to prayer until we look on in helpless amazement while another "surefire" program brings little results. It is not that prayer should replace our programs or strategies for growth, but it must *precede and permeate* them. Prayer is not inactivity; it is intense supernatural activity. It must be our *first* activity, not our last.

Prayer also produces meaningful service. Note that Nehemiah had a plan from the Lord, and he was steadfast to follow that plan. He did not simply sit at the base of the wall and pray, but he prayed as he sent the workers to the wall. Prayer must permeate the ongoing activity of our churches if it is to be empowered by God. Notice that Nehemiah recruited the people to join him by telling them how the hand of his God had been favorable to him (see Neh. 2:18). Not only did Nehemiah know that the power was from God, but also he wanted the people who followed Him to know the results had been given by God. This is a good rule for church growth activity today.

If prayer is one major theme in the Book of Nehemiah, praise and worship is the other. The phrase, "the great and awesome God" is repeated many times over in this book. It is a phrase of worship. When discouragement rose up to engulf the workers, Nehemiah would cry out: "Do not be afraid of them; remember the Lord who is great and awesome, and fight for your brothers"(4:14). When the wall was completed, Nehemiah gathered the people in the square and led them in worship, celebrating the activity of God through them. Chapter 9 is a lengthy hymn of praise composed for that day of celebration. Listen to the beginning lines:

> O may Thy glorious name be blessed and exalted above all blessing and praise! Thou alone art the Lord. Thou hast made the heavens, the heaven of heavens with all their host, the earth and all that is on it, the seas and all that is in them. Thou dost give life to all of them and the heavenly host bows down before Thee. (9:5–6)

The accounts of the disciples in the Book of Acts provide a

similar pattern. In our haste to read about the tremendous harvest at Pentecost, we leap over the preparation for Pentecost. Note Acts 1:14: "These all with one mind were continually devoting themselves to prayer, along with the women, and Mary the mother of Jesus, and with His brothers." Then the empowering of God came as He gave the Person of the Holy Spirit, and the disciples began to witness with great boldness. Peter's sermon produced God-sized results as about three thousand believers were added to the church.

The church birthed at Pentecost continued the same strategy; "And they were continually devoting themselves to the apostles' teaching and to fellowship, to the breaking of bread and to prayer" (Acts 2:42). Further, we are told there was gladness and sincerity of heart as the people were praising God. The formula sounds simplistic in our day of technological church growth, but look at the explosive growth. "And the Lord was adding to their number day by day those who were being saved" (Acts 2:47). Notice that the numerical growth of the church came naturally out of the transformed life of the church fueled by prayer and praise.

Because of the essential nature of prayer and praise, we will consider them in two separate characteristics.

Worship, the Wellspring of Church Growth

Many books and conferences on church growth address the issue of worship and church growth, but focus primarily on worship as an entry point for the unbeliever or first time visitor. Some have called worship the "front door" to church growth. This emphasis has grown with the focus on "seeker-targeted" or "seeker-friendly" worship services. Yet the emphasis on worship as a front door to numerical growth may have caused us to overlook other aspects of the role of worship in church growth. I would go so far as to say that authentic worship is the wellspring of most elements of church growth.

What Is Worship?

How do we begin to define worship? Warren Wiersbe defines it thus: "Worship is the believer's response with all that he is—

mind, emotions, will, and body—to all that God is and says and does. This response has its mystical side in subjective experience, and its practical side in objective obedience to God's revealed truth. It is a loving response that is balanced by the fear of the Lord, and it is a deepening response as the believer comes to know God better."[1] Evelyn Underhill defines worship as "the total adoring response of man to the one Eternal God self-revealed in time."[2]

Authentic worship is the believer's response to the self-revelation of God. When Isaiah saw the Lord sitting on a throne, lofty and exalted, with the train of His robe filling the temple, he responded with authentic worship. His response to the presence of God was awed praise mixed with contrite confession and repentance. He heard the seraphim cry out; "Holy, Holy, Holy, is the Lord of hosts, The whole earth is full of His glory" (Isa. 6:3). In response Isaiah cried out: "Woe is me, for I am ruined! Because I am a man of unclean lips, And I live among a people of unclean lips; For my eyes have seen the King, the Lord of hosts" (6:5). His encounter with the living God elicited his commitment to be God's messenger. "Then I heard the voice of the Lord, saying, 'Whom shall I send, and who will go for Us?' Then I said, 'Here am I; Send me!'" (6:8).

Worship originates with God and demands the response of His people. Isaiah's experience with Holy God led him to respond through confession, repentance, praise, and sacrificial service. True worship's primary goal is to give glory and honor to God, and it always results in the edification of the worshiper, leading him or her to serve the living God who is the object of worship. Thus worship involves both giving and receiving, commitment and blessing. True worship is balanced, involving the mind, emotions, and the will of the worshiper. It incorporates both attitudes, such as reverence, awe, and respect, and actions, such as bowing, praising, serving, and giving.

Robert Webber, in his excellent book on worship, has reminded us that worship is a verb. True worship, he declares, will always evoke an activity of response. It is something the people of God do individually and collectively to please God.[3]

Thus the singular motive for worship is to glorify and please God alone. This poses a word of warning. If we ever attempt to use worship for any purpose other than to glorify and honor God, then we have begun to move away from authentic worship. Worship may have several church growth ramifications, such as the edification of the saints and the reaching of the lost, but the primary focus of worship is the adoration of God. It is wrong to think that we can *use worship to grow our church*. We don't use worship. We worship! Worship's focus is singular—to adore God; its ramifications are many.

If worship is a divine encounter initiated by Holy God, then why do we treat it with casual disdain, both in our preparation and in our attendance? In worship we are not simply to observe the encounter of God with humanity, but we are allowed to be participants in this divine and unique experience. How then do we explain the relative boredom engendered by the average worship service? How do we explain the apathy with which it is treated by those who claim to serve the living God? What is missing in our understanding of worship and in our execution of that which we call the worship service?

The Elements of Biblical Worship

Worship has often been compared to a play. For every actor on the stage, a prompter stands ready in the wings to help should the actor hesitate or forget his line. In authentic worship the prompter is the Holy Spirit. Those on the platform are not the only participants in the play; they assist the congregation who is also part of the cast. Every believer assembled in the sanctuary is involved in the participatory drama of worshiping God, who, with the heavenly hosts, observes.

Remember, we cannot create a worship experience for our people. We can only provide the opportunity for genuine worship to occur and teach people to worship.

What are the elements which must be present to provide the opportunity for God's people to participate in worship? Franklin Segler describes ten elements of worship evident in the New Testament church:
- Music
- The reading of Scripture
- Prayers

- The people's "amens"
- The sermon or exposition of the Scriptures
- Exhortation
- Giving
- Doxologies
- Confession of sin
- The ordinances of baptism and the Lord's Supper[4]

For worship to be authentic it must focus on praising and adoring God. Using the modern terminology of "targeting," we must conclude that the true target of worship is God and God alone. Worship targets neither the believer nor the unbeliever, but the great and awesome God. Yet in many churches a performance mindset focused on appealing to the customers has replaced the overwhelming sense of awe and reverence engendered by being in the presence of Holy God. John MacArthur, Jr. has rightly warned that our duty in worship is not to please the non-Christian, but to please God.[5] We have somehow lost the awe of being invited to enter into the presence of the living God. As pastors, we can spend our time worrying about the technical quality of the service, rather than worshiping. As laity we can spend our time evaluating the performers rather than bowing before God in humble yet joyous adoration. In either case, we are robbing God and impoverishing ourselves.

The pastor is the worship leader even when he works in conjunction with other staff persons or laypersons who are gifted in worship leadership. This is not just a functional statement, but a practical one. I have learned congregants consistently watch the pastor for worship clues, even when someone else is directing the music or leading other elements of worship. If you are a pastor and don't believe this, focus your attention on something or someone in the congregation and watch the response of the congregation. They will look where you are looking.

Early in my ministry I often would sit on the platform, fidget with my preaching notes, glance often at my watch, and wonder how much of my preaching time the music was going to consume. Once I began to participate in worship, worship took on new significance to me and the congregation. I was always surprised how quickly it came time for me to preach. When I worship, I sense a greater empowering for preaching.

Let's look at a few of the elements of authentic worship. For the believer, worship involves praise through music, prayer, attention to the Word, offering, and commitment to service. Music, for many, is the central thread which knits the many elements of worship together. Music should not be selected with the intention of educating a congregation concerning the virtues of a certain style of music, but rather on its suitability for leading the people to focus on and adore God. The style of music might vary from context to context, and thus an attempt to argue that a certain style of music is the only appropriate music for a growing church is narrow and short-sighted. Music should be chosen that is culturally suitable and theologically sound. It then should be presented positively and powerfully. The music should never be regarded as a prelude to preaching or as filler intended to cover the awkward transitions in worship, but as an integral component for a worshiping family.

Prayer was central to New Testament worship, but it is often an afterthought in today's service. Some scrupulously time prayers making sure they do not exceed a certain length for fear they may appear boring on television or irrelevant to the seeker. Yet prayer is an opportunity to come boldly before the throne of grace in the very presence of the Creator of the universe. Prayer permits us to verbally acknowledge the presence of God, to stand before Him in praise, to confess our sins, to seek forgiveness, to offer ourselves to God, to ask provision for our daily needs, to intercede for others, and to offer thanksgiving to our gracious God. Prayer is personal conversation with God and ought never to be taken lightly. It provides an excellent barometer of the spiritual condition of a congregation. Prayer as we have already indicated is the umbilical cord for the supernatural empowering of the church to function in the spiritual realm.

Throughout the New Testament, reading Scripture was central to worship. The Word of God has a dynamic power inherent in it, and therefore we should never underestimate the impact of Scripture properly and powerfully read. I do not believe, as some suggest, that we should play down the role of Scripture in worship under the guise of targeting seekers. The Word of God has more profound power than any of our human strategies. Always pay attention to the presentation of Scripture. Whoever reads the Scripture should be well prepared so that it is read with feeling and focus. Short passages can sometimes be read in unison with great effect. Certain passages lend themselves to a dramatic monologue. Occasionally our choir would quote Scripture together as a part of or prelude to a musical number. Variety in the presentation of Scripture can be an effective way of ensuring that people hear and experience the powerful Word of God.

Preaching the Word is a centerpiece of worship. Preaching is declaring the truth of God in the power of the Holy Spirit. Paul expressed his conviction about the centrality of preaching in the first two chapters of 1 Corinthians. The Jews, Paul said, clamored for signs—some spectacular evidence of God's presence and power (see 1:22). Sounds a little like the "signs and wonders" movement in church growth. The Greeks, he continued, sought for wisdom (see 1:22). Thus Paul determined to preach the cross of Christ because it was the power and wisdom of God (see 1:23). Paul could have been tempted to meet the "felt need" of his day for dramatic signs and wisdom, but rather he chose to meet the real issue of human need through the preaching of the cross.

I am not suggesting that modern-day preaching should not address the relevant issues of our day—it should. I am, however, insisting that the measure of relevance is not determined by the world, based on some marketing survey, but by Scripture itself. The world order is irrelevant and passing away, but the Word of God abides forever. Know the needs of your congregation and community, but address those needs with timeless biblical truth. You cannot compromise any biblical truth because it may not square with the results of a marketing survey.[6] You must preach the full counsel of God's Word. Yet without an awareness of the needs, pains, and questions of your people, you may be applying medicine where there is no injury.

Preachers today must earn the right to speak and be heard. In the past we could introduce sermons with, "The Bible says" and expect people to listen. To earn the right to be heard, we may point first to the felt need or critical issue. This can be done in the introduction of the sermon. Contemporary preaching also requires regular application of biblical truth. Preachers cannot assume their listeners will make the application they think they should. Sermons that apply the truth of God's immutable Word to the pains of the congregation will prompt both human interest and supernatural response.

Do not hesitate to use drama, monologue, or other innovative ideas to bring variety into worship services. Sometimes the sameness of a certain worship pattern can cause people to become dulled to sensing God's presence and hearing His Word. When a new element to worship is introduced, make sure that it is done well, is appropriate, is not overused, and does not detract from the worship experience.

Occasionally I have had our laypeople plan and do a short skit as an appropriate introduction to the particular message I was preaching. On one particular Sunday, I began my sermon standing in one of the aisles with a softball in hand. I asked those seated to my left to specify its color. They responded, "White." I then asked those seated to my right the same question, and they responded, "Black." Both were correct since I had painted the ball so that it was half white and half black. I then threw it gently into the air spinning it and declared that it was actually gray. I then asked whether we had any right to insist that there were actually black or white issues having absolute answers. "Is abortion a choice or murder? Is homosexuality an alternative life-style or sin? We say one thing, the world says another. Who's right? Is anybody right, or is it another gray issue?" Needless to say I had everyone's attention as I began my sermon on establishing moral values.

We must be careful not to overuse such innovative elements or they will become trite. We must also be careful not to rely on them or to think our major task is to entertain those in the congregation because that is what they have come to expect. Hear me carefully—good, strong, biblical preaching can be entertaining, but our goal is not entertainment. I am afraid that in our haste to respond to some of the marketing studies, we may be tempted to overemphasize entertainment at the expense of powerful, moving, and convicting worship.

Not too long ago I was one speaker at an event that had several different worship opportunities. My audience was primarily Baby Boomers and Baby Busters. I used an appealing and contemporary introduction, but the bulk of the message was an exposition of Scripture with a call to commitment. After the service a string of young adults came to me thanking me for the emphasis. Several stated that my message was the first in which a speaker asked them to open the Bible or required them to follow a text. Because of the desire to appeal to the perceived needs and interests of these particular age group, those planning the conference had scheduled a lot of music, drama, and humor. These were all well done, but none spoke to the great need of those present like the powerful, preached Word of God. Remember what Paul wrote? "For since in the wisdom of God the world through its wisdom did not come to know God, God was well-pleased through the foolishness of the message preached to save those who believe" (1 Cor. 1:21).

Some marketers have found the offering to be an offensive element of worship, something to be down-played or removed altogether. Yet the offering was a high point of worship, both in the life of Israel and in the New Testament church. It was a time for recognizing God's ownership, human stewardship, and the graciousness of life itself. I believe that worship through the offering of ourselves and our possessions should still be a central and joyous component of worship. Rather than relegating it to an afterthought for the sake of the seeker—or perhaps more truthfully, the backslidden believer—we should seek to revitalize it and give it renewed meaning for our people.

Worship through giving our offerings should never be interpreted as the means for subscribing a budget, but as a vehicle for expressing our dependence upon God and our gratitude for His loving provision for all our needs. The giving of His tithe and our offerings is a sacrifice of a priestly people, and as such, it is our privilege and joy to bring Him the sacrifice of praise, good deeds, and sharing (see Heb. 13:15–16). Tragically we have divorced the giving of our money from its theological foundation and thus have trivialized it, making it little more than the punch line to a joke about being an essential element of a church meeting.

Lest you think the offering may be an impediment to the church's ability to attract the unsaved, remember that many unbelievers are struggling with greed and avarice and may be profoundly moved to witness the generosity of the people of God. Our uniqueness in this area of life may present a more powerful testimony to unbelievers than we could envision.

Finally, authentic worship always calls the worshiper to commitment and active response. In a real sense the call to commitment is the natural and spontaneous outflow of all the aforementioned components of worship. Here again many are tempted to de-emphasize the public call to commitment for fear of offending the seeker or Boomer. While Paul spoke of his willingness to become all things to all men in order that he might save some (see 1 Cor. 9:22), he in no way meant he would compromise the preaching of the gospel.[7]

Jesus did not hesitate to call persons to make public commitments in order to follow Him. The Boomer is no different than any unsaved person of any generation who does not like to be confronted with his or her sinful condition nor called to commitment. Yet the gospel is confrontational, and the presence of the Holy Spirit will lead Boomers and Busters alike to deep commitments. If we do not call for transformational commitment, we will get precisely what we ask for—shallow commitment to a "lite" gospel.

A recent edition of *Forum Files*, published by Leadership Network, reported that church attendance of Boomers is actually dropping. They also noted with alarm a growing consumerist mentality towards religion. Because people have changed from stewards to consumers, they are simply buying specific services.[8] This finding should not surprise us. We marketed for the Boomers by emphasizing the services our churches provided and minimizing the commitment the Lord desired. You will not get a commitment level deeper than that which you call for up front. Jesus constantly told His would-be followers to count the cost before they followed Him. The call to deep commitment will not turn Boomer and Busters away; it will turn them on.

Some use 1 Corinthians 14:20–25 and the prohibition of public displays of the gift of tongues to defend removing offensive elements, such as the call to commitment, from worship for the sake of the seeker. A careful reading of that same text reveals that the impact of prophesy on the unbeliever is laying bare the heart, disclosing sin, and recognizing the awesome reality that God is among the worshipers. True worship with its focus on God by its very nature calls the sinner and the saint to response. We may look at different ways to issue the call to commitment, but we cannot fail to confront sin and to draw the net of commitment.

We do not have to make the call to commitment offensive for it to be effective. For some the word *confrontational* is synonymous with *offensive*. Many persons inside and outside the church have been turned off by an emotional, manipulative invitation. Such an invitation reveals carnality at its worst because it suggests that we can't trust the Holy Spirit to call people to Christ. Give the invitation clearly, powerfully, and with certainty, and allow the Holy Spirit to grant the harvest.

I found it helpful to prepare the people for the call to commitment even before the worship service began. We frequently had many visitors to First Norfolk who were not familiar with the way we extended the invitation to respond to Christ's call to commitment. Before the choir entered the choir loft, I took a few minutes to welcome those present. If there were any unusual or different nuances to our worship service on a particular Sunday, I alerted everyone before the service. For example, if the congregants needed their bulletin for a chorus, I told them prior to the service so that no one would feel awkward. During these preliminary remarks I would say something like this: "Many needs and reasons have drawn us here. You will find that God's Word will speak powerfully to your life today. A part of the worship experience is our response to God's Word. We will provide an opportunity near the end of our service for you to make a public response as you feel led. You can do this by simply stepping into the aisle and meeting one of our pastors here at the front." I would then lead the congregation in a brief time of prayer and meditation while the choir entered. I would ask each person to pray about any decision they might need to make.

When I extended the invitation, I again tried to make it clear what a person needed to do to respond to God's call. I told them that trained counselors were prepared to pray with them in private and that no one would be singled out or embarrassed. After the invitation concluded and just prior to the benediction, I extended a final and less confrontational invitation similar to this: "Some of you may be visiting with us for the first time, and you weren't sure what was happening when people began to come down the aisles to respond to God's Word. The Bible teaches us that it is important for us to publicly respond to God. Perhaps you felt a need to receive Christ or to join the church or you may have a personal need for prayer today. After our final prayer, trained and loving counselors will be available to assist you. You can find them just to my left at the double doors." (I then pointed to their location and generally had someone there who would raise a hand.) Rather than playing down the invitation, we gave it even greater emphasis.

The Impact of Worship on Church Growth

How then, does authentic worship impact church growth? Perhaps the most obvious answer for some is that worship provides the church with the opportunity to reach the sinner. Kennon Callahan, for example, states that "now more often unchurched persons find their way first through the service of worship." James Emery White has focused on targeting the lost in his book, *Opening the Front Door: Worship and Church Growth.*[9] Both are correct in emphasizing that, in some circumstances, people will find it less threatening to attend an exciting and celebrative worship service before they attend a small group. The evangelistic impact of the worship service is certainly vital to church growth—and I will speak to this issue—but not as a first priority. Targeting the unsaved is not the first issue of worship; adoring and praising sovereign God is the first issue. The unsaved are not the primary participants of worship. In fact, I can find no theological support for the ability of the unsaved to join in worship other than as observers.

The participants in worship are not unsaved seekers, but the people of God. Therefore, it is proper to give first attention to the impact genuine worship has on the people of God.

First, authentic worship provides the supernatural empowering for the people of God. God promised to inhabit the praise of His people (see Ps. 22:3). When Moses was called to lead Israel out of bondage, he felt ill-prepared and incompetent to accomplish the task. The encounter with the great "I Am" assured him that the resources for victory were not his own, but were abundantly available from God Himself (see Ex. 3–4). Looking back on the growth at First Norfolk, I could point to numerous occasions where worship was a key element in assuring us of God's sufficiency to meet our needs. In one instance, we planned twelve worship services around various names for God. The understanding of the character and nature of God proved to be a catalyst for renewed ministry and growth.

Recently I received a church newsletter from Phoenix, Arizona that demonstrated supernatural empowering through worship. The article was written on August 23, 1993 by Gary Young, the pastor of First Baptist, Phoenix. Gary began the article with the bad news that his cancer had returned. In a moving letter that had the tenor of a "last testament," Gary talked about a transformation which had revitalized his church. "When and how did our church change? I believe it started years ago when God began convicting us about worship. . . . Our Statement of Purpose used to say: 'Win the lost, nurture the saved, meet human need.' Gordon (the minister of music) insisted that first we must worship God, then receive divine resources to do the rest. He was right. We refocused. When we did, the Holy Spirit was able to take more and more control of us through worship thereby producing more Christian maturity." Gary died September 20, a month after writing the article.

Second, God often communicates His strategy for His people during times of worship. Biblical examples abound, but let's focus on one from the New Testament. In Acts 13:1–3 we are told that the church at Antioch prayed and fasted and ministered to the Lord. While they were worshiping, the Holy Spirit told them to set aside Paul and Barnabas for the task of world evangelization. Worship is essential to church growth. This is God's strategy for your church reaching its world, too. We often reverse this divine plan. We develop our own plans, and then cry out to God to bless them lest they fail. If we first discover His plan, then we can be assured that it already carries His blessing. Some of you may be thinking, "What is he talking about? God isn't going to give us a strategy for reaching our community." That very thought indicates our anti-supernatural bias and the carnal state of our own thinking about church growth. We have not, because we ask not (see Jas. 4:12).

Third, authentic worship is the key to committed service. Isaiah's worship encounter is often pointed to as a premier example of adoring worship (see Isa. 6). He heard the seraphim call to one another: "Holy, Holy, Holy is the Lord of hosts; the whole earth is full of His glory" (v. 3). Yet that is not all Isaiah heard. "Then I heard the voice of the Lord saying, 'Whom shall I send, and who will go for Us?'" Isaiah's response came from his worship experience. "Here am I. Send me!" (v. 8). How often has your church's ability to grow been hampered by the lack of committed servants? Perhaps we should spend more time in serious prayer and joyous worship and less in anxious begging for live bodies to work in the children's division. After all, it is the Lord of the harvest who calls out the laborers (Matt. 9:38).

Fourth, worship is essential to the evangelistic ministry of the church. Allow me to first underscore the fact that a passion for the lost is born in the hearts of believers who encounter Holy God. I have already alluded to Isaiah's willingness to go and to the church at Antioch's readiness to send Paul and Barnabas as both emerging from worship. We shouldn't overlook the obvious connection between worship and the actual giving of the Great Commission. Matthew recorded: "And when they saw Him, they worshiped Him" (Matt. 28:17). Worship preceded the giving of the commission. Here we must inquire about the connection between the lack of evangelistic activity in the average church and the careless and apathetic forms of worship there. Are they not inextricably bound together? If worship is dull and uninspiring, can we maintain any zeal for evangelistic outreach? I would also inquire of those who claim to major on "quality worship" and yet who demonstrate no interest in evangelistic ministry. Whatever its style or quality, is such worship genuine?

Under the theme of evangelism, I would also point to the presence of unsaved in the worship service. It is true that in some situations the unsaved person may first attend a given church through an invitation to the worship service. This may be less threatening to some persons than entry through a small group. For this reason, do we alter the service to make it more seeker-friendly? I do believe the church should be sensitive to the unsaved who attend. We do not need to erect artificial or traditional barriers that might form an impediment to the gospel. Seeker sensitivity begins in the parking lot and must permeate every organization and element of the church. If we discover certain traditional elements of worship—such as the assumption that all the attenders know exactly what to do at every point in the service, or the way we recognize guests—are creating barriers, then by all means we must tear them down.

We cannot, however, compromise on the biblical distinctives of worship. I believe a powerful worship experience in which the people of God respond to the presence of God will do more to draw sinners to Christ than all the marketing strategies we can devise. It is true that unbelievers may leave not entirely sure they understood all that occurred. In truth, they can't understand our worship because they do not know our God! But they will sense that God was in our midst. Jesus promised: "And I, if I be lifted up from the earth, will draw all men to Myself" (John 12:32). When we present the crucified, risen, and exalted Christ in the power of the Holy Spirit, He will draw the unsaved.

What many proponents of seeker-targeted services have not recognized is the principle working behind the method. Remember, methods come and go and must be contextualized, but principles work consistently. The principle working behind the method of seeker services is the personal invitation. Church growth statisticians agree that between 79 percent to 86 percent of persons who attend a particular church do so because of the personal invitation of a friend or relative. The seeker service has worked, in part, because it is novel and exciting, and, in part, because we convinced our people they can invite their friends, and their friends will be comfortable when they attend our worship services. Do not assume people will simply flock to your door because you change the style of your service. You must still invite them to come.

Second, do not think the seeker service is a shortcut to evangelism and church growth which makes visitation unnecessary. Jesus commissioned His church to *go* and make disciples. He called His followers to go into the highways and byways and compel them to come in so His house could be full (see Luke 14:23). We have overlooked a significant theological truth. An unsaved person is spiritually dead and dead people don't walk. Every generation faces the temptation to exchange a "go and tell" strategy for a "come and see" approach. *The mandate is for the church to go, not for the sinner to come.* Don't misunderstand me. I believe in opening the front door through exciting worship. I think you should open the side door through Sunday School or cell groups. Punch all the holes in the church you can, and take the roof off in the process (that's biblical—remember the paralytic's four friends?). Yet if we are to reach the unsaved, we must first encounter them in the marketplace before we can invite them to visit our place.

Fifth, worship is critical to church growth because of its transforming impact on the lives of believers. We can think of the obvious issues of teaching, exhortation, and consolation that are a part of the worship experience. We could also point to the use of spiritual gifts of members in the worship service. Primarily, we should point to the transformation of life that occurs when an individual genuinely encounters the living God. Isaiah first became acutely aware of his own sin. Moses came down from the mountain with his face aglow. Paul was blinded by the presence of the risen Lord. Yet all alike were transformed. Genuine worship should be evidenced in the service, giving, and mission zeal of the local congregation. If we have truly met with God, we cannot leave without being molded into His image.

If we think now concerning the comprehensive definition of church growth—involving not only numerical growth, but also maturational growth which evidences itself in missions ventures and giving—we can see the inextricable relationship between worship and church growth.

Designing a Worship Service

In designing a worship service, we should think first about the style. Some confusion exists today because numerous terms are used, such as contemporary, innovative, seeker-targeted, traditional, to refer to particular styles of services. I have chosen not to use such terms to refer to churches or styles of worship services for several reasons. First, such uses will quickly become irrelevant. When an innovative method is copied and becomes the norm, it is no longer innovative. That which is contemporary at one moment in time is quickly dated in today's society. Second, terms such as innovative and contemporary can be divisive when used in reference to churches because they imply that a different style of church is neither innovative nor contemporary. Worship styles differ so greatly from one denomination to the next and from one part of the world to the next; what may be innovative in one place may be traditional in another. What God uses in one context may be little more than a powerless copy in another.

Rather than getting bogged down in terminology, look for what makes a difference in terms of worship and church growth. Kirk Hadaway studied extensive survey results to isolate principles that aided churches in growth. When he looked at the issue of worship in the growing church, he concluded that worship could impact the ability of a church to grow numerically. First, he detected a difference in the character of worship services in growing churches as compared with plateaued or declining churches. To the surprise of many, he concluded that no particular style of worship was characteristic of the growing church. Some growing churches were more structured or liturgical while others were more relaxed and casual. What did seem to matter could only be defined with words like exciting, celebrative, joyful, expectant, warm, spirit of revival, spontaneous, and even exuberant. Thus the spirit of the service is more important than its style or the type of music used.

Hadaway noted that the sense of excitement is enhanced by the crowded worship center of the growing church. In most instances the growing church paid careful attention to the appearance of the worship center, giving the clear message that worship is a matter of great consequence.

The content of the worship service in a growing church is a dynamic mix of congregational singing, prayer, choir anthems, announcements, testimonies, drama, and more. Hadaway noted that while the components are not all that different from most services in declining churches, the distinctive was in the power and movement of the service. It has been my own experience that a key element in powerful worship is the flow of the service. The various elements of the service are not disconnected entities but a portion of a larger tapestry. Dead spots and irrelevant intrusions are removed. The worshiper is spiritually swept along by the flow of the service.

Regarding the matter of preaching style in the growing church, you might find Hadaway's results surprising. He discovered little correlation between growth and the quality or style of preaching. I grew up when the emphasis among growing churches was on expository preaching, usually lasting thirty minutes and longer. Today some insist that preaching should be no more than twenty to twenty-five minutes and topical in nature, focusing on felt needs rather than on the exposition of the text. Here again we can get hung up on method, style, or the particular gifts of an individual preacher. You can find growing churches with pastors whose styles of preaching, lengths of sermons, and preaching abilities vary greatly. According to Hadaway, the preaching factors that did contribute to growth were the centrality of the Bible in the preaching event, and the absolute confidence of the preacher in the authority of Scripture combined with the ability to generate enthusiasm, communicate a vision for the future, and maintain high morale. You don't have to be a great pulpiteer or copy another pastor's style to grow a great church. You must faithfully utilize your preaching gifts, preach the Bible with authority, confidence, and enthusiasm, and exalt Christ.

Most of the debate concerning worship centers on the style and presentation of music. Some argue for gospel music, others contemporary, and still others liturgical. Some churches sing all their hymns from the hymn book while others use overheads or song sheets. You can find growing and declining churches alike who do all of the above. The key factor when it comes to music, according to Hadaway, is the quality of presentation. Ninety percent of growing churches rated their music programs as good or excellent. The music in the growing church is carefully planned but also has an element of spontaneity.[10]

What style of music is best for your church? No one can answer that for another church. Ask instead: What works best in our context? What sort of gifted musicians has God given us? Whatever style of music you choose, present it with quality and touch the full range of human feelings. Worship music should reflect the diversity of the congregation in hymns, anthems, and choruses. Most churches will find it necessary to use a variety of styles of music, and may want to blend choruses with anthems. Start simple and progress. Ensure that the musical instruments used for worship are regularly tuned. Insist on the very best quality possible in your given context and strive each week for improvement.

Six Steps to Changing Worship Styles

Perhaps you sense that your church needs to update and improve the worship experience. How do you make changes without alienating those who are perfectly happy with the current style?

1. *The change in worship styles must be initiated by trusted worship leaders.* If the pastor/staff has earned leadership respect in other areas of church life, the congregation will follow when meaningful and well-thought-out changes are made in worship. Leadership is not guaranteed by position, but earned through integrity in relationships. If your attitude is "my way or the highway," you had better have your bags packed. If your people sense your genuine spirit and know that you are a participant in worship, they are more apt to follow your lead when you suggest changes to improve worship.

2. *Move the congregation slowly and lovingly.* Remember that change is difficult for everyone, and when you suggest change in a worship style you are dealing with that which people consider sacred and immutable. You can turn a rowboat quickly and with little ill effect. When you want to turn an aircraft carrier, you need plenty of water and a wide berth. If you persist in turning the carrier too quickly, you will empty the deck of planes and render the ship impotent even though you head it in a different direction.

3. *Anticipate and deal with conflict.* The first time we used an orchestra in the worship service in Norfolk, a few people actually left. They were angered that we had brought rock music

into the church. The anthem that morning was from Handel's *Messiah*, hardly a rock and roll staple! Fortunately these persons were the exception rather than the rule. I would usually head off complaints by pointing out the obvious advantages of the variety of music we were using in our services. For example, I might notice that during a certain anthem some people were unmoved or perhaps antagonistic. Instead of ignoring the obvious, I would say, "Isn't this wonderful? Look at the diversity of our church. Some of you may not have liked that particular anthem, but did you notice that other members of our church were deeply moved? I am thrilled the First family is so open and loving that we can permit variety to meet the various needs of the members of our body." It is difficult to be negative in such a positive setting.

4. *Educate your people about worship.* People are often reluctant to make changes because they do not clearly understand the biblical or practical reasons behind the change. You may want to precede your worship changes with a series of messages on worship in the Bible. Many of the elements of worship we label as "non-traditional" have good scriptural warrant. The use of choruses, antiphonal music, various instruments, and dramatic portrayal are all found in Old Testament worship. Take your people to the Word, and allow the Holy Spirit to change them.

One of the most important things you can do to improve the quality of worship is to teach your people how to practice personal and private worship. Four steps appear to me to be basic: 1) a clear understanding of the person and character of God; 2) Scripture memorization aided by Scripture choruses; 3) an ability to do personal Bible study; and 4) instruction on how to pray. You can also assist your people by incorporating aspects of worship into committee and council meetings. Allow time for praise and thanksgiving before new business. Point out the activity of God in the various areas of your church's life. Give sufficient time for prayer to discover the plan of God.

5. *Keep quality in mind.* When you make a change, make sure that it is premiered with quality. If the change is an obvious improvement, there will be little complaint. In a majority of instances, you should not have to explain or draw attention to the change. If the change is so difficult that it requires detailed

explanation, the change may be too abrupt. If you need to alert people to differences in the service, do it prior to the service so that your explanation does not break the flow of the service.

6. *Use well-respected persons to help you introduce new elements to worship services.* One Sunday morning service we used the song, "Thank You," for the anthem. As the choir sang, actors and actresses from the church dramatized the words. A popular elderly lady in our church played the part of the teacher who was joined in heaven by the thankful people she had touched. The skit was well received because it was done with quality and involved respected layleaders in the church. Another option is to involve your youth to premier a new worship element on Sunday evening before trying it on Sunday morning. Sunday evening tends to be more relaxed and people will often respond to non-traditional elements when presented by youth.

You can move your congregation to accept new elements and different styles of worship, but make sure you aren't making changes just for the sake of change. If change becomes capricious or trite, it does not exalt the Father or grow the church. When worship focuses on experiencing and exalting the living God, believers will be empowered, and the lost will be brought to conviction.

Characteristic 3:

God-Connecting Prayer

The Role of Prayer in Church Growth

If the most critical element of church growth is supernatural empowering, then the fuel for all growth is powerful prayer. This seems so obvious as to be trite, yet the average pastor or church member has difficulty believing this is true. We may give lip service to it as truth. We may even want to believe it is true, but our practice and programming in the average church indicate we do not actually believe prayer is essential to all genuine church growth.

Look at the typical prayer meeting in most churches. It has degenerated into little more than an organ recital—a litany of prayers for ailing body organs: "Aunt Susie's liver, Uncle John's lungs, and Fred's colon." I am not making light of praying for physical healing. However, the truth is we spend more time praying to keep dying saints who are prepared to die out of heaven than we do to keep sinners out of hell. There is little passion to our praying and little confidence that it really does matter. We can object all we want, but the little time spent in prayer and the few who attend meetings for prayer tell another story.

When we confront an obstacle to our growth, our first thought turns toward programs, methods, and models. We are certain that a better outreach program would result in baptizing larger numbers of folks. If we could just get our people to sing choruses, we would attract the Boomers. If we had more money, another parking lot, a new bus, and the list is endless of the gadgets and gimmicks we think essential to the growth of our church. Now hear me carefully, I am not against methods nor organization. A church will not survive long without either, but we simply cannot rely on human strength and methodology to grow our church. We must experience supernatural empowering, and to do so we must give priority to prayer.

How fascinating that some who attempted to understand or imitate the tremendous growth of many churches in Korea choose to imitate their style of worship or use of cell groups. These may well be worthy of imitation, but they are hardly the source of the phenomenal growth. To understand the growth of the Korean churches or the tremendous evangelistic harvest now being experienced in many Third World nations, notice their dependence on prayer. Many Koreans arrive well before dawn to make their way to prayer mountain. Church history records a common thread through all church growth in every generation—prayer—concerted, focused, supernatural prayer. The methods and models will vary but prayer will be the constant. Thom Rainer in his book on church growth calls prayer the power behind the principles.[1]

The Biblical Pattern

The scriptural promises concerning prayer are well known to most Christians.

- John 15:7: "If you abide in Me, and My words abide in you, ask whatever you wish, and it shall be done for you."
- 1 John 3:22: "And whatever we ask we receive from Him, because we keep His commandments and do the things that are pleasing in His sight."
- James 4:2b: "You do not have because you do not ask."

It is apparent God wants to answer the prayers of His people, and we can be confident that we are praying according to His will when we pray about evangelistic church growth.

Could it be the primary reason so few churches are growing is prayerlessness? Have we simply not asked? Have we neglected His conditions concerning obedience to His Word and the resultant holy living?

God is looking for a people through whom He can demonstrate His mighty power (see Eph. 3:10). To experience supernatural church growth, we must have revival. God's conditions for revival have not changed. "And My people who are called by My name humble themselves and pray, and seek My face and turn from their wicked ways, then I will hear from heaven, will forgive their sin, and will heal their land. Now My eyes shall be open and My ears attentive to the prayer offered in this place" (2 Chron. 7:14–15). Do we want revival enough that we are willing to make prayer a priority in our personal and church schedules?

Notice that God does not simply call His people to prayer. God seeks a contrite people who will bow before Him in utter humility, recognizing their own unworthiness and His awesomeness. God waits for a people who will seek Him with utter abandon. Our goal is not to seek growth, but to seek Him. Finally, to know the full empowering of God, we must turn from our wicked ways. God desires to work through pure vessels. He demands holiness! Purity is more essential to church growth than any new program design.[2]

Perhaps the critical nature of prayer is summarized by two contrasting verses. "I can do all things through Him who strengthens me" (Phil. 4:13). "I am the vine, you are the branches; he who abides in Me, and I in him, he bears much fruit; for apart from Me you can do *nothing*" (John 15:5, author's italics). How much can be accomplished through supernatural empowering? ALL THINGS! What can be accomplished apart from supernatural empowering in Christ? NOTHING! It is not that we can achieve a limited amount without prayer; we can achieve nothing of eternal significance. The height of carnality is to hold to a form of godliness, but to deny the power of it (see 2 Tim. 3:5). When we attempt to grow the church devoid of prayer, we hold to a form of godliness, but we deny the supernatural power available to us.

The Prayer Life of Jesus

Our look at prayer would be inadequate without mentioning the prayer life of Jesus. This scene in Matthew's Gospel is familiar to us: "And after He had sent the multitudes away, He went up to the mountain by Himself to pray; and when it was evening, He was there alone" (14:23). The constant demands of ministry are physically and spiritually draining. Our Lord recognized these draining demands on His life and regularly found time alone for refueling through prayer. The reason that Jesus made prayer such a high priority becomes apparent when you look at His confession in John 14:10: "Do you not believe that I am in the Father, and the Father is in Me? The words that I say to you I do not speak on My own initiative, but the Father abiding in Me does His works." Notice that Jesus did nothing of His own initiative or empowering. If the perfect Son of God was totally dependent upon the Father for direction and empowering, what is the level of our need?

One other vignette might be helpful. Mark's Gospel is one of continuous activity and breakneck pace. The word "immediately" is characteristic of this Gospel. In the first twenty-eight verses of chapter one, Mark recorded these stories: the preaching of John the Baptist, the baptism of Jesus, His temptation, and His ministry in Galilee. But Mark's pacing did not to let up. Verse twenty-nine states: "And immediately after they had come out of the synagogue, they came into the house of Simon and Andrew, with James and John." Here Jesus healed Simon's mother-in-law creating such a stir that the whole city came out to see this miracle worker (see v. 33).

This context makes the next act of Jesus all the more significant. "And in the early morning, while it was still dark, He arose and went out and departed to a lonely place, and was praying there" (v. 35). That same morning the crowd returned, and the disciples panicked when they saw the throngs of people but no Healer. There may have been a barb of rebuke in Peter's voice when he finally found Jesus. "Everyone is looking for You" (v. 37). Jesus' response was unexpected to Peter and might surprise you: "Let us go somewhere else to the towns nearby, in order that I may preach there also; for that is what I came out for" (v. 38).

Why did Jesus want to leave when all the crowds had gathered at Simon's house? Our ego (the whole city was there) and our desire to do good (what about all the sick?) would have driven many of us back to the city. However, Jesus did not waver; He knew His primary task was to preach the gospel. Jesus spent time in prayer not only to experience the full empowering of His Father, but also to have the clear direction of His Father. Jesus could have experienced tremendous popularity and accomplished great good if He had spent His time on earth healing those with physical ailments. Seeing the great human need, He was tempted to do just that. Yet in the hubbub of constant activity, Jesus kept His perspective by spending time alone in prayer.

Not only are we dependent on prayer for empowering, we daily need God's direction found in it. When your church experiences growth, you will be pulled in many directions at once. After our first year of growth at Norfolk, we were inundated with ministry requests. Let's start a seaman's ministry! With three large college populations, we need a student ministry! What about a military ministry? We need to do something for the homeless! The list was endless and all the suggestions were good. Then came all the calls from those outside the church wanting a slice of my time or the resources of our church. All the requests were legitimate and I wanted to accommodate everyone. Without clear instructions from the Father, I would have mounted my horse, ridden off in all directions at once, and accomplished little.

If our Lord Jesus could do nothing apart from the Father's empowering, how much can we do? If Jesus needed daily direction from the Father, how great is our need?

The Disciples' Request

If you could be empowered to reproduce one activity of Jesus' earthly ministry to aid you in church growth, what would it be? Would you be tempted to ask for the power to heal? With the ravages of today's diseases, you could certainly make an impact for good. Think, too, about the media attention you would receive. People with AIDS, cancer, and all other forms of illness would be lined up at the doors of your church all hours of the day and night.

How about the ability to perform miracles? Think about the miracle of feeding the five thousand on a much larger scale. You could be instrumental in wiping out famine, and that would be just for starters. Such a ministry would draw worldwide attention to the church. It could certainly serve as a catalyst for church growth.

Both are tempting, but I think I might request that I be empowered to teach like Jesus. Every time He stopped to teach, huge crowds gathered around, standing or sittting for hours. He taught with such authority that lunch time seemed like an unnecessary intrusion. Quite a far cry from twelve noon Sunday morning at my church! Let me run five minutes over and people are banging their watches to see if they have stopped running. If I only had His teaching ability, I could grow a great church.

What was the singular request of Jesus' own disciples? "And it came about that while He was praying in a certain place, after He had finished, one of His disciples said to Him, 'Lord, teach us to pray just as John also taught his disciples'" (Luke 11:1). Remember this request came from Jewish men who had prayed from childhood. Yet they knew that Jesus' praying was qualitatively different from theirs. He prayed with intimacy and fervency. They knew that He was in constant dialogue with the Father, and that He received direction and empowering from the Father. They sensed that His prayer life was the key to all else they observed about His life and ministry.

If you could make one request for your ministry or church, would it honestly be, "Lord, teach us to pray"?

The Pattern of Acts

Most of us would agree that Acts is the textbook of church growth. Not only were great numbers of people being added to the church daily, but the number of churches was being increased on a regular basis. Acts is actually the second half of a two-part work that begins with Luke. Therefore, to understand the first chapters of Acts, begin with the last chapter of

Luke. "You are witnesses of these things. And behold, I am sending forth the promise of My Father upon you; but you are to stay in the city until you are clothed with power from on high" (24:48–49). The commission is linked to the command to wait. No ministry is to commence until they are clothed with power.

The Book of Acts continues this theme. Acts 1:4–5 repeats the emphasis on waiting and empowering. In verse eight the empowering is given specificity: "But you shall receive power when the Holy Spirit has come upon you; and you shall be My witnesses both in Jerusalem, and in all Judea and Samaria, and even to the remotest part of the earth." The empowering to fulfill the Great Commission is the empowering for church growth. Church growth is faithfully fulfilling the Great Commission in your given context and with a vision for the world.

Notice that the first activity of the disciples was prayer. "These all with one mind were continually devoting themselves to prayer, along with the women, and Mary the mother of Jesus, and with His brothers" (1:14). This was not a brief prayer meeting; they were continually devoting themselves to prayer. It is therefore not surprising to find the early church characterized by the same devotion to prayer. "And they were continually devoting themselves to the apostles' teaching and to fellowship, to the breaking of bread and to prayer" (2:42). The results of such praying included miracles and signs at the hands of the apostles, the sharing of possessions and the meeting of needs, unique fellowship, joyous praise, and daily additions to the church. This is the very description of the balanced growth we would all love to experience in our churches. It did not come as the result of a specific program, but as the direct result of supernatural praying. Our programs and methods are simply our way of organizing to accommodate the results that God gives supernaturally.

The pattern continues throughout Acts. Notice chapter 4. Peter and John were arrested for preaching the resurrection from the dead. When they appeared before the authorities who observed the confidence of Peter and John, they "understood that they were uneducated and untrained men, they were marveling, and began to recognize them as having been with Jesus"

(4:13). When Peter and John were released with a weak censure, they began to praise God (v. 24). Their one request: "grant that Thy bond-servants may speak Thy word with all confidence" (v. 29). In response to their prayer the place was shaken, and they spoke the Word of God with boldness.

The Pauline Example

Paul would certainly be considered one of the greatest church growth experts of all time. What did he consider essential for the healthy growth of the churches he planted? Let's look at the beginning of several of the Pauline letters.

- "I thank my God *always* concerning you, for the grace of God which was given you in Christ Jesus" (1 Cor. 1:4, author's italics).
- "For this reason I too, having heard of the faith in the Lord Jesus which exists among you, and your love for all the saints *do not cease* giving thanks for you, while making mention of you in my prayers" (Eph. 1:15–16, author's italics).
- "For this reason also, since the day we heard of it, *we have not ceased* to pray for you and to ask that you may be filled with the knowledge of His will in all spiritual wisdom and understanding" (Col. 1:9, author's italics).
- "We give thanks to God *always* for all of you, making mention of you in our prayers" (1 Thess. 1:2, author's italics).

Paul apparently believed that the most significant action he could take on behalf of the churches he loved was constant prayer.

What then was the content of his praying? If we could find a common theme, it might help us pray for our churches. Let me summarize these prayers in my own words.

Ephesians 1:17–24
That God may give you a spirit of wisdom and of revelation in the knowledge of Him so that you may know:
a. the hope of His calling
b. the riches of the glory of His inheritance in the saints
c. the surpassing greatness of His power toward us who believe.

Ephesians 3:14–20

For this reason, I bow my knees before the Father . . . that He would grant you to:

a. be strengthened with power in the inner man

b. experience the indwelling of Christ

c. know the love of Christ with all the saints

d. be filled up to all the fullness of God.

Benediction: Now to Him who is able to do exceeding abundantly beyond all that we ask or think, according to the power that works within us, to Him be the glory in the church and in Christ Jesus to all generations forever and ever. Amen.[3]

Colossians 1:9–10

We have not ceased to pray for you and to ask that:

1. You would be filled with the knowledge of His will in all spiritual wisdom and understanding so that you may:

a. walk in a worthy manner

b. please Him in all respects

c. bear fruit in every good work

d. increase in the knowledge of God

2. You would be strengthened with power according to His glorious might, for the attaining of all steadfastness and patience, joyously giving thanks to the Father.

Paul's essential prayer was that the believers in the church come to understand who they were and what supernatural resources had been made available to them. Notice the repeated emphasis on understanding, knowledge, and empowering. The need of the church is not for greater power, but for greater knowledge of the power already made available to us.

Further he prays for their worthy walk and personal fruitfulness. Fruitful living is directly tied to holiness. These would be effective patterns for our praying as we attempt to grow His church.

Paul taught the churches to pray for him and often related to them the results of their praying. In 2 Corinthians 1:8–11 Paul made reference to an affliction so great that he despaired of life. In that context he thanked the Corinthians for joining their prayers with the prayers of many for his deliverance. It is therefore not surprising that Paul frequently made prayer requests on his own behalf. Let's look at two:

- "And pray on my behalf, that utterance may be given to me in the opening of my mouth, to make known with boldness the mystery of the gospel, for which I am an ambassador in chains; that in proclaiming it I may speak boldly, as I ought to speak" (Eph. 6:19–20).
- "Finally, brethren, pray for us that the word of the Lord may spread rapidly and be glorified, just as it did also with you; and that we may be delivered from perverse and evil men; for not all have faith" (2 Thess. 3:1–2).

Paul desired prayer for an unfettered gospel and for protection for those declaring the gospel. Could it be that our lack of evangelistic results does not signal the need for a new evangelistic tool, but for a return to concerted praying for the powerful presentation of the gospel? Note that when Paul encouraged entreaties, prayers, petitions, and thanksgiving for kings and those in authority (see 1 Tim. 2:1–3), his concern was for peaceful conditions that would enable the church to declare the gospel. Why? Because he knew that God desires that all people be saved and come to the knowledge of the truth (v. 4).

Praying for Church Growth

Can we then formulate a specific pattern of praying for church growth today? I would suggest the following based on the biblical examples and teachings we have just considered:

1. Pray for persons in authority (around the world, in our nation, in our local communities, and in your church) so that peaceful conditions will reign, and the gospel will be spread.
2. Pray for safety and boldness for all those involved in the outreach program of your church.
3. Pray for the unsaved specifically and by name.
4. Pray that every church member will come to understand and appropriate the full resources available to them in Christ.
5. Pray that every church member will walk worthy of their calling and that the spirit of unity will be maintained.
6. Pray to the Lord of the harvest that He would impel laborers into the vineyard.

7. Pray for growth needs by name and with specific application. (For example, "We need four preschool teachers.")

Teach Your People How to Pray

We have somehow come to think that Christians inherently know how to pray. New Christians need fundamentals on praying as a first priority, yet few churches provide a basic course on fundamentals such as how to pray, study your Bible, and worship. The need for understanding how to pray does not stop with new Christians; it includes those who have been Christians for many years. All believers need to know how to pray more intimately and effectively.

If you are a pastor, you might begin by preaching a series on prayer. This could naturally lead to a study group on prayer using one of the many good books on prayer available to you through a local Christian bookstore. Don't be discouraged if only a few attend this first class; God often works through a praying remnant.

Knowing you will not get everyone into a class on prayer, you might want to give everyone a simple prayer outline—such as ACTS—to assist them in personal prayer. Print this in the bulletin and use it as your preaching outline.

Adoration (Ps. 100)
Confession (1 John 1:8–9, Jas. 4:8)
Thanksgiving (Phil. 4:6)
Supplication (Phil. 4:6, 1 Tim. 2:1)

While we should provide ample instruction on prayer, we should also acknowledge that prayer is learned primarily by observation and participation. If you don't believe that, just listen to your children pray. They will often use the same expressions and nuances you use when praying. This suggests that we should ensure that public prayers are worthy of imitation. If you have opportunity to pray aloud in your church, Sunday School class, or cell group, don't take it lightly. Pray honestly and transparently, not to impress, but to communicate with the Father. If you are responsible for calling on others to pray, call on those who have a powerful personal prayer life. You can also ensure that prayer is given priority time in various committee or board meetings of the church.

Organize the Church to Pray

Once the priority of prayer has been established and people have been trained, it is helpful to organize the church for prayer. There are many different ways to do this, and you must select the one that will work best in your situation. Do not think you must duplicate anyone else's prayer ministry.

Here are a few ideas that may get you started:
a. Organize prayer groups through Sunday School classes or other cell groups.
b. Use prayer chains.
c. Use days of prayer and fasting.
d. Develop a system of prayer partners.
e. Have regularly scheduled days for concerts of prayer.
f. Develop a prayer chapel that is accessible around the clock.
g. Have a prayer hotline.

Several resources will help you understand different ways of organizing your church to pray:
• David Bryant, *Concerts of Prayer* (California: Regal Books, 1988).
• Evelyn Christensen, *A Study Guide to Evangelism Praying* (Atlanta: Conger Printing, 1992).
• T.W. Hunt and Catherine Walker, *A Disciple's Prayer Life: Walking in Fellowship with God* (Nashville: The Sunday School Board of the Southern Baptist Convention, 1988, 1991, 1992).
• Larry Thompson, *Watchman on the Wall* (Nashville: LifeWay Press, 1992).

The method for organizing the church to pray is not nearly as important as the actual praying. When your church begins to pray—seeking God's face, turning from sin, following His direction, and experiencing His empowering—your church will grow. He desires for the church to grow and reach the lost world. He seeks a yielded and cleansed vessel. All church growth originates from the prayer closet. Prayer links our impotence with God's omnipotence. It links our human efforts to participate in church growth with God's sovereign power.

Characteristic 4:

Servant Leaders

Much attention has been given to visionary leaders and their leadership styles. You only have to browse the shelves of the nearest bookstore to find a plethora of books on leadership in the market place. I enjoy reading books on leadership and stories about various leaders. Some take a "good ole boy" approach while others are more high-key and direct. They range from the down-home image of Sam Walton, late chairman of Wal-Mart, to the turn-it-around genius of Lee Iaococca of Chrysler. Sam Walton would drive his pickup or fly his plane on his regular visits to his many stores. Iaococca would take to the television and sell his revamped organization to the public.

We can point to an equally diverse group of successful church growth leaders. As they tell their growth stories, all suggest a slightly different style of leadership. One seems to take charge and appoint the few committees which exist, while another hardly knows how many committees exist or how the budget works. One leads with powerful preaching, another has incredible administrative skills, another has charismatic personality, and still another leads with great people skills. Which are we to attempt to imitate? Should we lead the church like a Chief Executive Officer, a shepherd, a rancher, or a servant?

While church growth writers differ on the most effective leadership style, virtually everyone agrees that leadership is a key issue for church growth. Not only must the pastor be a visionary leader, the growing church must have a sufficient number of layleaders to staff its many ministries. Thus, some have called leadership the master key of church growth. It is true: if we are going to experience significant church growth, we must have enough capable, responsible, visionary, and dependable leaders. The church simply will never outgrow its leadership.

In a recent survey conducted by the Center for Church Growth, an equal number of Southern Baptist pastors from large churches and smaller churches were asked to rank the top five factors contributing to the growth of their churches. Both groups ranked pastoral leadership and vision as the number one factor.

The Biblical Concept

How does God intend to grow His church? That is a legitimate and obvious question at this point. Recall that we defined church growth as the church faithfully fulfilling the Great Commission in its unique context and with a vision for the world. Second, we underlined the truth that all authentic church growth is supernatural work and thus born out of powerful prayer and praise. If we now enquire as to the actual pattern of God in building His church, we find a consistent pattern throughout redemptive history.

God Works Through Human Instrumentation

God chooses to work His will on earth through yielded, human instruments. One of the most graphic, powerful stories of the Old Testament is God's supernatural deliverance of Israel from bondage in Egypt.

Pick up the story in Exodus 3 where Moses, tending his father-in-law's flock, had just been informed he was on holy ground. God identified Himself as the God of Abraham, Isaac, and Jacob. Then He revealed His plan: "I have surely seen the affliction of My people who are in Egypt, and have given heed to their cry because of their taskmasters, for I am aware of their sufferings. So I have come down to deliver them from the power of the Egyptians, and to bring them up from that land to a good and spacious land, to a land flowing with milk and honey" (vv. 7–8). So far so good! Moses was delighted to discover God had not been deaf to the cries of His own people nor blind to their misery. He was elated to discover God had a plan to deliver His people from bondage.

But what was that plan and how would it work? "Therefore, come now, and I will send you to Pharaoh, so that you may bring My people, the sons of Israel out of Egypt" (v .10)—an unexpected turn and not one which delighted Moses. Why would sovereign God use a human instrument, particularly one as weak as Moses? Moses immediately attempted to excuse himself under the pious garb of humility. "Who am I, that I should go to Pharaoh, and that I should bring the sons of Israel out of Egypt?" (v. 11). Moses' first question is irrelevant. The key to the delivery of Israel is not related to the ability of Moses but to the identity and authority of the One who was sending him. God thus assured Moses of victory with a promise: "Certainly I will be with you" (v. 12).

Moses then asked the right question. He inquired about the name of God. It is at this critical moment that God revealed Himself through the sacred name, Yahweh, often translated, "I AM WHO I AM" or "I CAUSE TO BE WHAT I CAUSE TO BE." God's remarkable name revealed both His sovereign power to change their plight and His merciful desire to do so. His name was the answer to every excuse and challenge Moses could mount. For example, when he complained he could not speak, the Lord replied: "Who has made man's mouth? Or who makes him dumb or deaf, or seeing or blind? Is it not I, the Lord?" (4:11).

The excuses we make for ourselves and our churches must sound equally feeble in the light of God's resources. "We're too small. We don't have the people or money. I'm not a very gifted leader. These people are stubborn. They don't want to grow." You can add to the list your favorites, but the answer to each is the same—I AM THAT I AM.

God has determined to build His church through human instruments which He created, redeemed, gifted, and placed in the body as He chose. Paul's confession in 1 Corinthians indicated He had discovered this truth: "I planted, Apollos watered, but God was causing the growth. So then neither the one who plants nor the one who waters is anything, but God who causes the growth" (3:6–7). Ephesians 4:11–16 is a classic passage that spells out the unique interrelationship of divine empowering and human instrumentation. The pastor-teacher is to equip the saints for the work of ministry with the result that "we are to grow up in all aspects into Him, who is the head, even Christ, from whom the whole body, being fitted and held together by that which every joint supplies, according to the proper working of each individual part, causes the growth of the body for the building up of itself in love" (vv. 15–16).

Nothing is as exhilarating as the realization that when we do our part to grow the church we participate with the exalted Christ in building His body. We are involved in supernatural activity with eternal implications. Nothing we do has greater significance than what God does through us to build His church.

Relationships and Functions of Leadership

One of the most essential passages for understanding the functioning of leadership in the church comes from one of Paul's earliest letters, 1 Thessalonians. Notice that Paul began this section on leadership by addressing the members concerning their relationship to those in leadership positions: "We request of you, brethren, that you *appreciate* those who diligently labor among you, and have charge over you in the Lord and give you instruction, and that you *esteem them very highly in love* because of their work. Live in *peace with one another*" (5:12–14, author's italics).

One of the keys to church growth is the appropriate functioning of the membership, which depends on healthy relationships within the membership. Healthy relationships within the body begin with proper relationships between laypeople and their leaders. Many churches fail to grow because a wall of separation that exists between leaders and laity.

Note that this entire passage and its discussion of the proper relationships in the body is placed in the context of the church's mission. We are called to esteem leaders highly for the sake of the work. When friction occurs between pastor and laity, we must remind ourselves of the significance of the mission of the church—to join God in fulfilling the Great Commission. We are empowered to deal with issues that impact eternity. For that reason, we must allow nothing, including personal preferences, to stand in the way of the proper functioning of the body.

All too often the work of the local church languishes because of dissension between the laity and the leadership. Only through mutual esteem based in God's love can we find the strength to live in peace with one another. When a church has a genuine encounter with God, relationships will be healed beginning with pastor and people.

Not only did Paul encourage healthy relationships for the optimum working of the body, he established three primary functions for the pastor who would lead his church in a biblical fashion. First, the leader is to care for the church by laboring hard among the flock (v. 12). "Labor among" signifies the hard work entailed in pastoral leadership. Laboring among requires not only rigorous physical labor, but also it requires that the pastor spend time with his people both caring for them and providing an example of ministry for others in the congregation to emulate.

The second key phrase, "have charge over" (v. 12), refers to oversight, leadership, and protection. The pastor is called to be the key administrator of the church. On three occasions this same term is used in the pastoral letters to describe the requirement that overseers and deacons must *lead* their own households to qualify for leadership in the church. Pastors must prove themselves faithful in the smaller context of their homes before being entrusted with the greater responsibilities of the church. Hebrews 13:17 gives us the same perspective on pastoral leadership: "Obey your leaders and submit to them; for they keep watch over your souls, as those who will give an account." The pastor will be held accountable by God for his spiritual oversight of the church. Laymen must support and submit to pastoral leadership for the work's sake. Numerous studies have demonstrated that growing churches are those that give their pastors the responsibility and freedom to oversee the mission of the church.

Note that the phrase "have charge over you" is qualified with "in the Lord." Administrative leadership is spiritual authority exercised in the Lord. It is an earned leadership forged in relationships—first, the pastor's relationship with his Lord and second, the pastor's relationship to his people. The pastor's authority is given by God and earned through humble service. The pastor is both leader and servant. This model maintains the unique paradox of servant leadership modeled by Jesus before His disciples. Jesus was clearly the leader of the disciples, yet He willingly stooped to wash the disciples' feet. Some pastors are willing to be servants, but they are reluctant to be overseers; others desire to be in charge, but are unwilling to function as servants. The fact that pastoral leadership offers the potential for abuse does not mean we can ignore the need for strong pastoral leadership. The pastor must fulfill this role if the church is to function properly, and the church must esteem and appreciate him for his work.

The third function is described by the phrase, "give you instruction" (v. 12). Responsibility for equipping the saints is given heavy weight in the New Testament. In Acts 6 the apostles refused to neglect the ministry of the Word to serve the table. The church called out mature, Spirit-filled men to minister to the needs of the widows so the apostles would not neglect prayer and the ministry of the Word. Paul listed "able to teach" as a qualification for anyone desiring the office of overseer (see 1 Tim. 3:2). In Ephesians 4:11–16, the pastor-teacher is given to the church by the exalted Christ to equip the saints for the work of ministry. This passage gives us a clue for understanding the vital connection between gifted members and those called to leadership. Leaders enable the believers to discover, develop, and utilize their gifts for the good of the body. The end result of such cooperative ministry is unity (v. 13), maturity (v. 13), doctrinal stability (v. 14), and the balanced growth of the body for the building up of itself in love (v. 16). Growing churches have recaptured the biblical vision of the servant-leader who is gifted to lead the congregation and equip the laity to fulfill their unique role in accomplishing the goals and mission of the church.[1]

Parenting the Church

Many different images have been suggested for the modern-day pastor, from CEO to rancher to player-coach. Each of these various images may contribute to our understanding of the function of the pastor, but I would like to suggest that the image of parent might be more comprehensive and biblical than those suggested above.

On several occasions Paul compared his ministry to the actions of a parent. In writing to the Corinthians, Paul had to deal strongly with their arrogant boasting about their powerful leaders. Paul tempered his strong rebuke with these tender words: "I do not write these things to shame you, but to admonish you as my beloved children" (1 Cor. 4:14). He continued by explaining that he had become their father through sharing the gospel. In this parenting relationship, Paul encouraged them to imitate him. In spite of his obvious fatherly compassion, he warned them that if they continued in their arrogance, he might have to discipline them. "What do you desire? Shall I come to you with a rod or with love and a spirit of gentleness?" (4:21).

Paul was forced to leave Thessalonica quickly and unexpectantly. He was concerned that his departure might be used by the opponents of Christianity to discourage the new believers. Notice how Paul described his ministry while in Thessalonica. "But we proved to be gentle among you, as a nursing mother tenderly cares for her own children. Having thus a fond affection for you we were well-pleased to impart to you not only the gospel of God but also our own lives, because you had become very dear to us . . . just as you know how we were exhorting and encouraging and imploring each one of you as a father would his own children" (1 Thess. 2:7–8, 11). He was like a mother in his tender care and like a father in his exhorting and encouraging.

In light of these emphases, it is not surprising that one of the qualifications for any person aspiring to the office of overseer is the ability to manage his own household. "He must be one who manages his own household well, keeping his children under control with all dignity (but if a man does not know how to manage his own household, how will he take care of the church of

God?)" (1 Tim. 3:4–5). Paul clearly compared managing the church with managing the home. If we keep this image in mind, issues such as affirmation, discipline, teaching, and leadership fall naturally into place.

Qualities of Leadership

Recently I attended a seminar titled "Managing People." About twelve people in management level positions were in attendance. Our convener asked us to list the qualities of effective and ineffective leaders for or with whom we had worked. You might find these lists helpful:

Effective Leader	Ineffective Leader
Humility	Self-absorbed
Vision	Lack of vision
Competent	Incompetent
Servant	Abuses power
Integrity	Deceitful
Trustworthy	Untrustworthy
Enabler-motivator	One-man show
Communicator	Poor Communicator
Good people skills	Focuses on tasks
Consistent	Lacks focus
Caring listener	No time for people
Knows limitations	Arrogant
Decisive	Indecisive
Takes risks	Afraid to fail

The American Management Association sponsored several carefully controlled studies during the 1980s which included over five thousand people. They asked this question: "What values (personal traits or characteristics) do you look for and admire in your superiors?" Notice the similarity of the qualities listed by members of the "Managing People" seminar and those discovered by the American Management Association listed in the next chart.[2]

Did it surprise you that honesty outdistanced all other qualities? People are looking for a leader who is honest and trans-

Characteristics of Superior Leaders

Ranking/Characteristic	Percentage of Managers Selecting
1 Honest	87
2 Competent	74
3 Forward–looking	67
4 Inspiring	61
5 Intelligent	46
6 Fair-minded	42
7 Broad-minded	38
8 Courageous	35
9 Straightforward	33
10 Imaginative	32
11 Dependable	31
12 Supportive	29
13 Caring	26
14 Cooperative	23
15 Mature	20
16 Ambitious	18
17 Determined	14
18 Self-controlled	13
19 Loyal	10
20 Independent	8

parent. If you are to lead your church in growth, you must, above all, be yourself! Look again at the list and notice that only numbers 2, 5, and 10 are related to skills or intelligence. The other seventeen are qualities that can be practiced and developed by anyone interested in leading their church or class to grow. A Carnegie Foundation study designed to determine what contributes most to a person's success found that only 15 percent of a person's success is determined by job knowledge and technical skills. A full 85 percent is determined by an individual's attitude and ability to relate to other people.[3] We can't excuse our lack of success by claiming we are not as skilled as other great leaders. While we cannot discount skills and abilities, we can develop the personal traits that will motivate others to follow us and labor with us.

When talking about leadership for growing the church, we must add another factor—the presence and power of the Holy Spirit to gift us and transform us, enabling us to grow the church. Remember that Moses felt he lacked the ability to lead Israel out of Egypt. He pointed specifically to his lack of speaking skills. God promised that He would be Moses' sufficiency. Not only has God gifted you through His Spirit to build His church, but He desires to build His character in you, just as He did in Moses.

The apostle Peter encouraged all believers to become full partakers of the divine nature since they had escaped the corruption of the world. Look at the list of qualities God desires to build in you:

> Moral excellence
> Knowledge
> Self-control
> Perseverance
> Godliness
> Brotherly kindness
> Love

"For if these qualities are yours and are increasing, they render you neither useless nor unfruitful in the true knowledge of our Lord Jesus Christ. For he who lacks these qualities is blind or short-sighted, having forgotten his purification from his former sins" (2 Pet. 1:8–9).

When Jesus talked about successful leadership, He held one image before His followers—the servant. "You know that the rulers of the Gentiles lord it over them, and their great men exercise authority over them. It is not so among you, but whoever wishes to become great among you shall be your servant" (Matt. 20:25–26). Jesus not only taught about servanthood, but He also modeled it. At the Passover just prior to His death, the Lord stooped and washed the feet of His followers. He then told them that He had performed this action as an example of how they should minister to one another.

Jimmy Draper, president of the Sunday School Board of the Southern Baptist Convention, underscored a critical feature of the paradox of servant leadership. He noted that Christians are a chosen people and a royal priesthood (see 1 Pet. 2:9) who are so captivated by Christ they joyfully become His servants and slaves. Recall the numerous references in Paul's letters where he referred to himself as a servant or slave. Paul's servitude was such that his response to the immature boasting of the Corinthians over leaders was a simple question and answer: "What then is Apollos? And what is Paul? Servants through whom you believed, even as the Lord gave opportunity to each one" (1 Cor. 3:5). We are simply vessels through whom God's power flows. Draper then observed that today we have a lot of slaves behaving like kings, when God's intention was to have kings serving like slaves! Remember, we have a flawless example of this leadership behavior—the King of kings took on Himself human flesh and became a servant.[4]

The servant model assures that leadership in the growing church is not an authoritarian power play, nor is it mere human ambition. But does the servant image mean we have neither ambition nor assertiveness? If we look again at the example of our Lord, we note that He was a servant, yet He was clearly the leader of the twelve. In relationship to the twelve, He taught, reprimanded, encouraged, and led. Servanthood as a leadership style does not mean we forfeit the administrative functions commanded in Scripture and seen in Christ's example.

It is interesting that the business world seems to have discovered that which Jesus taught two thousand years ago: "A new paradigm of leadership called 'Servant Leadership'—based on the philosophy of the former AT&T training executive, Robert K. Greenleaf—calls for leaders to be of service to others, to give more than take, and to serve others' needs rather than their own."[5] Peter Block, one of the most popular writers in the business field, just published a new book entitled *Stewardship* with this theme—choosing service over self-interest. It is surprising that many of us are more impressed to hear a business leader talk about servanthood as the appropriate model than to hear it from the lips of the Lord Himself.

Multiplying Leadership

No leader can build a church or a Sunday School class by himself or herself; leaders must multiply themselves by equipping others to be leaders. The goal of a good leader is to help others succeed, to see the equipping and management of others as vital ministry and not just as busy work. Scripture teaches that we are to set as a goal the maturity and ministry of all believers.

The pattern for balanced church growth was clearly established by Paul in Ephesians 4:11–16. It begins with the recognition that each Christian has been gifted by grace for service (v. 7). One of the gifted members is the pastor/teacher who is to equip the saints for the work of ministry. The pastor must understand that a primary task of pastoral ministry is developing other leaders to join in shared ministry.

Every member of the body is a leader; some simply have more responsibility than others. Look at the results of shared ministry—building up of the body of Christ, unity of the faith, knowledge of the Son of God, maturity, and theological stability. Paul summarized God's plan for growth in verse 16: "From whom the whole body, being fitted and held together by that which every joint supplies, according to the proper working of each individual part, causes the growth of the body for the building up of itself in love." Notice that growth is supernatural, that each gifted member plays a part, and that the body builds itself up in love. Who wouldn't want to pastor or belong to such a balanced church?

This balance is experienced only when members willingly take their places of service in the body and when pastors see the equipping of others for the work of service as their first priority. In fact, a central finding of a church membership study sponsored by the Lutheran Church–Missouri Synod was that growing, healthy churches had clergy and lay leadership working as a team.[6]

Many pastors like myself graduated from seminary with the idea that the "caring" pastor would visit every church member every year. On my first Sunday I announced my intention to visit all my families every year. I heard audible murmurs of admiration. Several members personally applauded my idea, assuring me that this was precisely what they expected the pastor to do. It didn't take me long to realize that accomplishing my announced goal would require five or six visits a week, every week of the year. I quickly realized that if I accomplished my stated goal I would fail in many of my other ministry objectives. Evangelistic visits would take a backseat, and time for study and administration would be scarce.

By my announcement and noble pastoral plan I would be perpetuating a concept that is neither biblical nor practical. This grand expectation of a "pastor-only ministry" has become ingrained in many of our churches and has virtually assured that they will remain small.

The other negative aspect of pastor-only ministry is that it prohibits many gifted laypersons from discovering and using their gifts for ministry. A pastor friend once boasted to me that he personally visited every prospect who attended his church. I told him he was both limiting the church's potential for growth and cheating his laypeople out of sharing in the joy of leading people to Christ. His pride was misplaced and truthfully, he was resentful because he had to spend every night visiting. This was neither biblical nor productive.

A recent and popular book on leadership is *Flight of the Buffalo* by James Belasco and Ralph Stayer. They compare an old an ineffective style of leadership to that of the head buffalo whose herd stands around until he shows them what to do. The authors prefer a new paradigm—flying geese, where every bird has to share the responsibilities to lead, follow, or scout in order to accomplish the goals of the gaggle. This style of leadership exemplifies four foundational principles: 1) leaders transfer ownership for work to those who execute the work; 2) leaders are responsible to create the environment for ownership where each person wants to be responsible; 3) leaders coach the development of personal capabilities; and 4) leaders themselves learn fast and encourage others to learn quickly also. Once again, the business world has discovered the principles of leadership clearly taught in the Word of God.

Carl George in his recent book, *How to Break Growth Barriers*, argues that the paradigm shift from the pastor doing the caring to the pastor seeing to it that people are cared for is critical to breaking growth barriers. George argues that for the church to grow the pastor cannot see himself as a shepherd who encounters each of his sheep nose to nose, but as a rancher who oversees the care of all his sheep through the skillful administration of other ranch hands. He notes that Paul used the image of shepherd only once (Eph. 4:11), choosing instead a wide range of images such as steward of Christ, teacher, example, priest, and helmsman to illustrate shared ministry.[7]

You do not have to abandon personal caregiving, but to enable your church to grow and embrace an Ephesians 4:11 model, you must become a developer and manager of caregivers. The term of overseer as applied to the pastor suggests such a management role.

Since the idea of the pastor as the professional, who is responsible for all ministry, is so deeply ingrained in many churches, you must move slowly in changing this attitude but deliberately or it will stunt your church's ability to grow. Consider preaching a series of messages on topics such as the pastor's role, the ministry of laity, and the mission of the church. It has been my experience that most laypeople, when given the choice of administration or hands-on ministry, will chose ministry. Take laymen with you on ministry calls and encourage them as they discover the joy of ministry.

Once you have made the decision to unleash your church by equipping and freeing others to serve, you must develop a strategy for doing just that. Jesus provided an excellent example in His training of the twelve to multiply His own ministry. A key passage is Matthew 9:35–10:42. Jesus was going about the cities and villages teaching, proclaiming the gospel, and healing diseases and sicknesses. In the context of ministry, He was moved with compassion for the needs of the multitudes of people who were like sheep without a shepherd. He then observed that the harvest was plentiful, but the laborers were few. To resolve this dilemma, He commissioned and sent His own disciples to multiply His efforts. Let's look at the seven steps Jesus used to equip them for ministry.

Step 1—Jesus modeled ministry. Jesus commissioned His disciples to do what He had continually done in their presence. In order to commission others, you must be willing to spend time with them and model ministry (see Matt. 9:35; 10:1).

You will not effectively model ministry without a serious time commitment to potential leaders. Jesus spent three years with His small group of disciples.

Step 2—Jesus shared His passion and vision. You cannot lead people and remain personally detached from them. Jesus shared with His disciples His compassion for the lost and His vision for a bountiful harvest (see 9:36–37). The study by the Lutheran Church–Missouri Synod found that growing congregations have clergy and laymen working together with a sense of mission which goes beyond the local congregation.[8] In other words, they have a shared vision.

Step 3—Jesus taught them to pray to the Lord of the harvest (see 9:38). If your church lacks a sufficient number of workers, it does not have a recruitment problem; it has a prayer problem. The Lord will thrust people into the harvest. Again, we must believe God's Word and practice supernatural praying.

Step 4—Jesus instructed His disciples (see 10:5). People will not do what they are not equipped to do. If the church expects people to share in ministry, it must offer opportunities for people to learn basic ministry skills.

Step 5—Jesus empowered His disciples and sent them out (see 10:1, 5). You cannot multiply ministry unless you are willing to give others authority and permission to do ministry. Do you ever give someone a job and then take it back if it is not done the way you would do it? We must empower people to do the work and then allow them the freedom to use their unique gifts working through their personalities to do it.

Step 6—Jesus provided the resources necessary to accomplish the task (see 10:16–23). As pastor or leader, you must instruct your fellow-laborers about their spiritual resources while providing them with ministry resources. Anyone laboring for church growth needs both physical and spiritual resources.

Step 7—Jesus observed, affirmed, and corrected His disciples. While we must give people the opportunity to try their own ministry "wings," we cannot leave them on their own. They need and deserve both correction and affirmation.

You may find it interesting that Peter Blanchard, one of the foremost business writers of our day, encourages business leaders to take similar steps in working with those under

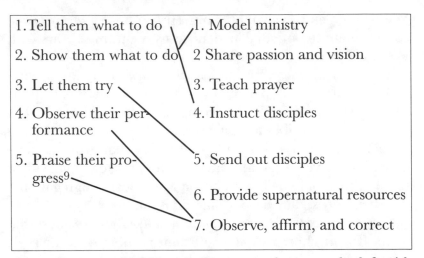

1. Tell them what to do   1. Model ministry

2. Show them what to do   2 Share passion and vision

3. Let them try   3. Teach prayer

4. Observe their performance   4. Instruct disciples

5. Praise their progress[9]   5. Send out disciples

6. Provide supernatural resources

7. Observe, affirm, and correct

them. Compare Blanchard's five steps, above, on the left with those of Jesus on the right:

Note the similarities and differences. All five of Blanchard's steps are included in the strategy of Jesus. There are, however, three unique differences. First, Jesus modeled ministry before He gave instruction. In my experience, instruction is more meaningful when it is preceded by modeling. Second, Jesus included two elements missing from Blanchard's list. Jesus shared His passion and vision prior to giving instruction. Without a shared vision, there is little motivation to receive instruction. We have all been disappointed when our well-conceived programs or courses were poorly attended because our people had little motivation to learn the material being offered. Finally Jesus provided supernatural resources which are unavailable through any business strategy, but readily available to His church.

The Key to Effective Leadership

If you can get along with people you can be an effective leader. Leadership is what you do in relationship with people, not something you do to or for your people. Church growth leadership is nothing more than working with and through people to accomplish the Great Commission. Thus the people of the church are the singular most important growth resource. To be an effective leader, you must believe in the value of people.

They are not subjects or simple laborers to be commanded. They are not objects on which to try our techniques or pawns to help the pastor achieve his growth goals. They are unique individuals created in the image of God. They are His precious gifts entrusted to leaders in stewardship; and thus, the goal of the leader is to enable each individual to fulfill his or her God-given potential. That's both a tremendous responsibility and opportunity. For this reason James warns against taking teaching-leadership responsibilities lightly (see 3:1). The teacher-leader has the opportunity and responsibility for helping other individuals to develop.

You cannot lead people unless you truly love people. I am constantly amazed with the number of people I find in leadership positions in the church who really don't like people. Somehow they like the task, or bask in the authority of the position, but really don't like the people they have been called to lead. I have been with pastors who were truly gifted and could perform well but had no people skills and no real interest in developing them. It is not likely they will be effective leaders. I have also pastored layleaders who were tremendously gifted but were never very effective in leadership because they had no real heart for the people. One teacher comes to mind who was a very gifted Bible expositor, yet he made it clear that he had no interest in visiting or knowing his class members. He came into the class, lectured, and left. We tried him in several classes with little long-term results because class members found him unapproachable. I would venture to say that most pastoral terminations are the result of poor people skills rather than issues of ability or theology.

Yet a word of balance is in order. The leader, out of his love for people, cannot avoid "rocking the boat" because he or she wants everyone to be happy or to like him or her. While on the surface it appears to create harmony, it usually renders the church ineffective. Unity bought with continual compromise is extremely thin. Giving direction and occasional confrontation does not mean that the shepherd loves his sheep less. In truth it would be most unloving if I as a father refused to give clear guidance and correction to my daughter Katie under the guise of wanting her to be my "buddy."

There are essentially two bases of authority for leadership. You can lead from position or from personal relationship. The positional base is focused in authority, position in an organization, a title, restraints such as a budgetary control, or the promise of reward or punishment. The personal relationship base is built on relationships with people, skills, reputation, and personal track record.

Positional	Personal
Position in organization	Relationships
Title-structure	Knowledge-skills
Control-budget	Reputation
Reward-punishment	Track record

Often both of these bases come into play, but the strongest leadership style in terms of effectiveness focuses on personal relationships. Each time you lead from position, you use up the resources of that base. Authority based on position or title is like a bank account from which you only make withdrawals. Pastors are frequently told to choose their battles well, because they only have "so many good fights in them." That means the leader should only appeal to positional authority or title in certain critical situations.

When you lead from earned relationships, rather than using up your account, you actually deposit additional funds in your leadership account. In other words, you build stronger relationships with the people you lead. They see your track record of good decisions made in the past and know through their personal relationships that you are a person of integrity and commitment. Many pastors, moving to a new church, make the mistake of using up their authority bank account quickly without having made any substantial deposits in their relational leadership account; they find themselves without a support base in the church.

A church typically gives a new pastor a short-term loan in both accounts. The amount of the loans is often determined by factors beyond the pastor's control. If the former pastor has abused the church, the new one may start with little, if any, bank account. Other churches give their new pastor a substantial bank account. My advice to new pastors—first, determine the size of your accounts; then, begin making regular deposits in the personal relationship account by spending quality time with your people.

For example, the new pastor who comes to a church like a streaking meteor and announces his intention of reorganizing the Sunday School, changing the style of worship, and streamlining the administrative process, may find it possible to make such changes, but to do so he will be required to make significant withdrawals from his positional account. The problem is that he has not had time to build up the personal account; therefore, if one of the changes made from position fails or faces opposition, he finds himself without sufficient funds and without friends.

The pastor will concentrate on building relationships for effective ministry. Stephen Covey, in his book *Principle-Centered Leadership*, talks of three forms of power—coercive power, utility power, and principle-centered power. The first two are positional forms of power. Covey favors principle-centered power which is based on personal relationships. Listen to his description: "A third level of responding is different in kind and degree from the other two. It is based on the power some people have with others because others tend to believe in them and in what they are trying to accomplish. They are trusted. They are respected. They are honored. And they are followed because others want to follow them, want to believe in them and their cause, want to do what the leader wants. This is not blind faith, mindless obedience, or robotic servitude; this is knowledgeable, wholehearted, uninhibited commitment."[10] You can build a substantial principle-centered leadership account if you will love and lead your people.

Is it ever appropriate to lead from position or power? Yes, in certain circumstances it may even be necessary. Let's look at the apostle Paul. Paul rarely appealed to his apostolic authority. In fact, he often chose not to demand his rights (compare 1 Cor. 9:1–18). Yet when he faced the critical issue of false doctrine, he readily appealed to the God-given authority which was his (1 Cor. 14:37; 2 Cor. 11:1ff). He used his leadership accounts wisely.

In one of my pastorates, I was faced with a critical situation that would have had long-term consequences for the direction and ministry of the church. The church had experienced rapid growth and we had found it necessary to hire several additional staff persons. The expenses from the rapid growth had created some cash flow problems. One Wednesday I received a call from an officer of the church. He asked to meet with me prior to Prayer Meeting. I thought nothing about the call until I discovered that other staff members had received a call to attend this unannounced meeting. Our personnel policies clearly spelled out the responsibility for pastoral leadership of the staff; thus the staff looked to me for guidance about attending this unusual staff meeting.

As I thought about the meeting, I knew that the issue was greater than cash flow. We had just made the transition to a larger staff structure where the staff reported directly to me. While the meeting was ostensibly about finances, the issue of staff accountability was being tested. I asked the staff to attend, but to follow my lead. When everyone was assembled, I requested my staff to leave. I then told the trustees who had gathered in my office that I would have been delighted to answer their questions about cash flow if they had sought the information. I also indicated that I would have gladly called a staff meeting if they had just requested it. The men understood what was at stake. They apologized and indicated that they understood that we were dealing with precedent. To my knowledge that was one of the very few occasions I found it necessary to lead from position.

Here again we might gain insight concerning the use of positional leadership by remembering our parenting model. Occasionally my daughters attempt to change the rules. One might want to stay out later than we allow. She may plead her case by arguing that other girls her age are allowed to stay out later than she is. In response, I may appeal to reason. Then I remind her of my fairness in the past. I may ask whether I tend to be unreasonable. She may ignore these arguments from relationship and continue to plead her case. In that situation I might respond: "Enough! I'm the parent and I make the rules. When you are a parent you can make the rules." The style of leadership must fit the situation and the person. Use this style of leadership sparingly.

Managing According to Need

Often management styles are divided into two primary categories: the autocratic and the democratic. Autocratic leaders are strong, tough, and demanding. They are often not well liked by many who serve under them, but they tend to have good bottom-line results. They generally lead from the authority base of position. The organization seems to win, while their people tend to loose. Democratic leaders are nice, easy-going, and grant a great deal of freedom. They are usually well liked, but often do not achieve measurable results. Their primary base of leadership is relational. Let's compare them:

Autocratic	Democratic
Focused on results	Focused on people
Task-oriented	Relationally-oriented
Hard-nosed	Caring
Tough	Tender
Often not liked	Usually well liked

Must we select one of these two alternatives? Do we have to choose between being liked and growing the church? Is it possible to obtain results and build relationships with people? Can we find some balance between caring for people and accomplishing the tasks of the church? If we build on the parenting model, I think we can find middle ground.

In 1 Corinthians 4:21 where Paul compared his leadership to that of a parent, he indicated that the Corinthians' behavior would dictate the leadership style with which he would respond: "What do you desire? Shall I come to you with a rod or with love and a spirit of gentleness?" In other words, the *situation* would determine whether he had to be tough or tender, lead from position or relationship.

A parent responds according to the specific need of the moment and the unique needs of the child. We have three girls who differ greatly in personality, age, and temperament. My oldest daughter Kristina is nineteen, a sophomore in college, and is a highly motivated achiever. My youngest daughter Katie is twelve, an extremely energetic and precocious seventh-grader. My middle daughter Rachael, to whom this book is dedicated, is a high school senior who has a tender and compassionate desire to make sure that everyone in the world loves everyone else. It would be poor and unfair to parent these three children exactly the same.

The other day I called Kristina at college. I was checking to see if she was planning to attend the football game that afternoon. She informed me that she had several conflicts related to her studies and the Bible study group she is leading. I expressed gratitude and pride for her discipline, but encouraged her to take some time to enjoy her college years. That instruction was appropriate for Kristina, but would have been totally inappropriate for Rachael. Rachael is so people-oriented that she often needs encouragement and even direction to spend adequate time with her studies and less at the ball games.

Often I make parenting mistakes by attempting to treat all my children alike because it's the "democratic" thing to do. Katie, because of her age and temperament, needs more directing than Kristina. Rachael needs support and encouragement. Many parents today have removed all restraints and avoided any system of reprimand because they want to be best friends with their children. This accounts, in part, for the rebellion and inappropriate behavior in many young children. As pastor, I frequently had parents allow their preteen children to sleep in on Sunday, saying, "I can't tell them what to do. What am I to do? They don't want to come." They had better tell young children what to do. They need and even desire direction. It is a parent's God-given responsibility to train them up in the way they should go. It is not inappropriate to be very directive and even authoritative in the development of a young child. Obviously there is a point in the maturation process where parents must release the apron strings and give guidance through earned relationships. The key to good parenting is to know what form of parenting works best in a particular situation and for a particular child, and then to adjust your leadership style.

Sometimes I hear the response: "It's not fair to treat children differently." I have even heard that from my children. "You're not fair! You let Kristina do whatever she wants to do. You never tell her to be in by eleven o'clock." Most children love to push our hot buttons on fairness. In truth, it's not fair to treat two different children in the same way. To be fair you must treat them according to their needs and their individual maturational levels.

The parenting model for pastoral leadership provides some important clues for leading the church. A new believer may need a more directive and authoritarian style of leadership in order to develop basic disciplines. The maturing Christian may need encouragement more than direction. Certain situations in the life of the church may require a change in overall leadership style as I mentioned above. Paul declared that if the church at Corinth continued their arrogant boasting and divisive behavior, he would come to them with a rod. The key to effectively parenting the church is to adjust the leadership style to the needs of the moment and the person or persons involved.

The Relational Model

While writing this characteristic I discovered the situational leadership model developed by Kenneth Blanchard, Patricia Zigarmi, and Drea Zigarmi. This model, spelled out in *Leadership and the One-Minute Manager*, illustrates well concepts that are appropriate to parenting the church. Blanchard argues that four basic styles of leadership are needed and must be employed according to the need of the person and the specifics of the situation. These four leadership styles are:

- *Style 1: Directing.* The leader provides specific instructions and closely supervises task accomplishment.
- *Style 2: Coaching.* The leader continues to direct and closely supervise task accomplishment, but also explains decisions, solicits suggestions, and supports progress.
- *Style 3: Supporting.* The leader facilitates and supports subordinates' efforts toward task accomplishment and shares responsibility for decision-making with them.
- *Style 4: Delegating.* The leader turns over responsibility for decision making and problem solving to subordinates.[11]

The *directing* style is used when decisions must be made quickly and the stakes are high, when leading inexperienced people who have the potential to be self-directive, and when leading someone who has skill but doesn't know the church, its priorities, policies, or ways of doing business. *Coaching* works best when leading an individual who has some competence but has lost enthusiasm because of disillusionment. These persons have started a task and found it harder than they thought. Thus they need someone to listen to their concerns, provide perspective, praise their progress, and involve them in the decision-making as much as possible to rebuild commitment. The *supporting* style is most effective with experienced people who are at times reluctant contributors. They want to be involved in decision making but don't always have faith in their own ideas and thus need recognition. The *delegating* style is appropriate with people who are peak performers, people who are competent and committed. They don't need much direction and often provide their own support.[12]

Thus the leader's priority concerns are to diagnose which style is most appropriate, treat the person fairly by using the proper leadership style, and then lead each person to achieve peak performance. Diagnosis cannot be made without spending time with the individual. This is why the pastor must love his people, spend time with them, and equip others to lead with him.

The manager must look at past performance with particular attention to competence and commitment. Competence is primarily an issue of skill and is easier than commitment to assess and develop. Modeling and instruction will help build competence. Commitment is enhanced as confidence and motivation grow. Confidence is the measure of a person's self-assurance, the feeling of being able to do a task well without detailed supervision. This is developed by instruction, affirmation, and opportunity to do the task. Motivation is a person's interest in and enthusiasm for doing a task well. This is developed through relationships where the manager shares his or her passion and vision.

Blanchard categorizes four development levels in individuals. An illustration of this is on the next page.[13]

The goal of a pastor is to use the appropriate leadership style and to manage in such a way that gradually competence and

THE FOUR DEVELOPMENT LEVELS ARE

HIGH COMPETENCE • HIGH COMMITMENT	HIGH COMPETENCE • VARIABLE COMMITMENT	SOME COMPETENCE • LOW COMMITMENT	SOME COMPETENCE • HIGH COMMITMENT
D4	D3	D2	D1

DEVELOPED ◄─────────────────────────────► DEVELOPING

confidence in the people are increased and every person reaches their own God-given potential, using fully their God-given gifts to enable the church to grow up into all aspects unto Christ. This is precisely the model described in Ephesians 4:11–16.

As I look back over my ministry, I think that some of the staff problems I encountered were caused, in great part, by poor diagnosis on my part. For the sake of fairness, I wanted to treat everyone alike. Yet the skill levels of the various staff members were often quite different. I also discovered that a staff person may be competent in one area of responsibility and undeveloped in another. When I assumed equal competence in all areas of responsibility, I failed to give sufficient direction in new or less competent areas of ministry, and some individuals felt abandoned in their new job responsibilities.

This process of leadership development should be utilized as layleaders are called out, trained, and equipped. When a new task is given, strong support and clear direction are essential. As competence is gained, the need for support and shared ministry becomes more critical. The layleaders will then require somewhat less direction. Ultimately, you will feel comfortable delegating certain areas of responsibility, giving the person the freedom to develop and manage the given responsibility. They, in turn, should be encouraged to raise up new leaders for service.

Two charts follow that will aid you in using the proper leadership style for the various development levels (see below[14] and page 99).[15]

DEVELOPMENT LEVEL	APPROPRIATE LEADERSHIP STYLE
D1 Low Competence • High Commitment	**S1** DIRECTING Structure, control, and supervise
D2 Some Competence • Low Commitment	**S2** COACHING Direct and Support
D3 High Competence • Variable Commitment	**S3** SUPPORTING Praise, listen, and facilitate
D4 High Competence • High Commitment	**S4** DELEGATING Turn over responsibility for day-to-day decision-making

Blanchard suggests five steps for increasing persons' confidence and thus moving them along on the developmental scale: 1) tell them what to do; 2) show them what to do; 3) let them try; 4) observe performance; and 5) praise progress.[16] When compared with the discipling model of Jesus (see, pp. 86–88), we noted three differences: modeling before teaching, the sharing of passion and vision, and supernatural empowering. Thus, while we can learn from this business model, we must not forget that in pastoring the church, or leading a committee, we have available to us supernatural empowering through prayer. We have resources available to develop competence and confidence that are not accessible to the secular world. In leading the church, we must rely on the Holy Spirit to give us discernment and provide empowering. If you neglect to train people to pray

SITUATIONAL LEADERSHIP II

THE FOUR LEADERSHIP STYLES

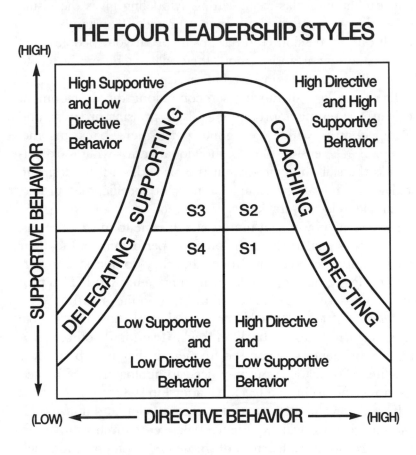

and to embrace and obey God's Word, you may develop an efficient management system, but you will not grow believers or Christ's church. Equally, we should not underestimate the power of shared vision and modeled behavior. Take people with you on a visit. Allow a prospective teacher to observe a competent teacher in a classroom setting. Modeling gives the visual image that instruction alone cannot provide. Constantly share the vision and passion God has given you. If your people don't share your dream and passion, they will not be motivated to learn skills or become involved in service.

The three keys to moving someone along the development scale are: 1) setting appropriate goals, 2) praising progress, and 3) reprimands which get good performers back in line. *Appropriate goals* ensure that the individual knows what is expected, has the skill to achieve what is expected, and the desire to achieve it. Thus appropriate goals must be specific, measurable, attainable, relevant, trackable, and agreed upon.

Praise is the power that motivates someone to make progress. The leader's goal is to catch someone performing up to their skill level and praise them. Notice that they do not have to perform perfectly, but up to their own competence level. This provides both positive feedback and motivation for growth.

Reprimands do not teach correct behavior, but only enable good performers to get back on track. If you find yourself having to reprimand a person too frequently, they may be in over their head. As leader, you may need to apologize for a missed diagnosis and go back a level in leadership style.[17]

If we lead volunteers or paid staff to develop and utilize their spiritual gifts, we will experience balanced church growth. To be effective we must learn to diagnose development, train, delegate, trust, and express gratitude for a job well done.

Express Praise and Gratitude

A survey of 25,000 non-management employees by International Survey Research Corporation of Chicago showed that "being treated with respect and fairness" satisfied employees most. Fifty-two percent of those surveyed ranked respect first. Pay and job security ranked second (48%) and third (46%).[18] Since pay and job security are non-issues with church volunteers, think how important the issues of respect and fairness are for the motivation of layleaders in the church. Fairness is achieved as we lead individuals according to their specific needs. Respect will come as recognition and gratitude are expressed for those who perform well.

We must be careful to give glory to Christ for the growth and to express proper gratitude to our people. I now belong to First Baptist Church, Woodstock, Georgia. The church has experienced incredible growth over the past several years under the leadership of Pastor Johnny Hunt. Johnny expects and demands a high level of commitment from the people, but they respond willingly because he frequently expresses gratitude and love. It is not at all unusual for Johnny to tell the congregation how much he loves them and how grateful he is to be their pastor. It is tragic that many pastors and leaders seem reluctant to express either gratitude or emotion.

At First Norfolk, we used volunteers, not only to teach and sing, but also for maintenance, yard work, and other such tasks. We regularly recognized these volunteers, not only by announcements from the pulpit, but also by special appreciation banquets. Yet the most powerful motivator was a personal word or note of thanks from those being impacted by the service. Praise is more effective when it is immediate, genuine, personal, and specific.

Your church can grow! God has given you, as leader, both tremendous opportunity and responsibility. Love your people and help them develop their full potential, and the church will grow naturally. I think this is what Paul meant in Ephesians 4:16; "from whom the whole body, being fitted and held together by that which every joint supplies, according to the proper working of each individual part, causes the growth of the body for the building up of itself in love." Note that growth comes from the Head, Christ, but is experienced as each part works according to its purpose and potential.

Characteristic 5:

Kingdom Family Relationships

Recently the long-running and highly successful television program "Cheers" called it quits. It was a show not well liked by many Christians, and rightly so, because it was set in a bar and often scorned biblical family values. Yet it apparently depicted "normal" existence for a large segment of our society. Why did the regulars come to the pub night after night? Was it because they were alcoholics and loved to drink? Actually bars somewhat discourage overindulgence since it gives them a bad name and disrupts the atmosphere. Why did they come? I think the theme song of "Cheers" said it all. Everybody is seeking a place where "everybody knows your name."

The world is crying out, "Is anybody there? Does anyone know my name? Does anybody care that I am alive?"

Out of curiosity I watched the much-touted last episode of "Cheers." I found it surprisingly and disarmingly honest. Sam and Diane were still deceiving each other about their happiness and still struggling to discover any sort of meaningful relationship. The other members of the cast began to filter out one by one to their own separate little worlds. The viewer received the impression that once the bar was closed, nothing existed that would bind the bar patrons to one another. The glue was the bar, nothing else. What they were all desperately seeking—community and fellowship—was sadly but honestly missing.

Words like loneliness, isolation, and alienation occur frequently in print today. America has become a transient society, and with that, many young adults have found themselves rootless and homeless. Often in the past people had a sense of community from their extended family who all lived within a few miles of each other. For many today the search for work has made this community no longer feasible. Now people feel isolated, a number in a crowd. The people surrounding them are faceless and anonymous acquaintances. The glue that could make them family simply does not exist at work, the health club, or the local bar.

A young Wake Forest student recently had the privilege of serving for a short time with Mother Teresa in Calcutta. When she asked Mother Teresa about the poverty, she responded that the worst poverty was "the feeling of abandonment, the feeling of being alone." She called this the poverty of the western world. People are "hungry not only for bread but hungry for love; naked not only for clothing, but naked of human dignity and respect; homeless not only for want of a room of bricks, but homeless because of rejection."[1]

Tragically people seeking community come to our churches and often find only a thin film of family promises without the substance of family relationships. One morning after I had preached on the theme of "God's Forever Family," a young married woman came to me in tears. She told me that she was one of those persons who felt isolated and lonely, even at church. She had been a member of our church for nearly two years and had regularly attended a young adult Bible study group. Her husband, who was not a Christian, did not attend with her, and thus she had found it difficult to discover and build relationships. The fact that we called ourselves "First Family" and emphasized fellowship made her feel even more alone. She wanted to break out, to know others, and to be known; but she was paralyzed by the idea of exposing herself to rejection. She had a twofold fear. She was afraid someone in her small group would speak to her, and she would then have to respond. But paradoxically, she was afraid no one would speak to her. Thus she often arrived late and left early to avoid any possibility of meaningful contact, and she remained alone.

Building and maintaining intimate community relationships in your church will not be an easy task. Larry Crabb and Jeff Jernigan warn that people enter our churches with built-in barriers to genuine community. They've never experienced it, and they've been taught to mistrust it. To them, community means uniformity, oppression, and control.[2] Thus many people have drifted toward ardent self-sufficiency and have eschewed any permanent relationships. Yet they have found this life-style desperately lacking and lonely.

People have an innate desire to belong, to know, to be known, and to be sheltered. On the opening pages of Scripture we are confronted with undeniable truth: "It is not good for the man to be alone" (Gen. 2:18). While this verse deals with marriage companionship, it points to a person's basic need for community relationships. In a recent report, given at the World Congress on Evangelism, George Gallup reported that people have renewed their search for more meaningful relationships. They are discovering the futility of going it alone.[3]

Healthy churches are committed to building kingdom community relationships. We will never build community if we allow people to remain isolated spectators of an audience. They must become members of the family. The church has the opportunity to reach and assimilate vast numbers of hurting and lonely people if we truly become the family we are called to be. But the world is not going to be impressed by our rhetoric on family; they must see the love of God modeled in an authentic, deeply loving, and committed community of believers.

The Biblical Fundamentals

Perhaps the best terminology for us to use to talk about kingdom community relationships is that of family. We have already looked at the pastor's role in terms of parenting; thus it is appropriate to look at community relationships in terms of family. The New Testament is replete with illustrations and terminology that compares community living to family relationships.

The Antioch Model

Beginning with our model church in Antioch, we cannot help but be impressed, as was Barnabas, with the visible presence of the grace of God evidenced by Jews and Gentiles sharing fellowship around the table. The barrier between Jews and Gentiles had existed for generations. It was not only a racial and cultural barrier, but it was a religious one as well. The Jews could give good biblical warrant for avoiding any social contact with the despised Gentiles. The fellowship between Jews and Gentiles was so startling a development that both Peter and Barnabas compromised this new found freedom when "certain men from James" came from Jerusalem to Antioch (see Gal. 2:11–16). Paul opposed Peter for his hypocrisy and corrected him by pointing to the grace of God, which had saved Jew and Gentile alike.

This humanly impenetrable barrier between Jew and Gentile was demolished in an instant through the power of the gospel. What could not have been accomplished through any human effort, grace had accomplished. Have we forgotten how radical the truths of Galatians 3:26–28 sounded in the first century? "For you are all sons of God through faith in Christ Jesus. For all of you who were baptized into Christ have clothed yourselves with Christ. There is neither Jew nor Greek, there is neither slave nor free man, there is neither male nor female; for you are all one in Christ Jesus." The church today faces similar barriers to fellowship, some as seemingly insurmountable as those of the first century, but we cannot forget the power of grace that broke down the barriers to fellowship in the first century is available today.

It is interesting, too, that the sense of family that permeated the church in Antioch was not limited to persons in Antioch. When the prophet Agabus prophesied a famine would impact the saints living in Judea, each of the disciples sent a contribution for the relief of the brethren living in Judea (see Acts 11:27–30). Why? Because they were family, and family members cannot ignore the needs of others in the family. One of the disturbing trends of our day that may have been fueled by the emphasis on "growing your church" is the lack of vision some have for the needs of the larger family. How can we consider a church to be a healthy, growing church if it does not manifest concern for the broader scope of God's family? Church growth is not a competitive sport but a cooperative ministry.

The commitment to family relationships in Antioch also required the concentration on nurturing and discipling new believers. Notice Luke's emphasis: "And it came about that for an entire year they met with the church, and taught consider-able numbers; and the disciples were first called Christians in Antioch" (Acts 11:26). The sequence of the verse is significant. These new believers who had been won to Christ from a pagan background did not resemble followers of Christ until they had been discipled for an entire year. Discipling is nothing more than parenting new believers as they grow to maturity.

The Saying of Jesus

The use of the term "brethren" throughout the Acts account and the Pauline letters is impressive indeed. Why did this fami-ly term become commonplace in the early Christian communi-ty? While we may not be able to establish a single reason, we certainly cannot overlook a significant event in the lives of those first disciples. "And His mother and brothers came to Him, and they were unable to get to Him because of the crowd. And it was reported to Him, 'Your mother and Your brothers are standing outside, wishing to see You.' But He answered and said to them, 'My mother and My brothers are these who hear the word of God and do it'" (Luke 8:19–21). Can you imagine the impact of Jesus' words on those early disciples? "He called us family. We are His brothers and sisters." Perhaps the disciples only realized the full impact of this saying as they gathered in the upper room awaiting the empowering of the Spirit. Luke told us that about 120 persons, men and women, were gath-ered. When Peter stood up in the midst of the disciples and began to speak, he addressed them as brethren (Acts 1:14–16).

The Acts Pattern

These early believers, Jews and Gentiles alike, were literally thrust together by their common conviction that Jesus was the Messiah and by their commitment to Him as the living and resurrected Lord. The Jews who became followers of Christ were cut off by former family and friends as they identified with what Jewish authorities deemed to be a dangerous and heretical splinter group that had departed from historic Judaism. You'll recall that they put Stephen to death and began a systematic persecution against the church in Jerusalem (see Acts 7:54—8:3). Paul, out of devout religious conviction, began to ravage the church, putting men and women in prison. Later Paul sought and received official permission to journey to Damascus to seek out those committed to the Way so that he could return them bound to Jerusalem (see Acts 9:1–2).

We can only surmise that the Gentile believers who abandoned the idolatrous religions of their family met with similar ostracism. Thus they were drawn together by common loyalty to Christ, and by the Spirit's power were made members of God's household. They formed family relationships which were deeper and more binding than any earthly relationships.

Any church seeking to develop a biblical pattern for fellowship cannot help but be impressed with the description of family unity the early church shared:

> And they were continually devoting themselves to the apostles' teaching and to fellowship, to the breaking of bread and to prayer. And everyone kept feeling a sense of awe; and many wonders and signs were taking place through the apostles. And all those who had believed were together, and had all things in common; and they began selling their property and possessions, and were sharing them with all, as anyone might have need. And day by day continuing with one mind in the temple, and breaking bread from house to house, they were taking their meals together with gladness and sincerity of heart, praising God, and having favor with all the people. And the Lord was adding to their number day by day those who were being saved. (Acts 2:42–47)

That passage is so moving and comprehensive that it nearly defies comment. Some Bible students have missed the impact of this passage by suggesting it pictures a communal pattern of life not practical today. The early church was not a commune. The early Christians did not dispose of all earthly property and retreat to some ranch in the Palestinian desert. We have no such picture in Acts or the Pauline letters. The text indicates the believers still maintained property rights and sold property and possessions as family needs dictated. The fact that the early believers continued to break bread from house to house further suggests that they continued their private lives and maintained personal property. However, their relationships became such that they literally began to live as extended family.

They met together on a regular basis for instruction, fellowship, breaking of bread (perhaps a reference to the Lord's Supper), and for prayer. Yet their fellowship extended beyond the confines of the assembled times together. They shared their possessions to help those whose needs were greater than their own. It is likely some of the early believers literally became homeless because of their commitment to follow Christ. They were ostracized by their birth families, but they were taken in by their new family. Such was the intensity of their fellowship that the regular gatherings for worship and teaching did not satisfy their family needs; thus, they were taking their meals together with gladness in various private homes.

The Teaching of Paul

Paul's life and teaching were profoundly influenced by his great Damascus road experience. We often focus only on Paul's great encounter with the Lord. We must, however, wonder how the days and weeks following Paul's salvation experience must have impacted him. He was now a man without a people. The early Christians knew him by reputation and feared him as a first century "terminator." With his commitment to follow Christ, he could not return to his former friends in Judaism. Remember that for three days after his conversion he was a helpless blind man. God sent Ananias to Paul to restore his sight and perhaps to introduce him to his new family. Imagine the impact of the first word Paul heard as Ananias lay his hands on him. "Brother Saul, the Lord Jesus, who appeared to you on the road by which you were coming, has sent me so that you may regain your sight and be filled with the Holy Spirit" (Acts 9:17). The use of the endearing term "brother" may have been more moving than the news he was to receive his sight. He had been adopted into a new family. After he regained his sight, he was baptized and fed. This new family met both his spiritual and physical needs and provided protection. We are told he stayed with them many days as he continued to grow in strength (see v. 22). Subsequently, his preaching produced a crisis and it was the disciples who lowered him over the wall at night (see v. 25). When he came to Jerusalem, Barnabas boldly introduced Paul to the Christian community which was still afraid of him. As the ire of the Hellenistic Jews increased, it was the brethren, his new family members, who risked their lives to send Paul away to Tarsus. Paul had experienced family protection.

I have already made mention of Paul's use of the parenting image to describe his relationship to his churches. This imagery promotes the concept of seeing the church as family. Paul, in Galatians, one of his earliest letters, instructed the believers: "So then, while we have opportunity, let us do good to all men, and especially to those who are of the household of the faith" (6:10). Believers form a new household that is established through like faith in Jesus Christ. While Christians must be committed to doing good to all persons, we have a special responsibility to do good to members of our own household.

Paul's Ephesian letter is replete with references to the church as body and as family. The first half of chapter 2 talks about the glorious work of salvation by grace through faith. The last half of the chapter deals with the results of salvation, that is, the workmanship of God. Paul made allusion to the uniting of Jews and Gentiles, two separate and alienated groups of persons, into one new person (see vv. 2:13–15). The imagery reminds us of the miracle of marriage where two persons become one flesh. Paul followed this discussion by using three illustrations for the new community which had been founded in Christ. The first is citizenship, the second is family, and the third is a holy temple (see vv. 19–21). We are fellow-citizens with one another; we are brothers and sisters in God's household, and we form a living temple for the indwelling presence of God's Spirit.

Paul concluded chapter three with an impassioned prayer for the church to become the full expression of God Himself. One facet of that prayer involved the discovery of the full expression of God's love with all the saints (see 3:17–19). It is interesting to note that individually we will never know the love of Christ which surpasses our knowing. It can only be known "with all the saints," that is, in the context of Christian community. Through our Christian family relationships we come to know experientially that which surpasses knowing individually. As we come individually to the family we each bring our own small portion of the brilliantly hued "love of Christ." As we place them together in the mosaic we call family, an exquisite pattern emerges.

In chapter four Paul called the believers to be diligent to preserve the unity which had been given by the Spirit. He then expounded upon the sevenfold basis of our family unity—"There is one body and one Spirit, just as also you were called in one hope of your calling; one Lord, one faith, one baptism, one God and Father of all who is over all and through all and in all" (4:4–6). We are one family because we are all born again of the same Father. As family we are indwelt by the one Holy Spirit, have one Lord, and are thus united in one cause.[4]

Teach Theological Basics and Model Family Living

The key to the development of family relationships in the church is the pastor, the father. If the pastor invests the time and energy necessary to become the pastor-father of the church, the church will begin to reflect his character as he, in turn, must reflect the character of the Lord. Let's look back again to 1 Corinthians 4:14–21 where Paul compared his ministry in Corinth to that of a father. Look at verses sixteen and seventeen: "I exhort you therefore, be imitators of me. For this reason I have sent to you Timothy, who is my beloved and faithful child in the Lord, and he will remind you of my ways which are in Christ, just as I teach everywhere in every church." Most early behavior is learned by imitation. Parents watch in amazement as small children imitate their actions and mannerisms as they develop and mature. Paul both recognized and encouraged this principle. He instructed the immature Corinthians to model their behavior after his as he modeled his after Christ.

This puts a heavy, but biblical, responsibility to be above reproach on any person who would be pastor or leader. This does not mean you must be perfect to be a pastor or to function as a lay pastoral caregiver in the church, any more than you have to be perfect to be a parent. Sometimes a parent has to say, "I was wrong; will you forgive me?" Children must see confession and forgiveness modeled, too. The key is that people will not learn to be family simply by teaching them the biblical basics of what it means to be members of the household of God. They must see and experience the dynamics of what it means to be family.

This is made more complex first of all by the fact that the church is made up of persons who are at different stages of spiritual development. Some are spiritual preschoolers who need constant attention. Some are developing adolescents with their emotional highs and lows. Second, the church family receives new children by birth (evangelism) and by adoption (transfer). Some adopted children may come from dysfunctional church families and may have never experienced healthy church relationships. Some may have been relationally abused by their former pastor-parent and thus have trouble relating to another pastor. The presence of adopted children or teenagers will always change family dynamics. Their healing and assimilation into the family requires the rest of the family to take time for consistently modeling healthy relationships.

If you are a pastor and your church is to become family, you must teach the biblical principles and allow the Holy Spirit to apply them individually. Keep the biblical context of family constantly before the church through your preaching and teaching. But you must begin the process of modeling family before it will become reality. Start with a few key leaders and parent them to maturity using the leadership pattern discussed in characteristic three. As they grow to maturity, teach them to parent-disciple others. Put mature, parenting leaders in places of leadership in your small groups so that the process of parenting can be extended throughout the church. You cannot produce a family climate in your church without effective small groups. These may include a combination of Sunday School classes and cell groups, but they must be structured so as to provide care giving for their members. In this fashion the church will "grow up in all aspects into Him, who is the head, even Christ" (Eph. 4:15).

What Is Entailed in Family Living?

What do we mean when we speak of the church as family? What are the dynamic essentials of family living? Definitions and descriptions of family have become more complex in recent days. During the discussion of sex education and family values in Norfolk, there was some debate on what was meant by "family." One suggested definition was: "People connected by birth, marriage, or adoption living in relationship under the same roof." That definition was not selected, but it might make a good starting point for our discussion of the church as family. We are related by birth and adoption, and therefore we must learn to live in relationship. Let's discuss nine components of family living:

1. The family is an ecologically balanced environment for the maturation of human beings. Edith Schaeffer first introduced me to this concept.[5] A balanced family environment promotes emotional, psychological, spiritual, moral, and physical growth. Environmental factors include oneness, security, responsibility, loyalty, faithfulness, generosity, trustworthiness, commitment, and endurance.

An ecologically balanced environment includes and provides for the whole life cycle development. In the healthy family there is the time of new birth, early development, the awkward adolescent and teen years, early adulthood, maturity, and finally death. The church as family experiences these realities in both the spiritual and physical realms. Through the program of evangelistic outreach, the birthing phase of life is duplicated. Any church that does not reproduce itself through evangelism is an unhealthy family system.

When a baby is born into the church through the evangelistic birth process, the intensive work of parenting a newborn begins. Many churches with an evangelistic thrust often think the hard work is completed when the baby is delivered. Any parent knows the toil is just beginning! Educators now tell us that the early years are formative for the development of personality and character. This is the period in which the emotional bonding that prompts healthy development occurs. It is a time of labor-intensive, one-on-one parenting. The nursing mother knows the intensity of the work when every three hours the newborn longs to be fed and held. Peter spoke of the intense hunger of newborn babes for the pure milk of the Word (see 1 Pet. 2:2).

We have all discovered many disillusioned persons who prayed a prayer or walked an aisle but simply never connected with a local church. Most begin to doubt the validity of their decision or the transforming power of salvation because they have not experienced a lifestyle change. In many instances, this confusion may have resulted from the lack of sufficient early discipling. Without this one-on-one parenting, bonding failed to take place. In my conversations with mature Christians who are continuing to grow in the Lord, all could name an individual who invested energy and time in the early developmental years of their spiritual life. We will consider this in greater detail in the characteristic on discipleship, but the most effective early discipling tool is one-on-one nurturing. As believers begin to mature, they may go through early periods of rebellion or disillusionment. They may become withdrawn and appear to have no desire to be with other family members. I can vividly remember these various stages with my own children. With certain children one stage can be so prolonged that you wonder if either of you will survive it. With other children they are momentary blips, or they don't occur at all. I remember when my oldest daughter went from being neat, organized, and outgoing to a somewhat reclusive slob. It was fortunately a passing phase, and we all survived it because we were committed unconditionally to family unity. We expressed our concern, gave her some space, and showed her our unconditional love.

As pastor of several different-sized churches in rural and urban settings, I have been amazed that human needs are so consistently the same. I have also been amazed to note how similar pastoring is to parenting. I have watched young adolescent Christians rebel and act out during that time of rebellion. Some would even declare their intention to "run away from home." I have seen, too, that when the church family remains consistent, concerned, and compassionate, they have the freedom to return.

The church will also experience the bittersweet joy of watching a child mature into young adulthood. I say bittersweet because it is the day we have worked and longed for, yet when it comes, it brings a small note of sadness as we cut the apron strings of dependence. Watching my oldest daughter leave for college was such an experience. While I was proud of her independence, I wanted her to need me just a little while longer. Yet in time, the maturing child and maturing Christian must be given the opportunity to find their own niche within the family. Many Christians remain stunted adolescents throughout their Christian lifetimes because they are not allowed or encouraged to find their place of maturing adult service. Leadership, service, and commitment in the church family are not simply issues reflecting the need of the church for volunteers, they are matters of Christian maturity and family participation.

If the church is to provide the ecologically balanced environment for Christian growth, there must be feeding, sharing, modeling, teaching, disciplining, delegating, and praising. Our ultimate goal? "Until we all attain to the unity of the faith, and of the knowledge of the Son of God, to a mature man, to the measure of the stature which belongs to the fulness of Christ" (Eph. 4:13).

2. There are six key relationships in the church family. If the church family is going to be healthy, we must continually monitor these six key relationships. A visual representation of the relationships is pictured on the next page.

The first key relationship is the pastor's to God. Ultimately, a church will not mature beyond the depth of the pastor's relationship to God. A quick reading of 2 Chronicles provides this critical insight: the conditions in Israel were inextricably linked to the relationships of the kings to God. When a new king is introduced, the Chronicler notes that he "did good and right in the sight of the Lord his God" (2 Chron. 14:2) or "he did evil in the sight of the Lord" (21:6). The conditions in Israel changed in response to the king's relationship to God.

Jehoshaphat provides one example. He began his reign with obedience to the Lord and prosperity resulted (see 17:3–6). Then he allied himself with Ahab and began a reliance on human wisdom (see 18:1ff.). This resulted in the disastrous bat-

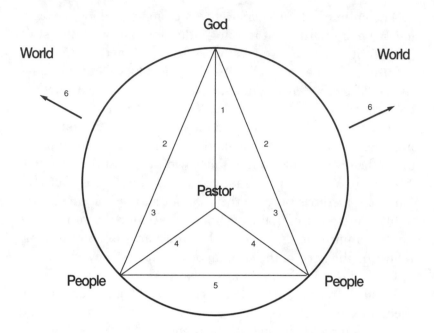

tle at Ramoth-gilead (see chap. 18). Jehoshaphat returned to the Lord when rebuked by the prophet Jehu. Listen to his prayer when invasion came from the Ammonites: "O Lord, the God of our fathers, art Thou not God in the heavens? And art Thou not ruler over all the kingdoms of the nations? Power and might are in Thy hand so that no one can stand against Thee" (20:6). The battle plan was literally for Israel to worship and praise God. The prophet Jahaziel spoke: "Do not fear or be dismayed because of this great multitude, for the battle is not yours but God's" (20:15). As Israel sang praises, the enemies destroyed one another (see 20:20–25). Unfortunately and unbelievably, Jehoshaphat responded to this supernatural victory by establishing an alliance with Ahaziah to make ships to go to Tarshish. The Lord then destroyed his works: "So the ships were broken and could not go to Tarshish" (v. 37). The king's relationship with God had a profound impact on Israel's prosperity. If you want to see this pattern of obedience and victory repeated, study the reign of Hezekiah in 2 Chronicles 29–32.

I am not suggesting that the pastor is like the king of Israel, but I do believe there is a biblical correlation between the health of a church and the spiritual condition of the pastor. Since church growth is a supernatural event, *the relationship of the pastor and the people to God is of greater significance than any program or strategy.* Remember how God fought for Israel? The same God desires to grow His church through you. If there exists even a hairline fracture in the pastor's relationship with God, it will be revealed by the stress of parenting the church. Often it will be revealed during times of victory and growth as with Jehoshaphat.

I grew up near Randleman, North Carolina, the home of the Petty racing enterprise. The metal frame garage near the Pettys' home contained some of the most sophisticated equipment available at the time for finely tuning a racing engine. I was fascinated to discover that they actually x-rayed key engine components. If a hairline fracture was discovered, they discarded what appeared to the unaided eye to be a perfectly good engine part. In truth, it probably would have performed acceptably for many miles at normal operational speeds. But when these same parts were exposed to high speeds and stress of a race environment, the fracture was exposed and the results were disastrous.

George Barna's recent study of today's pastors reveals that the pressure of pastoring is enormous and is increasing. Researchers have discovered that pastors make up one of the most frustrated occupational groups in our country. Four out of ten doubt that their present church experience is significantly deepening their relationship with Christ.[6] If that is the case, they are unlikely to lead in any significant church growth. The emphasis on numerical church growth has been, for some, the high-speed stress that revealed the unseen crack in the engine block.

Pastor, you cannot neglect your personal relationship with God and grow the church. The spiritual warfare implicit in supernatural church growth will put faith to the test. You can stand firm, but you must stay on your knees, in the Word, and with the family. I would highly recommend that you develop some system of spiritual accountability. I asked about a dozen men to meet with me on a regular basis and to hold me accountable in all areas of my life. They set the agenda for each meeting, and I gave them permission to ask me tough questions about my personal life. These meetings were both painful and joyous as the Spirit brought conviction and cleansing.

The second key relationship is that of the people of the church to God. The pastor does not stand alone in terms of responsibility for a proper relationship to God; it is required of all God's people. There must be a hunger to know God and to obey Him. This desire is fueled as God's people grow in their knowledge of Him. Worship and prayer, as already indicated, are essential to the spiritual growth of the people of God. We will look further at the need for discipling Bible study in characteristic 7. Here again, since church growth is a supernatural activity of God, *the growth of the church will be largely determined by the depth of the relationships of God's people to Him.*

I do not mean to imply that the megachurch has greater spirituality than a small church simply because it is larger. The success of church growth is not simply measured in numerical terms, but also in maturational terms. The rural church with a small population base could not expect to have the same numerical growth as the church in the densely populated metropolitan area. Remember, church growth is the local church faithfully fulfilling the Great Commission in its context and with a commitment to the world. *If we will pay attention to spiritual depth, the Lord will provide the increase to His church.*

The third and fourth key relationships are the pastor to the people and the people to the pastor. The work of many churches has been hindered by broken relationships between pastor and people. Some churches have been injured by an abusive or uncaring pastor and, in turn, many pastors have been hurt by their churches. Neither situation is pleasing to the Lord. Before any church can grow, there must be forgiveness and healing where necessary, and mutual love developed between pastor and people.

Note the directions Paul gave to the Thessalonians: "But we request of you, brethren, that you *appreciate* those who diligently labor among you, and have charge over you in the Lord and give you instruction, and *that you esteem them very highly in love* because of their work. Live in *peace with one another*" (1 Thess. 5:12–13, author's italics). Note the words "appreciate" and "esteem highly in love." Pastors need both the appreciation and love of their people if they are to be successful in fulfilling their God-given tasks. You may have noted the phrase "because of their work." The work of the church impacts eternity and for that reason, we cannot allow petty personality problems to destroy unity and peace. These mutual relationships permit the church to live in peace which is essential for healthy growth. If both the pastor and the people have been honest and serious about relationships one and two described above, then relationships three and four will develop naturally.

The fifth key relationship is the people to the people. Many churches are hampered in their growth because there are factions within the church fighting for their own agendas rather than focusing on God's agenda—the Great Commission. Paul had to rebuke the church at Corinth for their arrogant boasting about leaders and the dissension this had caused (see 1 Cor. 3). So serious was the conflict in Corinth that some believers were taking fellow-believers before secular courts of law. Paul was aghast. No matter who won the lawsuit, the church was defeated by the display of disunity and immaturity (see 1 Cor. 6:7).

In 1 Thessalonians 5, where Paul gave directions for the relationship of pastor and people, he also gave directions concerning the ministry of the brethren to each other. "And we urge you, brethren, admonish the unruly, encourage the fainthearted, help the weak, be patient with all men. See that no one repays another with evil for evil, but always seek after that which is good for one another and for all men. Rejoice always; pray without ceasing; in everything give thanks; for this is God's will for you in Christ Jesus" (1 Thess. 5:14–18). Notice that many of the pastoral care functions we often expect only of the pastor are actually responsibilities of all the brethren. Who should admonish new Christians acting like unruly preschool believers? Who should encourage discouraged new Christians acting like adolescent believers? The brethren!

We have already noted the dynamic link between knowing the full expression of Christ's love and the community relationship shared by believers in Ephesians 3:17–19. "So that Christ may dwell in your hearts through faith; and that you, being rooted and grounded in love, may be able to comprehend with all the saints what is the breadth and length and height and depth, and to know the love of Christ which surpasses knowledge, that you may be filled up to all the fulness of God." The incomprehensible love of Christ can only be known in its fullness *with all the saints.*[7] Here again, this fifth relationship will be healed if God's people are serious when they deal with relationship two above.

The final relationship is the church to the world. This was alluded to in 1 Thessalonians where Paul encouraged the Thessalonians to seek after that which is good for one another and for all persons. Our relationship to the world must be one of redemptive concern. The greatest good we can do through word and deed is to bring persons in the world the choice of a saving relationship with Jesus Christ and thus entry into His family. It will involve both social concern and evangelistic passion. Anything less would not be the full gospel. We will look at this aspect of family more fully in characteristic 6.

3. The family is a place where mutual care abounds. Paul modeled the concern required for family living. Writing to the Thessalonians, he stated: "Having thus a fond affection for you, we were well-pleased to impart to you not only the gospel of God but also our own lives, because you had become very dear to us" (2:8). Paul's love required that he impart his own life. We cannot give family care without first giving ourselves. The love required for mutual care is well described in 1 Corinthians 13. It is self-giving love that is the fruit of the Holy Spirit. It cannot be produced by human striving, but is experienced through yieldedness to the Spirit of God.

Paul most clearly described the outworking of such love in Romans 12:9–21. Our family love, he began, must be pure, having no hint of hypocrisy (see v. 9). The remainder of the characteristic is a commentary on the operation of pure love. In this passage, Paul used two different Greek words for love. One is *philadelphia* which means "brotherly love." The second is *philostorgia* which means "the tender care of a mother loving her own child." We could paraphrase, "Love the brethren the way a mother loves and nurtures her own child."

Our family concern will cause us to abhor evil and cling to good. Evil, simply put, is destructive to Christian fellowship. Thus, when we see evil about to destroy the vitality of a family member, we must intercede out of love. We cannot tolerate evil because it is destructive to individuals and their family relationships. Church discipline and the confrontation it requires issue out of family love.

One of the most pervasive evils of our day is divorce. It is a lose-lose situation. Everyone is hurt, including the church family. As pastor of a large congregation, I unfortunately saw my share of broken families. I often watched helplessly from the sidelines when no one asked me for help. Out of fatherly concern I decided to become proactive. When I would hear that a couple was struggling or contemplating divorce, I would call and ask for an appointment. Often my intercession fell on deaf ears, but to my surprise, all alike thanked me for my efforts. They would often say, "We wondered if anyone from the church cared." To put this in proper perspective simply ask yourself as a parent to what extent would you go to keep your children from destructive behavior?

Family love is not theoretical but intensely practical. It will cause us to give preference to one another in honor. This idea sounds radical in our culture where we have been trained to look out for number one. It is only in the context of family that we see individuals actually elevate the need of another above their own interests. This is an activity that must be learned through modeled behavior. Children see their parents sacrifice to provide for their needs and in turn learn to live sacrificially. Christians are motivated to live for others because in so doing they are serving the Lord (see v. 11). Such a servant spirit is not easy to maintain; thus, Paul underlines joy, perseverance, and prayer as the essential ingredients of servanthood.

Mutual care must be practical, embodying physical expressions such as contributing to the needs of the saints and practicing hospitality (see v. 13).[8] Think of the simple acts of concern such as notes, letters, and phone calls that abound in the caring family. Our church was organized for care through the Sunday School. Each class had a primary caregiver who organized others for caring ministry. As pastor, I rarely ministered to a hurting person who had not already been touched by the concern of a care leader. During the Desert Storm crisis, our care leaders and teachers had multiple opportunities to provide mutual care. Soon after the war began, my wife and my youngest daughter Katie rode their bikes to the home of a young, expectant mother. Her husband had already been dispatched, and she was alone in Norfolk. Paula offered the ministry of the Sunday School class which they had been visiting and simply said, "If you need me, feel free to call." We weren't expecting the call that came at 2:30 in the morning. "Paula, can you help me? I'm going into labor." It was a joy to observe the entire Sunday School class go into action to provide all the assistance necessary for this young lady whose other family lived a substantial distance from Norfolk.

As a pastor I have usually been on the giving end of care, but a few years ago my dad was diagnosed with a brain tumor. The response of our church family went beyond anything I could have anticipated. When I looked up and saw several men of our church walk into the hospital waiting room which was seven hours from our church, I cannot begin to describe the emotions I felt. These men truly were my brothers. Family care is essential to healthy community living.

When our churches begin to express mutual concern we will see our families grow stronger and more vital. Few persons will drop out of a church that expresses family care. Unsaved persons will be impacted by our love. It is true that the secular person doesn't care what you believe until they believe you care.

4. *Healthy family relationships require time and effort.* We cannot build healthy family relationships without the expenditure of time and effort. Human relationships are hard work. The Hemphill family is made up of five persons. Maintaining healthy relationships in this small family is a full-time job. The church family is a much larger, complex family made up of naturally born and adopted family members. Some persons who join church families have had good family experiences while others have been in dysfunctional church families. Each person brings his or her own agenda and needs. When a church family has a large number of new Christians, it will find the parenting is labor intensive. Do you remember how labor intensive it was when you had one preschooler in your home? Multiply that times the number of new Christians you have in your church and you will understand why church growth is physically and spiritually fatiguing.

Rich and Allison Culpepper planted a church in Connecticut several years ago. Our church was helping to sponsor their work, so we rejoiced in their regular reports of continued growth. The early years were demanding as the new family struggled to become established. Rich thought things would get easier as the church grew in size. Yet a growing family brings new demands such as the need for additional space. Rich's task was made even more demanding by the large number of people who were led to Christ through his ministry. While evangelistic growth is always exciting, the large number of new believers in a young church creates a unique demand. Rich and Allison have found themselves having to wear several hats and do several jobs at the same time because the new Christians had not yet grown to maturity.

I am concerned that some of the church growth designs that adjust church schedules to the supposed desires of Boomers for less time in a church setting have unwittingly sacrificed the time needed to build church family relationships. If we do not spend sufficient time together to build family relationships, we forfeit the opportunity to experience true biblical fellowship. We should be cautious to use time wisely and not waste family time with meeting for the sake of meeting.

Family time is precious and should be used for celebrating, feeding, nurturing, and strengthening relationships for family. For family to become reality, the small group structure of your church must be strengthened. Always carefully monitor the percentage of those regularly participating in cells, small groups, or Sunday School against those attending worship. It is easier to draw a crowd than to grow a family. Every church should strive for 100 percent of worshipers involved in the small group structure. Since many guests to our family celebration time will attend worship only for a short period of time, 100 percent is probably an unlikely achievement. If attendance in the small groups slips below 75 percent of worship attendance, we should take steps to improve the quality of care provided in the small groups. You may attract people through a large celebrative worship service, but you will not build family in that single context.

5. *For a family to grow, generosity must abound.* When the church at Antioch heard about the famine which would impact the believers in Judea, each of the disciples determined to send a contribution for the relief of the brethren (see Acts 11:29). When a church begins to grow, it will ultimately begin to face challenges to its generosity. If the people lose the spirit of generosity, growth will be impeded and finally stopped. When this occurs many

churches will actually vote, or informally decide, not to grow. Few churches would actually entertain a motion to close the doors to any new members—it would be difficult to pass a motion against the Great Commission. The language of the actual motion may be worded so as to conceal the real meaning and motive of the motion.

Perhaps you have heard or said words like these: "I can't understand why we place such an emphasis on evangelism; I don't know everyone now. Why should we go after more people when we can't find half of the ones on our rolls?" "If we get any larger, we're going to lose our intimacy." "I don't think we can afford to buy more land, build additional space, or hire additional staff now." "We shouldn't consider adding an additional Sunday School or worship service; it would require too much work and hurt our fellowship."

You recognize the fallacy of such thinking. God didn't establish the church to make us comfortable, but to fulfill the Great Commission. We aren't dependent upon any resources but His. Once church membership exceeds more than thirty-eight people it has already surpassed the number which most people are able to know intimately. The church family is made up of many small family groupings within the larger family. By organizing your small groups to provide for family intimacy, you can continue to fulfill the Great Commission and spend the time together that family unity requires.

If you don't develop a genuine sense of generosity, your church or class will cease to grow when it faces challenges that demand sacrifice. First Norfolk, like most growing churches, faced many such challenges. Over half of our members willingly parked off property every Sunday morning so that our guests and senior adults could park in the few parking places we could provide. Our people willingly gave up their classroom space when it was needed by another class. Teachers were willing to create new units so that small group care remained consistent and the church continued to reach the lost. I am convinced that the lack of a generous spirit has hampered many churches in their obedience of the Great Commission. Such disobedience then prohibits the flow of grace and ultimately leads to lethargy in the church.

6. The family encourages unity through diversity. When my second daughter was born, I was simply amazed at how different she was from our first. Not only did she look differently, but she behaved differently and had different tastes. At first it was hard for me to imagine she had been born of the same two parents and into the same environment. My dad quickly corrected me on the last point. Rachael wasn't born into the same environment as Tina. She had a sister when she was born. Her parents now lived in North Carolina, not England. Paula and I were older and somewhat wiser.

A family is always changing in its character. It must celebrate its diversity while, at the same time, working to maintain its unity. The body imagery in the Pauline letters underlines the value of unity in diversity. The body has many members, each with a unique function, and all vital to the proper functioning of the body. We must not expect the foot to perform like a hand. We cannot arrogantly boast that we have no need of any of the members God Himself places in the body. In truth God has so composed the body that He gives more abundant honor to the member lacking honor so that there is no division and the members then can care for one another (see 1 Cor. 12:12–27).

Edith Schaeffer argues that the family is the birthplace of creativity. It is a laboratory for discovery and experimentation. For creativity to flourish, an atmosphere of trust must exist. Two-way communication, which involves listening and talking, allows individuals to discover their unique giftedness. Such an atmosphere enables persons to try new avenues of creativity without fear of reprimand. Schaeffer argues that in such an atmosphere feedback which immediately follows an initial, creative presentation should be positive. If there is to be helpful criticism, it should come later and be aimed at edification.[9]

When our daughter Kristina was twelve years old, she went through a phase where she wanted to be a drummer. I can't honestly say that we were genuinely thrilled with her vocational choice! We were somewhat surprised since she had previously shown neither interest in the drums nor any ability to play them. Nevertheless, we allowed her to take drum lessons. Fortunately the phase passed. Her creative spirit remained unabated. Our family has a tradition of joining our extended family for the

Christmas holidays. We would generally meet at a cabin near the Blue Ridge Parkway. Kristina would organize the assorted nieces and nephews into a small drama group. They would create the costumes, choreograph the dance, and write and memorize what few lines were necessary for the show to go on. They would rehearse in the basement throughout the morning and then sell tickets to the adult family members to attend the opening (and only) performance.

The plays were short and simple, and would often have to be squeezed in between half-time of a televised game and dinner, but it was a joyous time for all. Kristina is now attending college on an art scholarship. She has immense talent and creativity. We're glad that she didn't remain a drummer, and I doubt that she will go into show business. However, we're glad we encouraged her to exercise her creativity and discover her unique giftedness.

The church must encourage creativity and provide the opportunity for experimentation in the context of loving community for members to discover their unique giftedness.[10] The discovery and use of one's spiritual gift(s) is directly related to family unity and love. The opportunity to attempt some area of service and fail without being a failure is permissible only in a family unit.

7. *The family teaches and models family values.* The greater majority of my personal values were learned in the context of my family. Sometimes these values were taught through verbal instruction, but most often they were learned by observation and imitation. It always brings me great pleasure when someone tells me I remind them of my father. I have always enjoyed serving others, but I can take no credit for my servant attitude; it came naturally from my father. It was his greatest joy to be of service to someone else. He would go to church early on Sunday mornings just to start the coffee pot for the men's class. I learned to tithe by observing my parents prepare their offering envelope. I developed a love for missions and a commitment to give to missions by watching my mom put her loose change in a container in anticipation of our annual foreign missions offering. My dad was scrupulously honest in all of his dealings with others and taught his children to be the

same. These values and others were never forced upon me; they seemed like natural expressions of our family.

If we want to teach love, service, sharing, humility, stewardship, and other family values, they must become a part of our family conversation and behavior. I fear we have often divorced issues such as service and giving from the context of family and thus they are viewed as duties to be done rather than values shared by the entire family. When one member of the family fails to fulfill his/her responsibility, the family as a whole is punished.

8. Family requires loving discipline. Paul's instructions for fathers in Ephesians 6:4 is equally applicable to the disciplinary needs of the church. "And, fathers, do not provoke your children to anger; but bring them up in the discipline and instruction of the Lord." Discipline in the church will always embody both affirmation and correction. People learn from affirmation and are redirected by correction. Most church discipline will be accomplished by an accurate and thorough teaching of God's Word. "All Scripture is inspired by God and profitable for teaching, for reproof, for correction, for training in righteousness; that the man of God may be adequate, equipped for every good work" (2 Tim. 3:16–17). We cannot compromise the teaching of God's Word if we are going to build strong churches full of mature Christians.

John White and Ken Blue in their book on church discipline argue that church discipline is anything the body of Christ does to train Christians in holiness, calling them to follow their Lord more closely. Training actually provides the context in which corrective discipline can be most helpful.[11]

If you want to understand church discipline, you need only to think about healthy discipline in the home. Healthy discipline majors on training and affirmation. Corrective discipline should only be applied when absolutely necessary, and it must be aimed at correction, not ostracism and punishment. It must always be accompanied with clear instruction and be given in the context of family love and security. *Deal only with the behavior; never attack the person.*

Our church was saddened by the news one of our faithful members had been involved in embezzling funds from her employer. It was a behavior pattern that had developed over time. Her response and the church family response were right on target. Her greatest concern was that her actions would bring reproach upon the body of Christ. She was grieved by her actions and came to the church leaders in abject repentance. She went to trial and was sentenced to a short jail sentence. The church rallied to her side and ministered to her and her other family members while she was in jail. Food was taken to the family, financial assistance was given, and loving concern was shown. It was a day of celebration when she was able to leave the jail and rejoin both her families. She didn't have to come slinking back to church; her return was seen as a joyous occasion and a time for celebration. Sounds strikingly like the story of the prodigal son, doesn't it?

9. *The family provides protection and healing.* I can remember many instances when I ran home for the protection it provided. I knew my home was a safe haven no matter what threatened me. My mom's arms and my dad's lap were so large and safe; nothing could harm me there. No childhood injury was so large it couldn't be healed by a little mercurochrome and a tender hug. The Bible speaks often about the need to care for the widows and orphans—those who need protection. This same protection must be extended to all family members. We must be careful that we not injure one another in our family relationships. The Lord sternly warns of severe consequences for anyone who would cause a child to stumble. The family offers protection whenever it is needed.

For many new Christians the church is the lap that provides warmth, protection, comfort, and healing. It is a safe haven and a center for healing those wounded in the battle. We can't get caught up in the "growth-at-any-cost" mindset and fail to provide a safe haven for the members of the family. Your church ought to be a place where God's people feel safe and protected, cherished and nourished, secure and loved, healed and challenged.

In Christ we are family by birth and adoption. We're going to live together for all eternity. It is high time we begin to behave now like God's forever family.

Characteristic 6:

God-Sized Vision

What ignites a church and propels it forward into unprecedented growth? Most pastors who have experienced healthy church growth readily agree that vision is the fuel for church growth. Robert Dale notes: "A healthy dream is a necessary foundation for a healthy organization. Nothing less than a Kingdom dream will turn a church toward healthy and aggressive ministry."[1]

The most frequently quoted vision-building verse is Proverbs 29:18. The *King James Version* reads: "Where there is no vision the people perish." The *New International Version* reads, "Where there is no revelation, the people cast off restraint." Vision, then, does not refer to the ability to formulate goals and work toward them, but rather to the work of the prophet. Thus the verse is pointing to the guidance or revelation of God. The word "perish" in the KJV is better rendered by more recent translations as "cast off restraint." The verse teaches that the nation or church that ignores God's Word can anticipate spiritual anarchy and lack of clear direction.[2]

This verse properly understood still stands as the anchor for this characteristic. Since church growth is a supernatural activity, it follows that a growth vision will come from God and be grounded in His Word. It is obedience to this God-given vision that gives the church restraint and provides direction.

When I first arrived in Norfolk, I was thirty-two years old and still wet behind the ears in terms of pastoral experience. God began to give us supernatural growth from the very first weeks of my ministry. It was the result of the long-standing prayers of many faithful prayer warriors. It was apparent the potential of this church in a metropolitan community was unlimited.

Numerous well-meaning people began coming by to encourage me to lead the church to begin ministries to the military, and to the college campuses, a Christian school, a daycare center, and the list continued to grow. All the ideas were good, and I wanted to please everyone, but it soon became apparent that we could quickly spread ourselves too thin and dissipate the energy, resources, and momentum of the church. It was during this time I accompanied our deacons on a retreat that became a prayer meeting. On this Friday night retreat, as we sought the guidance of the Lord concerning His direction for the church, the restraint and direction came that enabled us to focus our energies in such a way that He could grow His church in Norfolk.

Does your church have a vision that comes from God? Is it known, understood, and owned by the congregation? Do you focus your energies and resources based upon this vision? Does it influence scheduling, budgeting, and planning?

The Biblical Model

Our model church in Antioch had an impressive God-sized vision. "And while they were ministering to the Lord and fasting, the Holy Spirit said, 'Set apart for Me Barnabas and Saul for the work to which I have called them'" (Acts 13:2). The vision of the church at Antioch was staggering—*evangelize the world*. It began the Pauline missionary journeys throughout the known world. The church at Antioch had none of the resources available to us today to win the world to Christ. Win the world without mission boards, printing presses, radio, and television? A preposterous notion? No, a God-sized vision.

Notice, too, the context in which the vision was communicated. They were praying, fasting, and ministering to the Lord. They were prepared to hear from heaven because they had given priority to serious communication with the Father. Thus they came to worship in a receptive mode, and the Holy Spirit instructed them to set apart Paul and Barnabas to the mission task to which He had called them. If you do not yet have a vision for ministry, you haven't spent sufficient time listening to the Father.

Every great work of God began with a vision which originated with God but was communicated to a willing servant. Look, for example, at the freeing of Israel from Egyptian bondage. We are familiar with the story of the burning bush, but to understand the story we must begin at the end of Exodus chapter two. "Now it came about in the course of those many days that the king of Egypt died. And the sons of Israel sighed because of the bondage, and they cried out; and their cry for help because of their bondage rose up to God. So God heard their groaning; and God remembered His covenant with Abraham, Isaac, and Jacob" (Ex. 2:23–24). Prayer is the essential beginning for vision.

God sought out Moses, revealed Himself to him, and declared His intention to deliver Israel from captivity. "And the Lord said, 'I have surely seen the affliction of My people who are in Egypt, and have given heed to their cry because of their taskmasters, for I am aware of their sufferings. So I have come down to deliver them from the power of the Egyptians, and to bring them up from that land to a good and spacious land, to a land flowing with milk and honey'" (3:7–8). Notice that all supernatural activity, from the delivering of Israel to the growing of the church, is inaugurated by God in response to the prayers of His people.

God revealed His plan to deliver Israel through Moses: "Therefore, come now, and I will send you to Pharaoh, so that you may bring My people, the sons of Israel, out of Egypt" (3:10). Moses first acknowledged his unworthiness and then he began to make excuses. Every excuse was answered by the assurance of God's presence and empowering. Thus the deliverance of Israel was initiated by God, discovered through prayer, and accomplished through human instrumentation. It was the vision of freedom from captivity that provided the impetus for an enslaved people to respond to the leadership of Moses.

Another example of the power of vision is found in the book of Nehemiah. The Jewish people had been carried off to Babylonia as captives in 587 B.C. They were humiliated and disgraced by their captivity. Soon the armies of Persia conquered Babylonia, and King Cyrus released some of the Jews, allowing them to return to Jerusalem in 538 B.C. The first Jews to return began to reconstruct the temple, but they became discouraged as opposition erupted. They quit with little more than the foundation completed. A few years later Haggai and Zechariah appeared and challenged the people to finish the work. Sixty years passed, and more Israelites returned to Jerusalem under the leadership of Ezra to complete the rebuilding of the temple.

After the reconstruction of the temple, the focus of concern turned to the walls of Jerusalem which lay in shambles. The rebuilding of the walls was a matter of safety as well as national pride. Once again God sought a leader with whom to share His vision for rebuilding the wall.

The Book of Nehemiah opens with a moving speech by Hanani, who had came from Jerusalem to see Nehemiah. He delivered the shocking news that the remnant who had returned to Jerusalem was in great distress. Morale was low, the will to work had been broken, and the walls lay in ruin.

Nehemiah faced a dilemma. How should he respond to the information? He had a stable and comfortable job. His reaction was immediate: "Now it came about when I heard these words, I sat down and wept and mourned for days; and I was fasting and praying before the God of heaven" (1:4). Nehemiah first acknowledged the awesome authority of God, and then confessed his sin and that of the children of Israel. His first reaction was to pray.

Nehemiah was so burdened by the news of the broken walls that his concern showed on his countenance. Thus King Artaxerxes inquired concerning his sadness and discovered Nehemiah was burdened for the conditions in Jerusalem. The king then asked Nehemiah what he would request. Before responding, Nehemiah again prayed to the God of heaven (see 2:1–4). It was from this burden born in the cradle of prayer that God imparted to Nehemiah a vision to rebuild the wall. Vision for authentic church growth will always issue from a burden for the condition of the church and the lost who live around the church. It is our burden that calls us to pray, and it is in prayer that God imparts His vision for the church.

It was the clarity of this God-given vision that enabled Nehemiah to motivate the children of Israel to join him in the work. Notice in Nehemiah 2:17 that Nehemiah told the people about the desolate condition of the walls of Jerusalem and about his commitment to rectify the situation.

"Then I said to them, 'You see the bad situation we are in, that Jerusalem is desolate and its gates are burned by fire. Come, let us rebuild the wall of Jerusalem that we may no longer be a reproach.' And I told them how the hand of my God had been favorable to me, and also about the king's words which he had spoken to me. Then they said, 'Let us arise and build.' So they put their hands to the good work" (2:17–18). The people responded to the shared vision and put their hands to the task. The clear communication of God's vision to all the people of the church is the key to unified effort.

It was his settled conviction that the vision for rebuilding the wall had come from God that enabled Nehemiah to focus on the work in the midst of controversy and criticism. Nehemiah was ridiculed, his motives were questioned, and opponents placed roadblocks in the way. Nonetheless he persevered, driven by his vision.

Detractors will always challenge the vision of leadership. We hear it in phrases like: "That little congregation will never accomplish that." "They're just interested in numbers." "The pastor is on an ego trip." Visionary leaders cannot allow threats or idle gossip to discourage them from following God's direction. Those who are willing to follow God's vision to grow His church will face difficulties similar to those of Nehemiah. After the planning process is over and the hard work begins, many will wonder whether it's worth the cost. You may hear your own members say: "This is too big a task." "It costs too much." "This church is getting too big and impersonal." "The pastor doesn't care about me." The leader must rise above such criticism. He must stand tall on his knees if he is to see above the crowd. The leader keeps the vision alive and ensures the process of growth is ongoing.

Nine Characteristics of God-Sized Vision

How will you know when you have God's vision for your church? There are at least nine characteristics of a God-sized vision.

1. The vision originates with God. True vision is not centered in human beings, either the pastor or the people, but in God Himself. Vision is not the product of our own imagination or hopes; it is the discovery of God's design and plan for the church. Thus it begins with a supernatural encounter with Holy God. You must first know God experientially. *Experiencing God* by Henry Blackaby and Claude King is a workbook designed to help believers studying as a group capture God's vision and then join Him in His redemptive activity.

The key to vision discovery is prayer and fasting. "We have not because we ask not," explains James 4:2. If we are to find God's vision for our churches, we must be willing to ask and then to listen. Because we are activity oriented, our prayer times tend to be long on asking and short on listening. They tend to be more of a monologue than a dialogue.

2. God's vision will be centered in and supported by His Word. God will not communicate a vision contrary to His own nature and purpose. If your vision is a grandiose scheme centered in your own ego rather than based solidly in Scripture, you can be sure it is not of God and will not empower your church. You must always ask: "Does our vision finds its base in the revealed Word of God? Does it reflect the character of God Himself? Will it glorify Him?"

3. To bring a vision to reality, we must have supernatural empowering. If you can achieve your vision through some program or human strategy devoid of the power of God, it is not a God-sized vision. This does not mean you should not have a plan or use a particular program. God gave Moses a plan for leading Israel to the promised land (see Ex. 3–4). Nehemiah had a strategy for rebuilding the wall. Plans and programs are not to be despised, but they cannot replace supernatural empowering. You cannot rely on the program; you must rely on God.

4. Vision from God will be grounded in the Great Commission. The specific vision for your church must enable the church to better fulfill the Great Commission. To make disciples through going, baptizing, and teaching obedience is not an option for the church. Unless the church body is first committed to the Great Commission it is not likely to seek vision nor follow it. One of the most important series of messages the pastor can preach to prepare people for discovering vision is a series on the mission and ministry of the church.[3] Vision emerges when God's people have a clear understanding of the church's mission.

You may assume that everyone knows the Great Commission established the marching orders for the New Testament church. A recent Baptist state paper made reference to a survey taken throughout that state concerning the primary task of the church. Nine out of ten pastors identified the primary task as that of fulfilling the Great Commission, while only two out of ten laymen did so. They believed that the primary ministry of the church was to meet the needs of the members.[4] If we have not first accepted the Great Commission as the marching orders for the church, we will not know Christ's vision for His church.

5. Vision will lead the church to exalt Christ. We sometimes mistakenly think the church belongs to us. The church is the body and bride of Christ. He alone is the church's Head. Authentic vision for the church will exalt Jesus Christ alone. Any vision that draws attention to the pastor or the church is misdirected. In Ephesians 3, Paul recounted his call to ministry and his feeling of personal unworthiness. Yet through a gift of grace, God allowed him to unveil a mystery which had been hidden for ages in God, the Creator of all things: "In order that the manifold wisdom of God might now be made known through the church to the rulers and the authorities in the heavenly places. This was in accordance with the eternal purpose which He carried out in Christ Jesus our Lord" (vv. 10–11). This thought led Paul to an impassioned prayer for the church in verses 14–21 which concludes: "To Him be the glory in the church and in Christ Jesus to all generations forever and ever. Amen" (v. 21). When the church catches the vision God wants to accomplish and follows that vision with obedience, it will experience supernatural growth and thus bring glory to the Father and His Son.

6. *Vision requires radical obedience.* It is a terrible affront to ask for a vision from God and refuse to implement it. It would have been incongruous for the church at Antioch to decline sending Paul and Barnabas to do the work to which they had been called. We can not imagine Nehemiah refusing to return to Jerusalem. Yet many churches are lifeless and listless because they have been unwilling to obey the Head of the Church. For example, if your church has no passion for the lost and thus has no desire nor plan to reach them, it would be useless to pray for vision. Remember vision will be centered in the Great Commission and require radical obedience.

7. *Vision leads to natural growth.* Some churches seem to be struggling to find the right formula to make them grow. That is as ludicrous as a small child attempting to will his own body to lengthen itself. God is the author of church growth, and when the church is in proper relationship with Him, He will cause the increase. God will call the church to obedience to the Great Commission and then add regularly to their number as He did to the first century church. Note that natural growth is evangelistic growth. If you desire to see your church grow and yet have no passion for the lost, you need to go back to characteristic one. Stay on your knees until you have a burden that beckons you to go into the highways and byways and compel them to come in that His house may be filled (see Luke 14:23).

8. *Vision demands a willingness to change.* Nehemiah had to leave the comfort of his established position as cupbearer to the king in order to fulfill God's vision for his life. The church at Antioch was required to send two of their best known leaders on a missionary journey in order to accomplish their vision. It must have been quite an adjustment to do without the leadership of these two men. The good news is that vision helps the church to change because the change is now connected to a vision from God and the plan to obey that vision. Too often the demand to change seems capricious to many church members. Change can be more easily implemented if it is directly linked to a vision and the strategy to fulfill that vision. For example, it is easier to age-grade the Sunday School or change the style of the worship service if the church members see that such changes will enable the church to better fulfill the Great Commission.

9. *Vision requires family unity.* A vision can grasp a congregation and forge it into a unified whole. We have all witnessed the dynamics of a rather mediocre football team elevated to new heights because they caught a glimpse of the possibilities that lay before them. The movie *Hoosiers* recounted the seemingly impossible story of a small Indiana high school basketball team that overcame incredible odds to win the state finals. In order to accomplish their dream they had to become unified. Many churches lack family unity precisely because they do not have a family dream. Aimlessness leads to disunity.

Developing Congregational Vision

Vision begins with God, is centered in the Great Commission, flows through the core values of the community, addresses community needs, and can be accomplished through the full employment of the supernatural resources given by the exalted Lord. Verlyn Bergen illustrates vision development with the helpful graphic on page 138.

The purpose or mission statement of the church is the Great Commission. We can restate it in our own language, but we cannot depart from it. Core values describe the essential foundational truths by which behavior, actions, and ministry are conducted. The church's core values come from the infallible Word of God. We cannot compromise the principles of God's Word and build His church. Community needs can be discovered in many ways such as the study of demographic information and the use of surveys, but the most reliable system is through personal involvement in the community. A knowledge of community needs will enable you to provide the ministries that best fulfill the Great Commission in your own setting. The resources of the church are inexhaustible because they originate with God. The exalted Lord has gifted His church to reach the community in which He has placed it through gifted members. The resources for church growth are the gifted members of your church. Based on these fundamentals, the church can develop a clear sense of vision.

The church's vision is a clear picture of the church's preferable future, imparted by God to His church, based on a clear

CONGREGATIONAL VISION DEVELOPMENT

understanding of the nature of God, the mission of the church, the giftedness of the people, and the needs of your specific community. Vision deals with the future and provides a clear signpost that narrows the focus of the church and guides the activities of the church. A clearly stated vision increases commitment to ministry and thus gives empowering. It provides the restraint that focuses the energy of the church.[5]

Communicating the Vision

"Healthy congregations dream of a visible kingdom and work to organize and live out their dreams. Then, they tell and retell their stories."[6] Once the vision is known, the next step is clear communication of that vision. Vision will have little impact upon the church unless it is regularly and clearly communicated. George Barna notes: "the organizations that have efficient, clear, reliable means of communication tend to be successful; those whose lines of communication are underdeveloped, imprecise or otherwise restricted are more likely to experience stagnation or decline."[7]

The Pastor Is Pivotal in Communicating the Vision

If vision is to be actualized, it must be communicated with all God's people. Nehemiah shared God's plan with the people, and they confirmed it and agreed to work with him to see the dream become reality. The vision must be communicated through word and deed. People are inspired by words which are accompanied by passionate activity.

The pastor is the resident theologian and has a regular platform for articulating, interpreting, and incarnating the vision of the church. It is difficult to think that God would not communicate His vision for the church through His anointed leader unless this individual is out of fellowship with the Father. It is therefore important that the pastor keep the dream before the people and help them interpret the hand of God at work in their midst. These both must be grounded clearly and steadfastly in Scripture to avoid the possibility the pastor would impose his own dreams and goals on the church and then claim that they are from God. Many congregations are still struggling from leader-imposed visions that issued more from unbridled ego than from an encounter with God.

The pastor's greatest forum for communicating vision is from the pulpit as he opens and expounds upon the Word of God. When he allows the text to speak for itself to the needs of the moment, he will find that the Holy Spirit brings conviction and commitment. The pastor should also use other forums such as small group encounters in the Sunday School or with committees to keep the vision before the people. One-on-one communication with key layleaders is essential if the vision is to become part of the language of the church.

The pastor should not ignore the power of the written word to communicate vision. A regular article in the church newsletter can articulate the vision of the church. A vision statement on the bulletin and church stationery and posters or banners that herald the vision provide reinforcement. Use any and all opportunities to call the church to own the vision.

Dream Ownership and Consensus Building Is Essential

While it is difficult to think that God would bypass His anointed leader, it is equally hard to believe He would not confirm the vision through the body. This does not mean the congregation must be unanimous before it begins to act upon the vision. You will recall that Moses had only two spies out of twelve who believed God and were willing to take the land. In that instance God did not permit the people to enter the promised land because of their unbelief and disobedience. Nehemiah was plagued by insiders who ridiculed his feeble attempts to rebuild the wall. Nevertheless, he and the large majority of people were committed to the vision and persevered to rebuild the wall. It would, of course, be preferable that the church be of one mind as were the disciples in the upper room (see Acts 1:14). Unanimity requires a totally regenerate membership who are all walking in the Spirit.

Once God confirms the vision to the congregation, dream ownership and consensus building become high priorities. This requires regular, honest, and open communication. Invite the people of the church to join you in articulating the vision. Layleaders have a great impact on consensus building. This is particularly true in smaller churches where deep and enduring relationships have been established with key layleaders. The congregation needs to feel like the insiders or family members who are all working together for a shared vision.

A recent study commissioned by the Lutheran Church-Missouri Synod revealed that growing congregations see themselves in mission beyond their current membership and have lay and clergy leadership which share that vision. Based on this shared vision, they become action oriented. They are not willing to be limited by challenges of size, language, availability of resources, or criticism by others. In response to their vision, they are flexible in methodology for communicating an unchanging message.[8]

Develop a Vision Statement

A vision statement is a powerful tool for communication and consensus building. The vision statement gives specific direction for the completion of the mission of the church. It articulates a clear direction from God concerning the manner in which your church can best fulfill the Great Commission in your given context with a view for the world.

A vision statement is not sanctified imagination, but must reflect a clear communication from God. The vision statement does not create or cause the future—only God can do that—but it does enable communication in a succinct, articulate way God's vision for a church and its ministry.

A vision statement helps the church in four specific ways:

1. It provides direction for ministry. It keeps the church from operating on the "squeaky wheel" principle. It helps avoid both the tendency to grab for every fad in church growth and also the calcification which occurs when churches hang onto outdated traditions. You can evaluate programs and methods in light of your vision statement.

2. It can help to motivate people. Reading, seeing, and hearing it, they sense the church is moving in a clearly defined direction.

3. Thus, it can help to generate genuine enthusiasm for authentic and healthy church growth.

4. It can help identify the uniqueness of your church to others.

If you need further help in leading your church to discover its God-given dream, I would recommend *To Dream Again* by Robert D. Dale. Specific help for writing a vision statement is available in George Barna's book, *The Power of Vision*.

Anticipate Opposition

In the excitement to communicate vision, you may be caught off guard when someone expresses opposition to the vision and wonder silently or aloud, "How could anyone oppose something so positive? How could anyone stand against progress? How could any Christian be against winning the lost and growing the church?" Those are legitimate questions and ones with which you struggle, but the fact is—some will stand against the dream. They may appeal to reason, comfort, or potential cost, but in the end they oppose the changes necessary to be obedient to the dream.

You would have expected that everyone in Israel was delighted by the news that someone was concerned enough to rebuild the wall, but that was not the case. Opposition was immediate and persistent. Sometimes it became personality centered with the questioning of Nehemiah's motives. At other times it took the form of ridicule. Nehemiah fought opposition with prayer and remained true to the task. He refused to come down from the wall to fight a verbal battle with those who opposed him. He remained faithful to the dream.

Many pastors and many churches fail to follow through because they back away at the first signs of opposition. They choose to keep the peace rather than to realize their God-sized dream. This is a tragic and poor trade. It begins the process of compromise that weakens and finally destroys the opportunity for healthy growth. If you know the vision is from God, be obedient!

Allow for Checks and Balances

On the other side of the coin is the pastor or layleader who becomes arrogant and stubborn about their specific strategy to accomplishing the vision. They are unwilling to listen to others who express concern or desire to offer correction. Listen to the input of mature believers; God works through His entire family.

Paul had a clear vision concerning his mission to the Gentiles; nevertheless, he willingly attended the Jerusalem council (see Acts 15) and listened to the concerns of others. Paul was unwilling to compromise on the clarity and simplicity of the gospel that should be preached to the Gentiles, but he recognized the valid apprehension others had for the purity of the church. Thus, while he stood steadfast against any alteration of the message, he accepted the council's recommendations that maintained the purity of the church and prevented offense to the Jews. Paul was willing to accept checks and balances.

Sometimes we become so convinced of our own agenda that we fail to listen to the ideas and concerns of others. This only weakens the unity of the church. We must distinguish between the unalterable and the negotiable in structuring ways to accomplish the vision.

Stay Faithful to the Dream

The question arises, particularly in the context of congregational polity: What do I do if the majority of people do not support the vision? Here again, I suggest you go back to the matter of repentance, prayer, and fasting, and allow God to bring conviction. God alone can move His church. If you attempt to do the work of the Holy Spirit, you will become frustrated and disillusioned and soon leave the church.

We can also take a lesson from Moses in this instance. You remember his two faithful spies were outvoted by ten fearful disobedient spies. The people, in response to the fearful and fraudulent majority report, refused to possess the land God had commanded them to inhabit. As a result of their disobedience, an entire generation was condemned to wander uselessly in the desert. Moses, as their leader, accompanied them on this futile journey. What did he do with his wandering church?

First, he stayed with the people because he had a heart for them. As I read the accounts of the wilderness travels of the Israelites, I can't help but notice the constant groaning and complaining of the people. Moses must have frequently been discouraged and fed up with such a stubborn people. Yet we constantly see him interceding on their behalf before God. The pathos of the scene recorded in Exodus 32 stands etched in my mind. God was prepared to destroy Israel for making and worshiping the golden calf. Moses interceded for the life of his people, offering to die with them. From this incident, I glean this principle: *don't leave your post of service for any reason other than the call of God.* Stay until God changes the heart of the people or moves you. Don't attempt to move yourself because your people have not yet responded to God's vision.

Second, Moses transmitted the dream to another generation. He prepared a new generation of leaders to take the land. As a part of the preparation process, he restated God's law to this new generation. Mature leaders remain committed to the dream, even if results are not realized in their own lifetime. We have a limited and earthly view of eternal work. God knows our hearts and our work and will reward His servants equitably.

Third, Moses focused on God and allowed Him to build character in the people. Remember—church growth is God's business, not yours. You are only a vessel through whom God's grace is manifested. Don't fret or be disgruntled. It is required of the servant that he be found faithful, not successful in the world's terms. Our motivation is not to accumulate church growth awards now, but to lay up treasures in heaven. God may do more to build your church through your faithfulness to Him and His people than any single thing you will accomplish in ministry.

Develop Action Plans to Accomplish the Dream

Developing an action plan is an issue of obedience. It answers these questions: "How is the church to actualize the dream or vision? and "Who must be involved?" The church at Antioch sent Paul and Barnabas to evangelize the world. Paul soon developed a clear strategy to evangelize the major cities of his day. He began his work by teaching at the local synagogue and then establishing a local community of believers who would continue the task of world evangelization. Action plans ensure that the vision of the church will not dissipate.

Giving and serving tied to an action plan that emanates from a God-given vision is always more meaningful. A vision gives positive direction to goals and activities. Your church will develop its goals and plans in one of two ways. You can do no planning which means all of your goals are set by default, or you can do visionary planning. In the latter case, goals and plans are developed to enable the church to realize its vision. It is best when visionary goals precede budgeting and planning. In that way, budgets and action plans clearly reflect goals that concretize the vision.

Reward Actions that Move Toward Actualizing the Vision

Remember that learning takes place as you affirm correct behavior. Reward positive actions that help the church realize its vision. Make sure the reward is immediate, genuine, and public. Ensure affirmation is given for behavior that helps the church to achieve its stated vision.

For years in some denominations, Sunday School was seen primarily as an evangelistic tool. Recognition was given for activities that produced evangelistic results. In the early 1960s the vision for an evangelistic Sunday School was compromised and obscured in the minds of many. Many churches began to reward such things as largest attendance or highest average attendance. Rewarding these inappropriate goals actually worked to undermine the vision of an evangelistic Sunday School. It is easy to build a large class if you have no vision for the cooperative work of the Bible study organization. You can cling to all your members, refusing to send them out to other areas of service. You can resist all encouragement to create new units, or send people to other more appropriate classes. Ultimately you can pool a large group of people, but you will not have helped the Bible study organization grow and reach the unsaved.

By rewarding positive actions, you build positive role models in the church. Many churches recognize the individuals that participate in leading someone to Christ. Such an activity restates the mission of the church to fulfill the Great Commission and creates a positive role model for others to imitate. On one occasion at First Norfolk, we found it necessary to establish a third Bible study hour on Sunday morning to make space available to continue to reach people for Christ. This new hour for Bible study was 8:15 on Sunday morning. Some balked at the idea, arguing it was too early. One class of young adults caught the vision and volunteered to move to this earlier hour even though they had preschool children. Quite a sacrifice! The Sunday before they were to move, I had the entire class stand on Sunday morning and told the congregation of their decision. Their decision and the public praise led other classes to follow their lead.

Growing churches are characterized by vision. They hear from God, respond in obedience, reorient their priorities, devise an action plan that reflects their vision and enables them to accomplish their goals, and go to work.

Characteristic 7:

Passion for the Lost

What is the key to evangelistic results for the church as we advance toward the twenty-first century? Should all churches adopt the seeker-targeted worship service designed to make seekers—most often Boomer-seekers—feel comfortable? Should we organize our Sunday Schools for evangelistic outreach? Perhaps we will experience a greater harvest if we use need-based cell groups. Do we give up on person-to-person evangelism as a relic of the past? Should we bother training laity to do what they have no intention of doing? What do we do with traditional evangelistic meetings? Are events such as living Christmas trees on the way out or just being discovered by the rank and file?

All are legitimate questions and concerns because it is obvious the church today has lost its evangelistic edge. Church growth through evangelism has not even managed to keep pace with population growth. In truth, we have trailed population growth by 11 percent over the past thirty years. In the Southern Baptist Convention, a denomination which has gained a reputation for evangelistic fervor, no baptisms were reported by 5,771 churches in 1992, approximately 16 percent of its churches. A 1990 Southern Baptist Constituency Study revealed that 29 percent of Southern Baptist adult laity had talked with someone about Christ and 8 percent had led someone to make a decision to accept Christ during the past year. Yet 47 percent of active adult members had done nothing to bring a friend to church or introduce them to Christ.[1]

Something different must be done if we are going to be faithful in fulfilling the Great Commission in our generation. While the first questions posed may all be legitimate questions, they are not the critical ones. We have better programs and training tools than at any time in the history of the church and we are doing less with them. The issue of evangelistic church growth does not hinge on resolving the debate over whether the lost person is more likely to enter the "front door" through seeker worship, or the "side door" through need-centered cell groups. That reduces the issue to a matter of methods and models, and that is not the most critical problem the church of the twenty-first century must face. *The issue is not a failure of programming, but rather a failure of passion.* We have grown indifferent about the condition of the lost. We no longer have the concern that once drove the church to its knees and then into the streets. While it is not necessary to cling to the programs of the past, it is essential to restore the *passion* of the past that produced great evangelistic fervor.

My dad, who died of a brain tumor two years ago, pastored small churches in North Carolina for fifty-five years. He was diagnosed in February of 1991 and died in March of 1992. During his final year, I took every opportunity to spend time with Dad. I especially enjoyed hearing him talk about his early years in ministry. Many of the stories I had heard several times over, but they took on special significance during this last year.

One special event that will stand out in my mind is the day we loaded up our van and visited many of the churches that were a part of my parents' life. We saw the little Methodist church where they met. He directed me then to drive down an unpaved country lane, the same route along which he drove his Model-A Ford while courting Mom. At one point he asked me to pull over to the side of the road. There, with misty eyes, he recounted the story of his conversion. He told us how he had stopped in this same spot one Sunday evening nearly sixty years earlier, his eyes blurred and burning from the flood of tears, and surrendered his life to Christ. What compelled him to pull to the side of the road? He fell under deep conviction of his sinful condition at the precise moment that his parents and other leaders of the church had gathered in a brush arbor behind the church to pray for his salvation. He had joined the church as a lad, but he knew, and they knew, that he was not saved. The church leaders had never ceased to pray for my dad's salvation.

He went on to recount story after story of evangelistic fruit that came as the direct result of impassioned prayer. He told of old revival meetings and sawdust trails where hardened sinners came running to the altar. He recalled how his college professors at Mars Hill, a small college in North Carolina, were more concerned with whether the students were saved than whether they knew the course material. He reminisced how these great professors would pray passionately in class for lost students to come to Christ, and then they would personally witness to them.

Powerful stories of answered prayer are abundant on mission fields and from developing nations, but are seldom heard from the average American church. Have we become so sophisticated that all-night prayer meetings seem like a relic of a superstitious past?

The issue, again, is not method but empowering. Once an individual or a church develops a passionate concern for the lost, they will develop a plan for reaching them. The church should feel freedom to use any strategy that will enable them to fulfill the Great Commission, so long as it does not cause them to compromise Scripture.

To fulfill the Great Commission, a plan for evangelism must, of necessity, incorporate a strategy for *going* into the marketplace and engaging lost people on their turf. Second, it must ensure that those won are *baptized* into the life of the local church. Readers of this book may differ on the mode or significance of baptism, but all of us can at least agree that it involves incorporation and assimilation into the life of the local church. Finally, the church must have in place a discipling strategy designed to *teach them to observe all that Jesus commanded.* Evangelism and discipleship must be equally balanced if the church is to experience stable growth, leading to maturity and reaching its community and world.

A Look at Antioch

We have consistently turned first to Antioch as a model of a church God used to turn the world upside down. When we read the Acts accounts of this church, we are immediately impressed by the evangelistic fervor. Three times Luke indicated that large numbers were reached and equipped by the church in Antioch. "And the hand of the Lord was with them, and a large number who believed turned to the Lord" (11:21). "And considerable numbers were brought to the Lord" (11:24). "And it came about that for an entire year they met with the church, and taught considerable numbers; and the disciples were first called Christians in Antioch" (11:26).

It is significant that the church at Antioch was established by Jewish believers who had been scattered by the persecution in Jerusalem (see 11:19). There was not a single apostle in their midst! We would call these church planters "laity." Most were fairly new converts. As Jews who believed Jesus was the Messiah, they had become outcasts from their own families, forced to leave their beloved homeland as the result of the persecution that arose in connection with Stephen. Yet they didn't see their circumstances as a tragic inconvenience. They didn't blame God for their suffering. They enthusiastically preached the Lord Jesus everywhere they went (see v. 20). Luke mentioned another detail of some consequence—those who came to Antioch began speaking to the Greeks also. Their passion for the lost enabled them to reach across barriers that had once been dividing walls. The Lord honored their passion and placed His hand on them, and as a result great numbers were saved.

As I visit growing churches across our country, I find many methods and models for doing evangelism. The methods of evangelistic churches differ as greatly as the settings and styles of pastoral leadership. Yet they all have one common denominator—the pastor and the church have such a passion to see the lost come to know Christ, they are driven to take the message to their community. Prior to the development of methodology, we must rediscover the passion and the power.

Develop a Sound Theological Foundation

Many members of mainline evangelical churches behave as if everyone is going to heaven. We may not claim to believe in universalism—the doctrine that all will be saved—but we certainly function as if that were the case. In recent years we have seen a depreciation of doctrinal teaching in many churches, and we are already beginning to reap the harvest of a lack of biblical conviction.

The study by Johnson, Hoge, and Luidens, which looked at the decline of mainline denominations, is instructive at this point. They studied specifically the decline in the Presbyterian Church USA and determined the primary reason for the decline was the laity's lack of conviction that Jesus alone was the means of salvation. The researchers found that parents in these churches preferred for their children to be Presbyterians, but were not concerned if they joined another religious group as long as they became good people. It was, the researchers concluded, this theological "lay liberalism" that led to the precipitous decline in the Presbyterian Church USA.[2] A comprehensive study of the growth of various religious groups in America by Roger Finke and Rodney Stark came to a similar conclusion: "Not all denominations shared in this immense rise in membership rates, and to the degree that denominations rejected traditional doctrines and ceased to make serious demands on their followers, they ceased to prosper."[3]

The Presbyterians do not stand alone in the theological vacuum. Most churches struggle to get a handful of folks for a doctrinal study and yet pack the sanctuary for a special event. While big events may be key entry points for reaching the unsaved, we cannot grow a balanced church on a steady diet of performance-driven events. We must base all church growth and evangelistic activity on a sound theological foundation. There is a close correlation between evangelistic activity and sound theological teaching. One will not long endure without the other.

Here are *eight key* doctrinal building blocks for a theology of evangelism. They may not be exhaustive, but they will build an evangelistic foundation.

1. We must understand the condition of the lost. Unless we have an established conviction about the plight of persons outside of Christ, we will never be motivated to develop and sustain an ongoing emphasis on evangelism. We must believe and teach that reconciliation to God in Christ is not something that makes life nicer, or suffering more palatable, or the individual a better person—it is life itself. Without Christ there is neither life nor hope. We must believe that people without Christ are lost, that hell is their eternal destiny, and that Christ alone is the answer. Anything short of this conviction leaves the church without the passion to reach beyond itself.

A simple reading of Romans 1–3 gives anyone a sure picture of the lost condition of both the irreligious and the religious. The picture of human beings in the last verses of Romans 1 sounds like the headlines in the newspaper or the lead stories on the evening news:

> And just as they did not see fit to acknowledge God any longer, God gave them over to a depraved mind, to do those things which are not proper, being filled with all unrighteousness, wickedness, greed, evil; full of envy, murder, strife, deceit, malice; they are gossips, slanderers, haters of God, insolent, arrogant, boastful, inventors of evil, disobedient to parents, without understanding, untrustworthy, unloving, unmerciful; and, although they know the ordinance of God, that those who practice such things are worthy of death. (Rom. 1:28–32)

When Paul addressed the condition of the Jews, he inquired whether they were any better than the Gentiles, and answered with a collection of Old Testament passages: "There is none righteous, not even one; there is none who understands, there is none who seeks for God; All have turned aside, together they have become useless; there is none who does good, there is not even one" (Rom. 3:10–12).

It was this understanding of the human condition that caused the apostle Paul such grief and sorrow that he could wish himself separated from Christ for the sake of his fellow Jews. It was his conviction that all those who had been reconciled to God were now given the ministry of reconciliation that drove Paul to beg people to be reconciled to God (see 2 Cor. 5:18–21).

When a life is at stake, people respond instinctively to the crisis. The fireman hurls himself into a burning building to rescue a frightened boy. A mother darts in front of an onrushing automobile to grab a stray child. An average swimmer jumps into a rushing stream to grab a drowning stranger. What is it that prompts such heroic acts? One thing—*the sure knowledge of the consequences if they do not attempt the rescue.* If evangelism is to become natural in our churches, we must have a full knowledge of the *consequences* if we fail to reach out.

By the way, a clear understanding of the condition of lost persons will drive the church out of the building and into the marketplace because *dead men don't walk.* If unsaved people are dead in their trespasses and sin (see Eph. 2:1), we can't leave it up to them to find Christ. Since the Bible teaches that not a single lost person seeks for God (see Rom. 3:11), we must become the seekers.

2. We must believe that Christ provides the only access to the Father. This verse is familiar to most Christians: "Jesus said to him, 'I am the way, and the truth, and the life; no one comes to the Father, but through Me'" (John 14:6). Peter echoed this same truth when confronted by the rulers, elders, and scribes: "For there is no other name under heaven that has been given among men, by which we must be saved" (Acts 4:12).

If we believe Christ alone grants access to the Father, then we have a mandate to witness. For example, without such a conviction, we are not likely to think that people of other religions need our witness. Surveys show that 64 percent of Americans believe all religions pray to the same God. That revealing statistic may explain why only 28 percent of adults believe they have a responsibility to share their religious beliefs and 25 percent strongly feel they have no such responsibility.[4]

3. We must believe the fields are ripe for the harvest. When I visit a church that has declining baptismal and attendance figures, I often find they justify the figures by citing the poor quality of the soil around the church. They complain that "these people are just not responsive." Still others blame their lack of growth on the large number of churches in their area which has led to the depletion of the harvest. It may be true that some areas of the country are less responsive than others; and it may be we have followed the lead of fast food establishments and built all our restaurants across the road from existing restaurants, but there are still plenty of lost people who need Christ in every area of our nation.

It has been my experience that in every location where some churches are complaining about the lack of responsiveness, other churches have found the fields ripe for the harvest. Most pastors in the Chicago area would never have suspected that a church like Willow Creek, focused on reaching the secular person, would have such tremendous results. Bill Hybels saw ripe fields rather than rocky soil.

Rick Warren, drawn by a passionate concern for the lost of California, has built one of the nation's great evangelistic churches in a place where many thought such church growth was impossible. Leland Herriford when he was sixty-four, accepted God's call to a dwindling community in Modena, Missouri. Leland didn't see a declining, impossible rural setting, but only a great opportunity to build an evangelistic church. Ed Young, Jr., began a church in the affluent Las Calinas section of Dallas. Still meeeting in a rented theater, they are running over fifteen hundred and reaching secular, seemingly unreachable people.

I was speaking at New Orleans seminary recently and met a young pastor, Chris Stephens. He had gone from his seminary training to a little country church in Jennings, Louisiana, a place where no one could build a church. The population in his community is eleven thousand and 90 percent are Catholics. Apparently he failed to look at the demographics because this church, running twenty-five in Sunday School when he came in 1990, is now averaging three hundred and has led the association for three years in baptisms, baptizing over sixty a year.

Stan Frye failed to notice that the Conover, North Carolina area was so overchurched it would be impossible to find large numbers of lost people who needed to hear about Christ. His church has grown from forty members to one thousand in four years under his leadership. The church has baptized 353 in the last four years, baptizing 127 this past year. Stories like these could be repeated hundreds of times in virtually every area of our country. They provide ample evidence that the harvest is plentiful.

Demographic data can certainly be a helpful tool to assist any church in knowing best how to reach their community. Some, however, have used it as an excuse for their lack of evangelistic results. Such churches have the dread disease of paralysis by analysis. They spend more time analyzing their community than presenting the gospel to the lost. Let me assure you that the fields around your church are ripe for the harvest. More people are receptive to hear the gospel than we have trained witnesses to share the gospel. I submit as my evidence the findings of the Head of all church growth, the Lord Himself: "Then He said to His disciples, 'The harvest is plentiful, but the workers are few'" (Matt. 9:37). Our lack of evangelistic results cannot be blamed on the poor quality of the soil or the viability of the seed, the problem is still the same—*the workers are few.*

A look at the findings of pollster George Gallup confirms that the fields are ripe for the harvest. Gallup found that 58 percent of Americans indicated they would probably return to church, 63 percent believe that the Bible is the literal or inspired Word of God, and 77 percent pray to God occasionally.[5] We are not living in a post-Christian era, as some fear: we are living in an era of religious superstition. The rapid spread of cultic and New Age teaching gives powerful testimony to the huge spiritual vacuum that exists around the world. The church that would effectively sow the good seed of the gospel will experience a bountiful harvest.

4. The Great Commission is not a divine suggestion. This may be the single area in which theological confusion has caused the most damage to the evangelistic ministry of the church. Most pastors arrive on their church field with the assumption that the members share his conviction that the church takes its marching orders from the Great Commission as recorded in Matthew 28:19–20. This is an unwarranted assumption. A recent survey revealed that just the opposite is true. Nine out of ten pastors surveyed indicated that the primary concern of the church was to reach the unsaved and unchurched. In response to the same question eight out of ten church members felt that the primary ministry of the church was to meet needs of the members. Only two in ten saw the primary purpose as reaching unchurched people.[6] If the pastor and the people are working from such widely diverging purpose statements, confusion and frustration will be the order of the day.

Why do churches exist? Leith Anderson lists five options: 1) the denomination; 2) the church building; 3) the pastor; 4) the members; or 5) the community. Anderson argues that today's church survivors and thrivers will be the churches who exist for others.[7] I am in complete agreement with Anderson's evangelistic emphasis, but I find his five suggestions incomplete. The church exists for God alone! It was founded by His Son (see Matt. 16), redeemed by His death, empowered by His resurrection and the sending of His Spirit, and one day He will return for His glorious bride.

This is not just an issue of semantics; it is a key theological issue. If the church belongs to God alone, He has the right to fashion its ministry and purpose. He has done that succinctly in the Great Commission which contains a singular command— to make disciples. The three participles in the verse—going, baptizing, and teaching—support the original command. These three define how the church is to fulfill the purpose statement given by our Lord. Note that the first directive involves the church going to reach the unsaved. I fully agree with Leith Anderson that too many churches today have neglected an essential priority of the Great Commission. They have retreated into unholy huddles and have turned on the "No Vacancy" sign.

Notice, however, that there are two other disciple-making strategies—baptizing and teaching people to obey the commands of Christ. Baptizing refers to the incorporation of the believer into the community of faith, the local church. Chuck Colson has strongly underlined this necessity in his book, *The Body*: "Evangelism should always be designed to bring the convert into the local church, where the work of discipleship can be done."[8] The church must also be committed to teaching believers to obey the commands of Christ. Bill Hull argues that the disciple-making church holds the key to world evangelism. When the church makes disciples, two good things happen: 1) Christians become healthy and reproduce; and, as they multiply, 2) the world becomes evangelized in God's way.[9]

Here the issue of balance becomes critical to healthy church growth. If we maintain that the church exists only for reaching unbelievers, we ignore the discipling needs of believers and thus weaken the church. Several church activities, by definition, are for believers. For example, worship is for believers since they alone can participate in an event based on a personal relationship with God. Fellowship is for believers since family members alone experience the deeper level of relationships that come from our common birth. In one sense, the church serves believers since believers only can fully participate in its activities. Yet the activities of the church designed to build healthy relationships and develop mature believers exist so that the church can be used of God to reach the world. Chuck Colson correctly observes that evangelism naturally flows from worship and fellowship. He argues that evangelism is the by-product of spiritual life flowing from a healthy body being nourished by the Head.[10] Churches that claim to have dynamic worship and wonderful fellowship and yet have no commitment to reaching the lost need to look again at the Great Commission.

The healthy church must maintain the balance between outreach and discipleship with the ultimate goal of obeying Christ in faithfully fulfilling the totality of the Great Commission.

5. *Every Christian is called to be a witness.* While the evangelical church has not always acted on this truth, it has generally agreed that all believers should be trained to share their faith. This is no longer true. In recent days several church growth writers have argued that only 10 percent of the church body has the gift of evangelism; therefore, training efforts should be concentrated on this 10 percent. Gary McIntosh and Glen Martin write: "Here we find, as previously stated, approximately 10 percent of the church body who are the soul winners and have the gift of evangelism."[11] Similarly Robert Logan talks about the tools to equip believers without an evangelistic gift.[12] I'm confident that none of these men intend to imply other church members have no responsibility for reaching the lost, but that has been precisely the application in many churches. It has given some Christians the theological excuse they have been

looking for to avoid the challenging task of sharing their faith.

This assertion that only 10 percent of believers have the gift of evangelism has been defended both by observation and by an appeal to the dispersal of spiritual gifts. Some have observed that only about 10 percent of the laity in the average church are involved in its outreach ministries. First, we must challenge the idea of basing our strategy on observation rather than revelation. There are many things we could observe about the church that do not correspond with the written revelation of God. We don't keep lowering the standards to conform to the apathy of carnal believers.

The argument based on spiritual gifts at least appeals to theology rather than observation. The conclusion that 10 percent of believers have the gift of evangelism was based on the results of a spiritual gifts inventory given in a large number of local churches. Only about 10 percent filled out the inventory in such a way to indicate that they had the gift of evangelism.[13] Inventories are at best imprecise tools, and much depends on the wording of the questions and the explanation made by the presenter. The very fact that "witnessing" and "confrontational evangelism" are seen by many to be overly aggressive and outdated could easily prejudice the results. I personally am not surprised to find that many people would answer questions about witnessing in a negative fashion based on the knowledge of how few actually witness. We could also wonder how many Christians would claim to have the gift of giving (see Rom. 12:8). If we discovered that to be equally low, would we then develop a strategy to train only that small percentage of folks to tithe?

Let's look at the key passage in question, Ephesians 4:11. It is here that the gifted evangelist is listed. The Ephesian letter was a companion letter to Colossians, written to counter false teachings impacting the churches in proconsular Asia. For that reason, in this letter Paul focused on the gifted leaders given to the church by the exalted Lord. "And He gave some as apostles, and some as prophets, and some as evangelists, and some as pastors and teachers, for the equipping of the saints for the work of service, to the building up of the body of Christ" (Eph. 4:11–12). The evangelists in this gift list are compared with the apostles, prophets, and pastors-teachers. The parallelism is crucial to a correct understanding. Paul was referring to gifted evangelists, like Billy Graham in our day, that are given to the church in the same manner as the pastor/teacher or prophet. These gifted leaders are given by the exalted Lord for the establishment and development of the church so that the gifted members could be equipped for the ministry of service.

The Great Commission includes everyone who has accepted Christ. Those who know Christ are under divine mandate to bear witness to their personal relationship with Christ. In 2 Corinthians Paul made it abundantly clear that everyone reconciled to Christ has been given the ministry of reconciliation:

> Now all these things are from God, who reconciled us to Himself through Christ, and gave us the ministry of reconciliation, namely, that God was in Christ reconciling the world to Himself, not counting their trespasses against them, and He has committed to us the word of reconciliation. Therefore, we are ambassadors for Christ, as though God were entreating through us; we beg you on behalf of Christ, be reconciled to God. (2 Cor. 5:18–20)

It is every believer's privilege and calling to be an ambassador for Christ. For that reason, we should follow the instruction of Peter: "But sanctify Christ as Lord in your hearts, always being ready to make a defense to everyone who asks you to give an account for the hope that is in you, yet with gentleness and reverence" (1 Pet. 3:15).

The doctrine of the priesthood of believers, cherished by many evangelical groups, anticipates the witness of all believers. The Old Testament priest functioned so as to bring persons into the presence of God. Listen to Peter's description of the people of God: "But you are a chosen race, a royal priesthood, a holy nation, a people for God's own possession, that you may proclaim the excellencies of Him who has called you out of darkness into His marvelous light" (1 Pet. 2:9). God desires to possess us so that we will proclaim His excellencies.

It is true that some members of the body are more verbal than others and thus will often find personal witnessing more natural, but that doesn't mean all Christians cannot give a verbal witness. Effective witnessing is based on supernatural empowering, not natural tendencies. When the Holy Spirit came upon the early Christians, they spoke boldly about Christ. The total witnessing effort of the church will be a team activity. We can learn to work together in bearing an effective witness that takes full advantage of the unique experiences and strengths of all church members. This is the benefit of family evangelism. We can teach several methods of witnessing and provide numerous opportunities for engaging the unsaved community. We can teach our people to invite their friends to church, to share their testimony, and to network their personal witnessing with other family members. For example, in First Norfolk we had several Jewish persons who accepted Christ as Savior. When I had opportunity to witness to a Jewish person, I would often take these persons along. We had alcoholics who had found Christ and full release from their addiction. They were very effective in leading people in a similar condition to a saving knowledge of Christ. This practice takes advantage of the positive aspects of homogeneity, the principle that the gospel flows most effectively through a kinship or friendship unit. While we must work together as a family evangelism team, we must challenge all believers to be witnesses and train them to be effective.

6. *The Holy Spirit empowers us to witness.* We are immediately reminded of the promise of our Lord as recorded in Acts 1:8: "But you shall receive power when the Holy Spirit has come upon you; and you shall be My witnesses both in Jerusalem, and in all Judea and Samaria, and even to the remotest part of the earth." The Holy Spirit provided the enabling power for Jesus' disciples to do greater works than He had done (see John 14:12). These greater works involved the supernaturally empowered witnessing of all believers. We see an example of this in Acts 4:31: "And when they had prayed, the place where they had gathered together was shaken, and they were all filled with the Holy Spirit, and began to speak the word of God with boldness." The companions (4:23) certainly included more than the inner circle of apostles. Recall that the church at Antioch was established by the empowered witness of those who had been

scattered by persecution (see Acts 11:19–21). According to Acts 8 the apostles remained in Jerusalem and the scattered believers were bearing witness to Christ.

In Ephesians 5:18 Paul directed his readers to be continually filled with the Spirit. In that context he compared being filled with the Spirit with being intoxicated with wine. While Paul discouraged drunkenness, he used the comparison to great effect. When a person becomes intoxicated their bodily functions are controlled by the effect of the alcohol—personalities are altered, the speech slurs, and bodily movements are impaired. When believers are filled with the Spirit, He will influence their behavior, their speech, and their functioning. When Christians argue that they don't witness because it doesn't come naturally to them, I respond: "It isn't natural; it's supernatural!" When the Holy Spirit indwells you, you are empowered to do the supernatural. Witnessing doesn't require the gift of evangelism; it requires a yielded believer indwelt by the Holy Spirit.

7. God gives the results through us. One of the most encouraging truths about witnessing is that God will give supernatural results. The early church was enjoying wonderful fellowship breaking bread from house to house and they had favor with all the people. Their behavior and speech was such that "the Lord was adding to their number day by day those who were being saved" (Acts 2:47). Do you remember Paul's testimony concerning his work in Corinth? "I planted, Apollos watered, but God was causing the growth" (1 Cor. 3:6). If you and your church will be obedient to spread the seed through witness, and water that seed through building relationships, the Lord will give the increase. The farmer knows that ultimately the fullness of the harvest is out of his hands. He is dependent on the rain and the sunshine. The potential for evangelistic harvest for your church is assured by God, but we must be faithful to do our part by sowing the seed and watering the ground. Here again we see the linking of divine sovereignty and human responsibility. God has chosen to bring his evangelistic harvest through human instrumentation.

8. Believers must obey and accept ownership. Matthew 9:35–10:23 gives us an insightful look at the sending forth of the twelve. Jesus was going through all the villages, teaching and preaching and healing. He was moved by the needs of the people who were distressed and downcast like sheep without a shepherd. He first instructed His disciples to pray to the Lord of the harvest to send workers out into the harvest. Prayer forms the basis for the response of the twelve. Jesus then gave them authority and instruction before sending them out.

The first essential witnessing action of the believer is to obey. Witnessing courage actually comes from obedience. Witnessing requires faith that God will provide the resources and give the harvest, and thus it demands obedience. We must obey even when we do not feel competent.

Why do so few obey the command to go into the harvest? That may well be the most critical question of this chapter. No doubt it is vitally linked with the little time we spend in harvest praying. We cannot enter the presence of Holy God on behalf of the lost without being moved by His compassion for the lost. Yet, even as we pray for the lost, there seems to be something missing.

This summer, while meditating on this text, I was forced to ask myself the question: "Why did Jesus feel such compassion for the lost, and I feel so little?" I knew if I was moved by compassion I would of necessity be more involved in personal witnessing. The Lord used an event in the life of our family to give me the answer to my question.

We recently built a new home, and in landscaping the back yard I installed two small water gardens. I had barely finished the work and filled them with water when I had to leave home for another series of growth conferences. One evening when I called home, my middle daughter Rachael asked if she could stock the ponds with fish while I was gone. I knew the ponds had not sufficiently cured to make them safe for the fish, but I was feeling a bit guilty for being away from home, and thus I relented. I did, however, instruct her to buy the cheapest gold fish she could find. I knew they probably would not survive very long.

The next evening when I called home, Rachael excitedly told me of her beautiful fish. Somehow I knew that cheap gold fish couldn't be that beautiful, but I was afraid to ask and I didn't want to dampen her enthusiasm. A few days later I returned home and was greeted by two exuberant daughters. "Daddy, come see our fish!" The fish were indeed lovely. They should have been; they were expensive Koi, a decorative Japanese fish. The girls began to tell me the names of the fish and who owned each fish. That's right, there were five fish, one each for the individual members of our household.

That evening I noticed that a couple of the fish had begun to swim somewhat erratically. Not a good sign! The next morning I discovered our first casualty. I told the girls of our loss and their first question voiced in stereo: "Whose fish died?" When I responded it was mine, they both breathed a sigh of relief. The first death was soon followed by others. The last fish to die was Rachael's. When I broke the news to her, she was deeply saddened. Her fish had died! What made the death of this fish so tragic? One factor—ownership—it was her fish.

Suddenly I saw the passage in Matthew in a clearer light. Jesus was the shepherd, and they were His sheep that were distressed and downcast. That is why He was moved with compassion. *The key that moves us to obedience in witnessing is ownership.*

Do you remember the story of Jonah? God called Jonah to go to Nineveh. He was as thrilled to go to Nineveh as most of us are to show up for Monday night visitation. Reluctantly he obeyed and God gave a bountiful harvest. Jonah, however, was not rejoicing over the harvest, he was pouting on the hillside because Nineveh had repented and the plant he had been using for shade had died. The Lord asked him if he had good reason to be angry over the death of a plant. Jonah responded: "'I have good reason to be angry, even to death.' Then the Lord said, 'You had compassion on the plant for which you did not work, and which you did not cause to grow, which came up overnight and perished overnight. And should I not have compassion on Nineveh?'" (Jonah 4:9–11). Ninevehites had been created by God but blinded by sin. They were His. Compassion is tied to ownership.

Look again at the ending to the story of the prodigal son (see Luke 15). The father was rejoicing because his son had returned, but the elder brother was angry and pouting. The elder brother never referred to the prodigal as his brother, but only as his father's son. The father corrects him: "But we had to be merry and rejoice, for this brother of yours was dead and has begun to live, and was lost and has been found" (v. 32). Until you accept the ownership for your community and the lost around your church, you will not be moved with compassion to reach them. Ownership and obedience are essential elements to effective evangelism.

Developing the Climate for Evangelism

Developing an evangelistic church is not so much an issue of finding the right program and strategy as it is developing an evangelistic climate. The evangelistic church is permeated with the desire to win the lost and expand the family. The passion for evangelism grows when the climate is right, and this in turn will lead to the development of an appropriate evangelistic strategy. Our first priority must be to understand and develop the climate.

Seven Essential Elements of an Evangelistic Climate

1. Conversation about evangelism is natural. The evangelistic church talks naturally about soul-winning. It is heard from the pulpit, Sunday School teachers, and other laymen of the church. It is embodied in the prayers of the church and is seen frequently in its printed materials. It literally saturates the church. Evangelistic conversation begins with the pastor, but must be embraced by the church if is to become climatic.

2. The evangelistic church is marked by a pervasive spirit of love. The pastor and church members openly express their love for the Lord, for one another, and for the lost. There exists a deep level of caring in the fellowship of members.

3. A spirit of expectancy and excitement permeates the evangelistic church. Church members come to church each Sunday expecting the Spirit of God to give a regular harvest of souls. You can sense the excitement when you walk onto the grounds of the church. Such an expectancy depends on weekly sowing of seed by the pastor and church members. As a pastor it is easier to give the invitation with a sense of expectancy if you have brought someone to church that you have led to Christ during the week.

4. A sense of urgency motivates the people to be serious about outreach. Most Christians know they should witness but are lackadaisical in their commitment. A sense of urgency comes from a clear understanding of human lostness and the absolute necessity of salvation.

5. The evangelistic church has strong, conservative theology. Activity is ultimately based on doctrine. I have cited, on several occasions, the study by Johnson, Hoge, and Luidens that indicated the best predictor of church growth was orthodox Christian belief. Declining churches, they discovered, had developed a theological system that rejected the exclusive truth claims of Christianity and the doctrine that God consigns anyone to hell. This lay liberalism was not found to be an energizing faith, and therefore its advocates rarely attempted to convert anyone to their point of view.[14]

6. The evangelistic church expects God to work supernaturally. Many churches are paralyzed by their inability to believe God can supernaturally change lives. We hear it in phrases like: "This community is impossible to reach." "He will never change."

7. A team spirit and a shared vision mark the evangelistic church. The pastor is not viewed as the "hired gun" responsible for all evangelistic activity. The laity understands that all believers are responsible for fulfilling the Great Commission.

Creating the Climate

If your church doesn't have such a climate, you must take immediate steps to remedy the situation or any suggested plan of evangelism will fail because the proper motivation is lacking. Follow these thirteen steps and you will see the environment change:

1. Teach the theological basics to develop conviction. Preach a sermon series or teach a series of lessons on the doctrine of salvation.[15]

2. Start evangelistic praying. If you are a pastor or lay leader, do not be afraid to pray publicly for the lost. Start prayer groups that focus on praying for lost people. Most church prayer meetings are little more than "organ recitals." We pray for Aunt Susie's liver and Uncle John's lungs and other assorted body organs. Some of these dear saints are worn out and dying to go to heaven, but we keep praying they will hang on. Yet we seldom pray for the lost people all around our churches who are dying and going to hell.

3. *Create a can-do attitude.* Many churches spend most of their time explaining why they can't reach their communities instead of looking for innovative ways to win the lost. Quit talking about the problems, and start looking for solutions.

4. *Saturate church communication with evangelistic emphasis.* Use personal contact, church newsletters, Sunday School classes, and committees to talk about the need to reach the community for Christ.

5. *Model evangelistic behavior.* If verbal communication is not supported by life-style, it will not produce results. You can start by taking someone with you on a visit. If you are not trained to make an evangelistic visit, simply ask a friend to learn with you. Take a simple tract such as the *Four Spiritual Laws* booklet and ask for permission to read it to a lost person. As you grow in your witnessing skills, you may want to get additional personal training in a course such as *Evangelism Explosion, Continuous Witness Training,* or an equivalent provided by your denomination.

6. *Start evangelistic activity.* Activities such as a regular night for visitation or the scheduling of an evangelistic meeting can greatly assist in creating an evangelistic climate. When Kirk Hadaway looked at churches that had been able to break out of a plateaued situation, he discovered the single largest reason for growth was evangelistic activity.[16]

Even if the particular evangelistic activity does not reap a great harvest, it will help to build climate.

7. *Encourage the people to bring their friends.* If we accept the finding that 76 to 89 percent of people come to a church because of the invitation of a friend or family member, then we should encourage our people to bring their friends. One fourth of all unchurched people say they have never been invited to church, but would come if they were invited.[17] Create sufficient quality in worship, Sunday School, and special events that people will want to invite their friends. If your people are having their needs met through the ministries of the church and have a genuine concern for people, they will bring needy

friends. We've been told: "Friends don't let friends drive drunk!" To that I say, "Friends don't let friends go to hell!"

8. Put greeters in the parking lot and at the doors. Recently a friend recounted his first visit to First Norfolk. He had been reluctant to attend because of the size of the church, but when he arrived someone directed him to a parking space reserved for visitors. When he reached the door, he was warmly welcomed by a greeter. "It was like they had been expecting me," he said. Chuck Kelley makes this same point visibly by contrasting the hotel room with a spare bedroom in a friend's home. Often when invited to use a spare bedroom you find that the closet and drawers are stuffed with out-of-season clothes. The guest is not provided with a personal phone and has to share the bathroom with the teenage daughter. The hotel, on the other hand, has empty drawers and closets, a clean bathroom, and a private phone. The hotel is clearly saying: "We've been expecting you; we're glad you're here; stay as long as you like." The spare room says: "We don't usually have guests, you're welcome, but don't stay too long." You have the uncomfortable impression that your visit is an inconvenience to the family. Does your church project the atmosphere of a spare bedroom or a hotel room for sinners?

9. Equip laity to share their faith. The climate for evangelism will not spread until the laity become personally involved. Find a method with which you are comfortable and start training!

10. Set evangelistic goals. What are the most prominent goals in your church? What creates most discussion and receives the most publicity? For most churches the answer would be the finances. Is money the most critical issue of your church? Set goals related to conversions and keep people aware of how well they are doing toward reaching those goals. Before you argue that such a goal is carnal and contrived, I would warn you that most churches set giving goals. Why should we apologize for setting goals that are in line with the Great Commission? If you fail to set goals for evangelistic growth, you actually set goals of no growth by default.

11. Highlight decisions made through the witness of laity. You can have the person used of God to lead someone to Christ stand with the new believer when introduced to the church family.

You can include the name of the witness along with the name of the new member in the church newsletter.

12. Care for the needs of believers. If the church members do not feel loved and cared for, evangelistic activity will often decline. This matter will be discussed more completely in the next characteristic.

Develop an Intentional Strategy

Every church must have an intentional strategy for reaching its community. You don't need to clone the outreach program of any other church. Your program should be designed with the knowledge of your unique community and the gifts and resources of your church. Nevertheless, several basic elements must be in place for any strategy to be effective.

The Five Essential Components of Evangelistic Strategy

1. Discover prospects. The church must discover those who are prospects for the gospel and then create avenues to reach them. The best prospect discovery system is always personal invitation by a member of your church. If you simply train your people to be sensitive to the needs of those around them, they will discover more prospects than you might imagine. You might ask one of your small groups to list people they know through work, social clubs, and neighborhoods that do not presently attend church. New residents to the community are always good prospects. Some churches have used need-related surveys to discover prospects. You can customize these for your specific community, but remember to focus on the discovery of ministry needs. Adults often respond well to neatly dressed youth. You can either ask a few survey questions at the door or ask the occupant to fill out the survey card and hang it on the door to be picked up at a later time. People who have attended your church for any function are often receptive prospects. Many churches miss excellent opportunities to discover prospects by failing to register guests who attend special events such as concerts, Vacation Bible School, or choir specials.

The ways to discover new prospects are endless. Ask a group of laity to suggest ideas. They live, work, and recreate with the people the church is commissioned to reach. You will find that they will suggest many innovative methods of finding prospects. If laity are allowed to suggest ways to find prospects, they will be highly motivated to participate in the actual projects.

2. Equip laity to present the gospel in the power of the Holy Spirit. Many good methods and programs exist to train people to witness. Some provide training over a period of several weeks, while others can be done in an evening. Find one that suits your church and your own gifts and get started. Another option is to start by simply taking two friends with you on an actual visit. If you use a tract or marked New Testament, show them how to use the same tool. Witnessing is learned better through example than through lecture presentation.

In characteristic 3 we looked at Jesus' strategy for equipping His disciples. You can follow His example in training fellow members to witness: model the behavior, share your passion, teach them to pray, instruct them in witnessing procedure, empower and send them out, provide the necessary resources, and observe, affirm and correct.

If you do not currently feel comfortable with your own witnessing ability, find someone to train you. If you can find no one in your church, ask a mature believer in another church to help you or go to a conference on personal witnessing. Learn how to witness and then multiply your efforts by equipping others.

3. Take the good news to your community. Jesus' training methodology and teaching clearly indicate He expected His disciples to take the message to the lost world. The Great Commission begins with an emphasis on going. The parable of the dinner in Luke 14:15–24 concludes with the command: "Go out into the highways and along the hedges, and compel them to come in, that my house may be filled" (v. 23). In Luke 15 we discover three parables about lost items. The shepherd searches for his sheep, and the woman turns the house upside down looking for her coin. In both stories the stress is on the joy experienced in discovering the lost items. The third parable of the lost son is distinctive in that no one sought for the boy. The father, who represents the Heavenly Father, could not seek for the lad. Yet there is someone who could have gone—the elder brother. Because of his refusal to go, he could not participate in the joy of his brother's return. The elder brother was not a bad sort of fellow. He had stayed at home and tended the farm and obeyed his father: "Look! For so many years I have been serving you, and I have never neglected a command of yours; and yet you have never given me a kid, that I might be merry with my friends" (v. 29). In spite of his service and obedience, he could not share his father's joy because he was unwilling to leave home and look for his brother. True joy is experienced when we participate in the search for God's lost children.

Recently much attention has been given to the worship service as an outreach tool. Terms such as "seeker-targeted," "seeker-driven," and "seeker-sensitive" have become commonplace. The evangelistic church will use every means possible to reach the lost, and thus it cannot overlook the presence of unsaved guests in the worship service. I am grateful that those who have written on the seeker service have challenged us to improve the quality of our worship services, remove artificial and traditional barriers that unnecessarily make guests feel awkward, and to hang out the welcome sign at the hotel for sinners. We would do well to heed these challenges.

Many churches with a seeker service have maintained good balance, but some persons hearing their success stories in conferences have copied the method without maintaining the same balance. Therefore, I would like to interject into this discussion a few words of caution: *First*, you can't dilute authentic worship and develop a healthy church. Worship must first be directed to God and thus exalt Christ. An unsaved person can't worship, but saved persons must, or they will fail to grow and reproduce. Don't starve believers. *Second*, a seeker-targeted service is simply another term for an evangelistic service. When I was a boy, many churches had evangelistic services on Sunday evening. They were remarkably similar to seeker services today—with choruses, an informal atmosphere, and an emphasis on inviting guests. Such a service has proven hard to sustain on a weekly basis over a long period of time because people are less motivated to invite their friends after the novelty wears off. You must continually emphasize personal invitation or be prepared to discard this as a growth method when it no longer works. *Third,* most churches who do such a service successfully do not depend on this service as their only outreach effort. If you use such a service, don't shut down other avenues for reaching people. *Fourth,* the seeker service is a method of growth, not a principle. The principle at work behind the success of the seeker service is the personal invitation. *Fifth,* if you decide to attempt such a service, do it with quality, do not compromise scriptural principles, and provide an excellent worship experience for believers. Monitor the attendance of both to ensure that believers are being fed, and you are reaching the unsaved. *Sixth,* do not allow the seeker terminology to confuse the thinking of your church about who the true seekers are. God has always been the seeker—He sent His Son to seek and save the lost. The church has been commissioned to go and seek the lost. The presenting of the gospel to the unsaved will take place primarily in the world and not in the church.[18] Do not allow seeker terminology to dull the commitment to outreach. The seeker mindset might delude us into thinking that sinful, fallen humanity is seeking God. We cannot swap a "come-see" strategy for a "go-tell" one and be faithful to the Great Commission.

4. Challenge the lost to commit to Christ. Every witnessing strategy must have a plan for drawing the net. Many Christians do well at developing witnessing relationships and even at sharing their testimony, but fail at the point of invitation. Once the gospel has been presented in the power of the Holy Spirit, it is only natural to invite a decision.

5. New believers must be assimilated and nurtured. The Great Commission does not conclude with the instructions to go. If we are going to be faithful to the Great Commission, we must baptize (assimilate) and teach new Christians to obey all that Christ commanded. Some churches focus only on giving birth to new believers and fail to develop believers. Ultimately this leads to frustration as large numbers of conversions are reported, but no visible results are seen because these persons are not incorporated into the local church and thus do not become reproducing Christians.

Develop a Personalized Strategy

No one knows your church and community like you do, therefore you should design the outreach strategy that will work best in your context. Feel free to borrow and adapt. Keep balanced and be intentional. Here are a few suggestions as you begin to develop your personalized strategy:

1. *Effective evangelism is usually a combination of many factors.* Successful churches do not rely on a single method for reaching people; they use multiple strategies. The more hooks you get in the water, the more fish you are likely to catch. Be creative! Don't be afraid to try a new idea. If it doesn't work, bury it and move on.

2. *Learn all you can about the people you are trying to reach.* Good fishermen are usually well informed about the fish they are attempting to catch. It would be foolish to use a lure designed for bass if no bass inhabit the pond you are fishing. Most denominations now provide demographic information to assist you in knowing your community. Nothing, however, will replace hands-on experience. Get out and meet the people you are trying to reach. Talk to them; find out what their needs and aspirations are.

3. *Develop a presence in the community.* Do people know your church exists? You may be surprised to know how many folks have grown so accustomed to your church building that they ignore its presence and ministry. This is true in any size community. You might consider sponsoring a community event to develop presence. Invite the community to use your facility. In Norfolk we invited the Navy to use our fellowship hall for their sessions prior to the deployment of a ship. This exposed a large number of people to our church for the first time and began to create receptivity. Think creatively! Groups exist that will need, on an occasional basis, a place to assemble. Every time you get the community onto your property or into your building you are breaking down barriers and developing presence. Remember your building is nothing more than a wrapper around the church's ministry. Use it as an effective outreach tool.

Yet to develop presence, we must do more than invite people to come to us—we must be part of the community. Christians should be trained to see every community relationship as a possible avenue for winning someone to Christ. This, too, must be modeled by the pastor. The pastor is the one person who most visibly represents the church. You can look for unique opportunities to develop presence. Volunteer to help in sports leagues, pray at a ball game, or join a civic club. The list is endless; you should be guided by the community needs and your own interests.

For example, Johnny Hunt, the pastor of First Baptist Church of Woodstock, Georgia, is interested in stock car racing. He began to attend races at the dirt track in his community. Soon he was invited to pray before races. The owner was so impressed with Johnny's concern for the community that he removed a sign advertising beer and put up a sign with the church logo at his own expense. The church has since had a Sunday service where race drivers and fans were invited to attend and then recognized in the service. You can do similar things to create a presence for the church in you community. Have fun!

4. Develop a regular visitation night. Organized visitation should always be a part of the total outreach program of the church. Start by visiting the people who visit your worship services, Bible study groups, or special events. Any person who fills out a visitor or registration card should be visited. People are not naive. If they give you their name, phone number, and address, they will expect your contact. You may prefer to call visitors and set appointments. This saves time and ensures that you do not visit at an inconvenient moment. Other churches have had good success going unannounced on a particular night. Try both ideas and see which works best in your area.

You are no doubt aware that some writers argue visitation is no longer effective. There are eight good reasons you should have a visitation program: 1) It helps to create the evangelistic atmosphere. It reminds everyone of the responsibility of the church to reach the community; 2) It develops a team spirit. People begin to see that evangelism is not the sole responsibility of the pastor; 3) A regular visitation program creates an arena of personal accountability. People left to visit on their own usually will not visit at all; 4) It gives the participants a vision for supernatural activity. God will give you results and people will thus see the hand of God; 5) Visitation is an essential seed sowing activity that will enable you to see an evangelistic harvest through other events. Don't depreciate the impact of visitation even when you do not see immediate results. Trust the Word of God to have its ultimate impact; 6) A visitation program provides a training opportunity for teaching people to witness; 7) Visitation will help sensitize your people to the actual needs that exist in your community. The Christian often becomes isolated and insulated from the real world. Visitation can help to break down that isolation; 8) Visitation still works! Results from national Continuous Witnessing Seminars and regional WIN (Witness Involvement Now) schools of evangelism held by the Southern Baptist Convention reveal that when an attempt is made to present the gospel by a trained witness, one out of every three lost persons will allow an immediate presentation. For every four times the gospel is presented one person prays to receive Christ.[19]

5. *Use events to discover prospects.* While you cannot rely on events to grow your church, they can be an important part of your total outreach program. A big event such as a musical presentation or special guest speaker helps to develop community presence. The success of the evangelistic event depends on a personal invitation by church members and the immediate follow-up to those who attend. Many churches virtually waste big events by not registering guests or providing for any follow-up response.[20]

6. *Ministry-based evangelism.* Often we make an artificial distinction between social ministry and evangelism. The Bible knows no such distinction. Social ministry which expresses no concern for the spiritual condition of persons is incomplete, and evangelism which shows no concern for the physical and social needs of people presents a partial gospel. Evangelism provides a wonderful opportunity to meet needs and share the gospel. Meeting needs opens the door of receptivity. Ministry-based evangelism will be normative for the church of the twenty-first century. Every community has unique needs and your church is gifted to meet some of those needs. Determine the needs of the community, examine the gifts operating through your members,

and design a ministry to meet needs and present Christ in the power of the Spirit.

First Baptist of Leesburg, Florida, has over fifty ministries and baptizes over three hundred people a year in a community of twenty-five thousand. Pastor Charles Rosel explains that the ministries began at the initiation of church members. This church did not experience anything like this rate of baptisms until they began ministry-based evangelism.

The entire Greater Boston Association of Southern Baptist churches was built through ministry-based evangelism. While the association grew from seventeen congregations to fifty-seven congregations, baptisms were recorded at the phenomenal rate of one baptism for every eleven church members. Compare that with the ratio of one to forty in the Southern Baptist Convention as a whole. One church, Grace Baptist Church in Marlboro, Massachusetts, started with fifty-five people and grew to over three hundred in eight years. The pastor, Mark Acuff, invited the mayor to speak on what a new church should offer in service to the community. In return, the mayor appointed him to a social services committee. Another church, the Haitian Baptist Church of the New Jerusalem in Dorchester, grew from thirty to five hundred under the leadership of Tony Kebreau by offering ministries such as English as a second language, citizenship classes, and benevolence.

The Tree of Life Missionary Baptist Church, an African-American church in Gary, Indiana, grew from no members to over six hundred in thirteen years. This church has rehabilitated twenty-seven apartments for low income families. The city has just given a full block of HUD houses to the church for them to refurbish. This church has established a program for troubled teens where they teach carpentry skills and conduct Bible study. They have seen many of these ministry recipients come to know Christ. Joe Ratliff, pastor of Brentwood Baptist Church of Houston, Texas, attributes their phenomenal growth, from five hundred members in 1980 to ten thousand in 1993 to their exciting worship combined with need-based ministries, from literacy counseling to in-home care for AIDS patients. Brentwood even established its own credit union to meet the needs of those shut out of the city's mainline banking system.

Stories such as these could be repeated all over the country from churches of differing denominational affiliations. All are providing social ministries with a marked difference—the good news of Christ. The cup of cold water is accompanied by an offer of living water. Your community may not have the same needs as any of those just mentioned, but it does have needs that will provide a door of opportunity to minister in Christ's name.

7. *Schedule an evangelistic meeting.* Many churches are experiencing good results from evangelistic meetings. The keys are thorough prayer preparation, excellent pre-meeting planning, personal invitations to the lost, and a gifted evangelist. Choose an evangelist who has a proven track record in churches similar to yours. Make sure to schedule well in advance and follow through on necessary pre-meeting planning. Critical pre-meeting components often omitted are prospect discovery, evangelistic praying, and personal witnessing throughout the community. Evangelistic meetings will often be the harvesting tool for the seeds sown through witnessing.

I was recently with Pastor Dan Brandel from Idaho. Going to a new pastorate, he found a church that had had a rapid succession of pastors and an accompanying decline. Soon after coming he introduced the church to evangelistic witnessing techniques and a year later he scheduled an evangelistic meeting. The members assured this pastor that revivals would not work in their area, yet out of love for their new pastor, they acquiesced. The church prayed, a prospect list was developed, the people visited, the evangelist came, and twenty-four people were baptized into the life of the church.

8. *Staffing for evangelism.* As the church grows and needs additional staff, many churches consider adding a staff person whose primary responsibility is outreach evangelism. I do not recommend this because I think the pastor must be the key leader in the evangelism program and all staff members should be integrally involved in the total outreach strategy of the church. If, however, you do decide to add a Minister of Outreach, make sure everyone on the staff and in the church clearly understands that the outreach ministry requires their participation.

9. *Budgeting for evangelism.* The church's budget will reflect its priorities. If you are going to be effective in reaching your com-

munity, you must provide the resources. While you should interpret the entire church budget in terms of the Great Commission, you should include an amount for direct local evangelism that is equal to your giving to other mission causes, and not less than 10 percent of the total budget. This will ensure that you continue to reach you local community and also build a strong base for reaching the world. Include money for outreach events and training materials.

10. Evangelistic concern should extend to the world. The truly evangelistic church cannot neglect the plight of the lost around the world. It should be involved in teaching missions, giving to missions, and challenging the people to do mission work around the world. Some churches have focused all their energies and resources on reaching their own community. While such a strategy may provide impressive local church returns, I do not think it is an effective Great Commission strategy.

Total church growth demands we go into all the world. If our giving patterns are any indications of our commitment to reach the world, there is need for concern. The U.S. population is 4.7 percent of the total world population. The giving to Christian causes in mid-1993 was 175 billion dollars, of which 9.6 billion went to global mission causes.[21] In other words, we spent 94.5 percent of the money given to spread the gospel on 4.7 percent of the world's population. How can we look at the facts and declare our serious commitment to *church* growth?

Contextualized Witnessing

Our personal witnessing is more effective if we first determine the level of responsiveness of the person to whom we are witnessing. Each individual is at a different point based on their personal background and previous encounters with believers. Here is a visual representation of the levels of responsiveness.

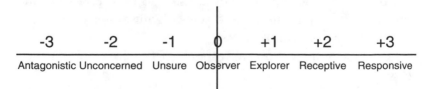

-3	-2	-1	0	+1	+2	+3
Antagonistic	Unconcerned	Unsure	Observer	Explorer	Receptive	Responsive

Try to view people somewhere on this continuum from -3 to +3, and attempt to move them in a positive direction with each encounter. I would also encourage you to expect the Holy Spirit to provide positive movement through the gifts and opportunities He has given you. Do not underestimate a person's potential to move through several stages in one witnessing encounter. For example, Paul moved from being antagonistic to being responsive in a single encounter with the risen Lord (see Acts 9). Some witnesses make the mistake of moving too slowly or delaying their verbal witness to a person who does not appear to be responsive.

If you look at the chart as a whole, persons in the minus category will look first to see the *salt* of Christian behavior before they are likely to respond to the *light* of our verbal witness. My word of caution to you is this: Raise the flag of Christian witness as quickly as possible in your developing relationship for two reasons. First, if you develop a friendship with an unsaved neighbor and never mention your personal relationship with Christ, it becomes increasingly more awkward to do so as time progresses. If you fail to mention your concern for his or her salvation for several months, he or she may question the legitimacy of your friendship when you later introduce the topic. Second, he or she can legitimately wonder why you failed to warn him or her earlier if eternity is at stake. You should raise the flag as early as possible. This does not mean you have to share your entire witness. In truth, the antagonistic or unconcerned person probably will not permit such a presentation. You should not, however, conceal your personal commitment to Christ or your desire to see your friend know Christ. Those who attempt to remain undercover agents for Christ rarely lead their friends to Christ.

When witnessing to anyone in a negative category, you should practice active listening and live a consistent Christian life. Be sensitive to the unbeliever, listen to their concerns and objections, but don't hesitate to splash living water on them at any available opportunity.

Let's look at a few positive responses to persons in each category:

• Build a personal relationship with those who may be *antag-*

onistic toward your witness and show them unconditional love. Do not respond negatively when they strike out at you or your beliefs.

• The *unconcerned* person often responds as you meet a personal need. Look for those teachable, reachable moments as you continue to build your witnessing relationship.

• Individuals who are *unsure* have begun to ask questions about life and may respond to the witness who engages them in dialogue about life. They may be unsure because of some event in their own life or that of a family member. Help them to interpret these events from a biblical perspective. You may want to give a well-chosen book about the questions of greatest concern to them. They may attend a need-related support group.

• The *observer* is developing an openness to the gospel. This person often responds to your invitation to attend a special event or a need-related support group or possibly a study group. Continue your dialogic witness. Dialogic witnessing requires that you answer the questions about life the unsaved person is asking. You thus engage them in dialogue at the point of their concerns.

• The *explorer* is open to attending a Bible study group. Realize that the explorer may still be looking into other systems of thought. Don't be defensive if they compare Christian belief and New Age thinking for example. You need not worry; the Christian world view will hold up to scrutiny and prove itself superior to any other world view. If the observer or explorer attends church with you, they will not be likely to fill out a visitor's card or registration pad no matter how you greet guests.

• The individual at +2 is *receptive* and thus will probably fill out a visitor's card. Anyone who fills out a visitor card should be visited in his or her home by a team who has witness training. This person is very close to being *responsive*. Harvesting witnessing tools such as CWT and EE are particularly helpfully for preparing people for these in-home visits. This does not mean that such tools cannot be used in witnessing to persons at other levels of responsiveness. Here again we must be prepared to witness and be responsive to the work of the Holy Spirit as the Word of God does its supernatural work.

We could illustrate the full witnessing process as follows:

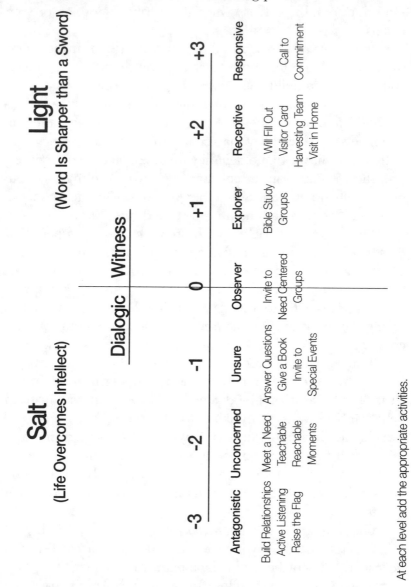

	Salt (Life Overcomes Intellect)			Dialogic Witness		Light (Word Is Sharper than a Sword)		
	-3	**-2**	**-1**	**0**	**+1**	**+2**	**+3**	
	Antagonistic	Unconcerned	Unsure	Observer	Explorer	Receptive	Responsive	
	Build Relationships	Meet a Need	Answer Questions	Invite to	Bible Study	Will Fill Out	Call to	
	Active Listening	Teachable	Give a Book	Need Centered	Groups	Visitor Card	Commitment	
	Raise the Flag	Reachable	Invite to	Groups		Harvesting Team		
		Moments	Special Events			Visit in Home		

At each level add the appropriate activities.

I discuss this method of witnessing in greater detail in the book, *Sharing Life's Answer with a Friend.*

The growing church will have a passion to reach their community and their world and will use any available means and opportunity to do so.

Characteristic 8:

Maturation of Believers

Today the church is frequently compared to a business. Increasingly business concepts and models are being applied to church growth methodology.

Dr. William Crabb objects to such thinking when it comes to the bottom-line issue of purpose for existence. The business, he notes, exists to produce a product. Without a product that produces a profit, a business would not survive. "In the local church, the 'product'—or more precisely, the aim—is to promote and facilitate growth of people toward Christlikeness." Thus people are not resources to perform functions, but people for whom Christ died, given in stewardship to be grown into His image.[1]

Healthy churches place a high priority on promoting the growth of people toward Christlikeness, which is the fundamental issue of the discipling ministry of the church. Bill Hull defines discipleship: "The intentional training of disciples, with accountability, on the basis of loving relationships." "Intentional" demands that we have a clearly planned strategy. "Training" implies a prescribed course of study and a process designed to help people reach certain goals. The phrase, "with accountability" recognizes the fact that people need help keeping their commitments to God. The final phrase, "on the basis of loving relationships," demands that community building must be a high priority of the discipling church.[2]

I frequently hear pastors and laity contrasting the discipling church with the evangelistic church as if they are separate entities or even in opposition to one another. It is true that some churches focus a majority of their energies and resources on winning people to Christ and give little attention to the assimilation and development of these new believers. They boast of impressive evangelistic results, but worship and or small group attendance remains plateaued. The back door of the church is open wider than the front door. While we could commend such a church for their zeal to reach the lost, we could hardly endorse such a strategy as being faithful to the Great Commission.

Other churches, either in reaction to such zeal or out of apathy for evangelism, have placed virtually all their resources and efforts on growing the saints to maturity. They often boast they are not driven by the concern for numbers, but are interested only in quality and maturity. Once again, we would applaud the concern for developing mature believers, but we could not be impressed with discipling that does not produce evangelistic concern. A Christian who expresses no concern for the condition of the lost could hardly be considered Christlike.

The Great Commission commands that the church be involved in the process of making disciples which means they must embrace both evangelistic activity and ministry to believers leading to maturity. Authentic evangelism requires the assimilation of the new believer into the church; assimilation, in turn, necessitates discipleship which ultimately leads to effective

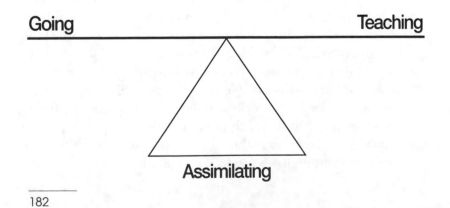

Going   **Teaching**

Assimilating

evangelism. The assimilation process is the crucial balancing point between going and teaching in the Great Commission.

When a church takes seriously the Great Commission, it will develop a balanced strategy which includes evangelism, assimilation, and teaching. These three facets of discipleship will continually feed each other. Bill Hull makes the point clearly: "'at home' disciple making is the key to world evangelism. Unhealthy churches at home lead to weak missions abroad, but when the church makes disciples at home two good things happen: Christians become healthy and reproduce, and as they multiply, the world becomes evangelized God's way."[3] We could illustrate the process as a circle of continuous ministry:

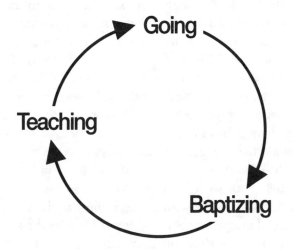

The Church at Antioch

If we take one last look at Luke's description of our model church, we will notice a curious passage. "And he left for Tarsus to look for Saul; and when he had found him, he brought him to Antioch. And it came about that for an entire year they met with the church, and taught considerable numbers; and the disciples were first called Christians in Antioch" (Acts 11:25–26).

This passage occurs after the second reference to large numbers of people turning to or being brought to the Lord.

The tremendous evangelistic harvest presented the church with a discipling demand. Barnabas first recruited assistance, going to Tarsus to look for Saul, and then he began the lengthy task of teaching the new believers to observe all that Christ taught them. The text mentions that they met with the church for an entire year. Discipleship is an ongoing process, not a quick fix.

The sequence in this text is also interesting. Luke mentioned that the believers in Antioch were first called Christians after noting that Paul and Barnabas taught them for an entire year. Many of the persons who became Christians in Antioch had come from a Gentile or pagan background. The earliest disciples in Jerusalem had all come from a Jewish heritage. Many of the fundamental issues of Christian moral values have their foundational basis in the Ten Commandments, and thus the Jewish believers found much common ground in Christian teaching. Many of the fundamentals of Christian behavior were already in place for the Jewish Christians. The pagan converts, on the other hand, had no such background; thus, the discipling process had to begin with foundational issues. It may well have taken a year of teaching before some of the converts from paganism truly began to resemble Christ.

Notice, too, that after the year of teaching, when the Jerusalem believers were threatened by famine, each of the Antioch disciples shared with those believers living in Judea. These Gentile believers now considered Jewish Christians they had never seen to be their brothers and sisters. The teaching of Scripture had produced a positive effect.

The Acts Model

Any discussion of discipleship in the modern church would be incomplete without first looking at the model of the early church as outlined in Acts 2:41–47. The tremendous evangelistic harvest of three thousand souls created a challenging opportunity for the emerging church. How then did they respond to this influx of new believers? Notice the emphasis on the continual process of disciple making: "were continually devoting . . . everyone kept feeling . . . they began selling their property and possessions, and were sharing them . . . day by day continuing with one mind . . . they were taking their meals together . . . the Lord was adding to their number day by day."

Discipleship is a process, not an event. The process of discipleship involves several factors if it is to be balanced.

1. *They added the converts to the body* (v. 41). Biblical discipleship requires attachment to the body of Christ through the means of a local church family. Thus a first step in discipleship is incorporating a new convert into the body of Christ.

2. *They devoted themselves to apostolic teaching* (v. 42). Discipleship involves cognitive learning, particularly of strong doctrinal teaching.

3. *They devoted themselves to one another in biblical fellowship* (vv. 42, 44–47). Discipleship is based upon producing healthy believers in the context of healthy relationships. This will not happen without a commitment of time and energy. They were together day by day, and they were eating together. Many churches are looking for a quick-fix discipleship plan that has low time demands. You'll be hard pressed for biblical examples. Their fellowship required practical expression through loving sacrifice.

4. *They devoted themselves to worship* (vv. 42, 47). Praise, the breaking of bread, meeting in the temple, and prayer are all mentioned in this text. It is likely that the phrase "breaking of bread" refers to the Lord's Supper. Worship is essential to discipleship.

5. *They were respected throughout the community* (v. 47). The behavior and moral values of these growing Christians earned them favor with the people.

6. *They continued to emphasize outreach* (v. 47). The early Christians sowed the seed of the gospel both through their behavior and their witness, and God kept adding to their number daily.

This Acts model gives us all the basic ingredients needed to develop a balanced discipleship ministry in today's church. Now look at applying these components to our own church families.

A Family Model for Discipling

Throughout this book I have utilized family imagery to refer to the church fellowship and the church leaders in relationship to their people. The parenting model thus became the focus of the leadership characteristic. I think it is helpful to carry this imagery with us in the discussion of discipling believers. The parent's role in the home is actually a discipling role and thus the parallels help us develop a model that will assist the local church in meeting the unique needs of each person who is added to the fellowship.

To begin the discipling process, you must first determine where a person is in his/her personal spiritual development. You may be thinking this is too obvious to warrant discussion, but such is not the case. First, we have already indicated that churches add children both by birth (evangelism) and by adoption (transfer). Those who come by transfer from another church may or may not be well developed in their faith. They need not be treated as spiritual infants, but it would be equally wrong to assume they are fully-developed Christians. We must determine their level of development and then offer them the right opportunities for further development.

Second, we cannot assume that all those who come to us by birth have the same needs. I had the advantage of growing up in a strong Christian home. Many of the basic skills for Christian growth were well in place in my life before I actually made my personal commitment to Christ at age nine. For example, I already knew to read my Bible daily and to tithe. I had been trained both by my parents and my older siblings. This was normative behavior in my home. Many individuals who are won to Christ and come from a strong, functional Christian home may have many of the discipling components already in place. However, those who are added to your fellowship from a non-Christian environment may not have had any exposure to these basic skills. Discipleship is most profitable when it begins with the most basic needs of the individual.

We would not consider training an infant and an adolescent in the same way, and yet many churches have a single discipleship strategy for everyone who comes into the church. The infant primarily needs nurturing and bonding. The infant is held closely by the mother who nurses him/her. Yet we put infant Christians in a discipleship class to be nurtured with a group. This may account, in part, for the large number of new believers who never seem to survive long enough to attach themselves to a body of believers. The newborn Christian needs to develop a close, one-on-one relationship to a mature Christian who can meet the intensive personal and survival needs that are experienced by every infant. Children who accept Christ out of a mature Christian home may have most of these infant discipling needs met by their own parents. This is an ideal situation. If, however, you have a young person or adult who has accepted Christ and has not had the benefit of being raised in a Christian home, the church must ensure a personal discipler for initial bonding to occur.

The maturing child on the other hand needs to develop some basic life skills for themselves such as feeding, clothing, personal hygiene, and the fundamentals of obedience. They must be encouraged and affirmed as well as corrected. They have to accept ownership for their personal actions and learn to solve personal problems. This phase of discipling requires personal attention as well as regular encounters with one's peers in small groups.

The youth, developing from adolescence to adulthood, is moving toward productivity. Here learning becomes more cognitive. The basics become automatic and are the foundation for all advanced learning. Character, relational skills, and ministry or leadership skills must now be built on the foundation of basic life skills. The ultimate goal is mature adulthood where the individual is living in healthy relationships, contributing to the family, and reproducing themselves through evangelism.

We could make a simple representation of these discipling needs, starting with the most basic on the foundational level and building to productive life skills.

Reproductive Ministry
Ministry Skills
Character Through Relationship
Foundational Doctrine
Basic Life Skills
Self-Worth
Nurturing—Affection
Bonding/Security

At this point you may be thinking, *I'm having enough problems parenting the few children I have at home. How can I possibly tackle an entire church?* Here again the key is to disciple people who can in turn disciple others. You must learn the process, develop the necessary program, and empower others to accept leadership responsibilities. One other word of encouragement—the textbook of all discipleship is the Bible which is supernaturally powerful. If you faithfully follow a biblical model and teach biblical truths, you will experience good results. Here's a discipling truth to underline: "All Scripture is inspired by God and profitable for teaching, for reproof, for correction, for training in righteousness; that the man of God may be adequate, equipped for every good work" (2 Tim. 3:16–17). Be of good courage; you have all the resources you need to disciple all the believers God will entrust to your care.

Infancy, the Formative Stage

We now have a clearer understanding of the importance of the preschool years in a child's development. Matters such as personality development and even intelligence seem to be greatly impacted by those critical preschool years. Frances L. Ilg and Louise Bates Ames, in their book, *Child Behavior*, write: "Each and every part of the child's nature has to grow—his sense of self, his fears, his affections and his curiosities; his feeling toward mother and father, brothers and sisters and playmates; his attitudes toward sex; his judgments of good and bad, of ugly and beautiful; his respect for truth and justice; his sense of humor; his ideas about life and death, violence, nature, and deity."[4]

This understanding of early child development has led many parents to change their patterns of parenting preschoolers. One of my staff members took this matter of early imprinting so seriously that he began to read to his son while the baby was still in the womb. He not only read the standard nursery rhymes and selected Scripture passages, he talked with his embryonic son about sports. I'm sure this good friend is depending on a basketball scholarship to the University of Kentucky for his son! Knowing him, he may be looking for a healthy retirement from his son's earnings as a professional athlete. While he may have been joking about some of his aspirations for his son, he was serious about making the most of those early months and years in his son's development.

If we are going to develop mature believers, we, too, must take these first months seriously. Unfortunately in many churches infant believers are either neglected or placed in a classroom setting with other spiritual infants in the hope they will be discipled in a structured setting. No caring parent would arrive home from the hospital, place an infant son or daughter on the floor, and boldly announce: "Okay, honey, we have done our job. If you get sleepy, your room is down the hallway, second door on the right. When you get hungry tonight, there is milk in the refrigerator. By the way, don't wake your mom and me until about seven. We're really tired." Doesn't work that way, does it? The infant is totally dependent and demands immediate attention. Baby Christians are equally dependent and need careful, constant attention.

Bonding Is Essential

Bonding with the parents reassures the newborn that he or she belongs and is secure. This is not a difficult matter to accomplish, and it doesn't take specialized skill; it does, however, require time and a willingness to touch. Infants need to be held and cared for in order to meet their bonding needs.

When the church gives birth to a new believer through evangelistic activity, the first priority must be attachment to the family through bonding. Lyle Schaller discovered that from one-third to one-half of Protestant church members do not feel a sense of belonging.[5] We have simply not paid sufficient attention to the matter of assimilative bonding.

What should be the first step? I believe baby Christians must first be discipled one-on-one. New Christians need to be linked to someone who can be their discipling partner. This discipler must, like Paul, provide the gentleness of a nursing mother (see 1 Thess. 2:7). This tenderness, so appropriate to those first months of an infant's life, will soon need the parenting actions of the father—encouraging, exhorting, and imploring (see 2:11). When the infant convert fails in the struggle against the old nature, there must be a tenderness that shows unconditional love. But there must also be the encouragement to do better, the exhortation to go on in development.

The image that readily comes to mind is that of a young child learning to walk. They smile as they turn loose of the chair and make those first wobbly steps. Panic and fear are etched on the faces as they lose balance and fall. The cries of pain and disappointment are heard as they strike the floor. A loving parent then sweeps the crying child into caring arms and wipes away the tears with calm words of assurance: "You'll be okay. You're doing better. We're so proud of you." As the child becomes more adept at walking, then encouraging, exhorting, and imploring become more vital than a simple display of tenderness or the child will continue to fall simply to get the attention of the parents. In the early stages of Christian infancy there must be a balance between tenderness and encouragement.

Over the years I have asked men and women who are now being used of God to make an impact in the Christian community as to how they were discipled. Virtually all have responded by telling me about a key individual who discipled them. Rarely do they mention a particular discipleship tool or even a class in which they participated. They first mention the person who gave them personal attention and watched over their development in those formative first months of their Christian lives.

It is essential that this discipling/bonding encourager be a growing Christian who is available and combines the parental elements of tenderness with encouragement, exhortation, and insistence that the infant grow to maturity. Parenting and discipling are both time-consuming activities, but both are essential if we are going to develop balanced maturity in our homes and in our churches.

Each church will need to develop its own strategy for providing for the one-on-one discipleship necessary for the bonding of new believers. Some will want the person who leads an individual to Christ to be responsible for early assimilation. This will create some difficulty for the church that uses an evangelism training tool such as Evangelism Explosion or Continuous Witness Training both for training in evangelism and for the outreach program of the church. If, after a profession of faith is made, the evangelistic team stops their evangelistic activity until bonding has occurred, the training process is disrupted. As a pastor, I virtually dismantled one outreach program by insisting that the evangelism team be responsible for early assimilation of anyone they led to Christ. Such a strategy inhibited the continual learning process for the trainees. In some cases, it may work well for the evangelist to be the early assimilator, but not everyone has the temperament to be effective in the early bonding ministry.

We discovered that we could best accomplish our Great Commission goals by tying evangelism and assimilation discipleship to our small group structure through the Sunday School. We age-graded all adult classes to take advantage of the principles of homogeneity and receptivity. Homogeneity simply recognizes that Christian witness travels with greater receptivity through a kinship or friendship unit.[6] In each adult class we had an outreach leader who, in many cases, was also an evangelism trainer. Thus evangelistic visits were made by the appropriate age-graded small group. Each of these small groups should be organized to have a sufficient number of care leaders with primary responsibility for the nurturing ministry of the church. When a person receives Christ, he or she can then be assigned to a care leader for assimilation discipleship. This means the evangelism team and the caregivers will be together with the new convert in the same small group family context. Use of a simple tool like *Survival Kit for New Christians* will prove to be a helpful tool for this process, but the key is one-on-one nurturing.

Imitation Begins Early

Early formation of patterned skills is often accomplished through imitation. We are not trying to clone look-alike believers, but we must take seriously the process of imitation mentioned so frequently in Scripture. In 1 Corinthians 4:16 Paul exhorted the Corinthians to imitate him. In 11:1 of the same letter he wrote: "Be imitators of me, just as I also am of Christ." A simple look in a concordance will reveal other references to imitation of behavior as a key discipleship tool.

I mentioned earlier that I learned many of the basic Christian life skills at home by simply observing other family members. Prayer, Bible study, stewardship, and worship patterns were ingrained in me from early childhood. You will discover the same will be true for many converts who come from a strong Christian home. This is an optimum discipling situation. When an adult receives Christ, the church must assume the responsibility for assuring that the new believer has a mentor early in his/her spiritual life. Ideally this should be the same person who provides for the assimilation needs, too. This simply means that the best way to teach someone to pray is to pray with them. The same will be true for other basic skills such as worship and Bible reading. Remember, the Bible is the essential tool for discipling. At this stage new believers will long for the pure milk of the Word so that they will grow in their salvation (1 Pet. 2:2). New believers need to receive the Word from the pulpit and in small group settings, but it is also helpful to have a mentor who can help apply and explain the Word.

Exhorting, Encouraging, and Imploring Will Help Develop Positive Self-Esteem

A child begins early to develop a sense of personal identity and worth. It is tragic when a child is constantly told they will never amount to much, when they are beaten back at every point of development, and never receive the necessary encouragement that allows them to develop a positive self-image. Unfortunately some churches major on strong, corrective teaching with little attention to affirmation and encouragement. This does not mean we ignore issues of correction when necessary. It does require, however, that we acknowledge that learning occurs primarily through positive affirmation of approximately right behavior by the developing Christian. For example, a dad teaches his child to throw by first modeling the right way to throw. The child's first attempts will fall far short of the mark. Yet the dad will lunge for the ball and simultaneously yell, "Good throw!" It is this positive feedback that provides the stimulus to improve. After the child has developed sufficient skill to throw reasonably well, the dad may find it necessary to correct an improper throwing motion or bad habits developed through laziness. At this point correction is both necessary and helpful. This same pattern will yield rich dividends in discipling infant Christians.

The three words "exhorting, encouraging, and imploring" (see 1 Thess. 2:11) are all positive in their approach. The first two are very similar and suggest encouraging toward a particular type of conduct. The third has a greater sense of urgency and authority. Discipling a new Christian is no light matter and should be taken with the same seriousness as parenting a child. Our sense of worth comes from God alone, but our sense of self-esteem is constructed by significant others who help us understand God's Word and develop our own spiritual personalities.

When we see discipling in these family terms, we will then see that all of our contacts, ministries, and activities both in the church and beyond become discipling events. Discipleship is not so much a program as it is a way of life for the church concerned about developing believers. The Old Testament community gives us a good basis for such a model. "And these words, which I am commanding you today, shall be on your heart; and you shall teach them diligently to your sons and shall talk of them when you walk by the way and when you lie down and when you rise up" (Deut. 6:6–7).

Early Childhood—The Developmental Stage

Since discipleship is a continual process, we do not neglect the foundational elements established in infancy as the believer grows; instead, we build upon them. The sense of personal identity and worth established through the security of belonging and being loved will now need to be developed in a personalized manner. Thus the discovery of one's unique identity and giftedness becomes the basic need in the developmental stage of discipleship. In the developmental stage, the basic life skills—such as feeding and clothing oneself, personal hygiene, sharing, and personal responsibility—must be learned and developed so as to become habitual.

In infancy, virtually everything is done for the baby. In childhood, the growing child begins to make choices for himself or herself. Children who continue to grow in a natural and balanced manner become more responsible. Assuming responsibility means that the issues of obedience and corrective discipline play a heavier role now in the discipling process. During this phase of development, the imitative learning pattern is complemented with more cognitive learning opportunities. This demands both basic doctrinal instruction and interaction with persons other than the one-on-one discipler. Group learning activities become essential, and in such contexts, character and relationship skills are hammered out. We might draw the parallel to early elementary school learning experiences where cognitive learning is combined with the development of interpersonal relationship skills.

Mastering Basic Skills
Is Fundamental to Childhood

The developing child must now be taught how to take care of basic life needs. Every parent can remember the frustrating days when more food ended up on the kitchen floor than in the child's mouth. Yet parents couldn't give up on the task of teaching the child to feed himself because, as simple as it is, eating is essential to survival.

Taking care of personal hygiene needs and clothing oneself are ongoing struggles in early childhood. I can remember being sent from the table time and again to wash my hands. I had run my hands quickly through the water and dried them on Mom's clean towel. The evidence was on the towel! Why were my parents so insistent on using soap and actually removing the dirt? I was going back out to play right after dinner and my hands would get dirty again. The most agonizing ritual of childhood was learning to wash behind your ears. When I failed to wash to Mom's satisfaction, she would take the wash cloth and remove two layers of skin with the dirt. I have more pleasant memories about learning other basic skills. I can still vividly recall the night that I learned to tie my own shoes. I practiced in church while Dad was preaching. When I finally got all the loops in the right place, I nearly celebrated out loud. Remembering where I was, I bridled my glee just in time.

Yet learning personal hygiene was far easier than learning to relate to others. This required sharing my toys and my space, painful experiences requiring repeated learning opportunities that often ended in temper tantrums and my being confined to my room. Slowly the need for friends outweighed my desire to get my own way. I was clearly maturing.

What are the basic life skills of the Christian life? We would certainly need to list prayer, Bible study, Scripture memory, worship, stewardship of life, witnessing, and obedience leading to holiness. Because many pastors and mature laypersons developed these basic skills as they grew up in a Christian home or environment, many churches tend to neglect these basics. For example, I learned the books of the Bible in Vacation Bible School. Most of the Scripture I know by heart I learned in Bible drills conducted in Training Union. What opportunity do we provide for new believers without such a background to learn basic Christian life skills?

Some skills such as worship and prayer are learned through participation. A mature believer can sit with a new convert and assist during a worship service. The pastor should regularly preach messages teaching people how to worship. The church might provide a small pamphlet that will help people to understand the various components of worship. I believe authentic worship is lacking in many churches because we have developed no system for training people how to worship. The basics of prayer are learned as the one-on-one discipler prays with the new believer. Then these skills can now be augmented by discipleship courses on prayer.

Do not make the mistake of assuming new believers will learn to study the Bible without guidance. For several years I taught the new members' class in our church. I noticed that when I invited people to turn with me to a certain book of the Bible, often they would uncomfortably thumb through the Bible, searching in vain for the text. Some new believers did not know the Old from the New Testament. It dawned on me that asking them to find, read, and understand a text for themselves was like someone asking me to read a computer manual and run a program without having any prior knowledge of computers or computer terminology.

This may well account for the fact that 60 percent of all Americans attend church at least once a month, but of those only 12 percent read their Bibles. A national survey conducted by the Church of God revealed:

- 25 percent of church members admit they never pray
- 35 percent never read the Bible
- 60 percent never give to missions
- 70 percent never assume responsibilities in the church
- 85 percent never invite anyone to church
- 95 percent never win anyone to Christ[7]

There are many tools available to help teach these basic skills. At the developmental level these skills can be taught by a personal mentor and in small groups. Make sure to cover all the skills and provide for repeated learning until the behavior becomes an ingrained practice. A Stanford University study revealed that it takes hearing something seven times in order to form an opinion. It takes an additional seven times to internalize what's heard. A person must hear a truth at least eleven times in order to change a false conception. Combine this finding with the results of the Princeton University study that shows that 21–28 days of doing the same thing is required to form a habit and you see the need for patient and habitual training during this developmental stage.[8]

Our failure to take seriously the teaching of basic life skills has led to spiritual impotence in the average Christian's life, and this in turn has created weak churches that have little impact on American society today.

Discovering a Sense of Personal Identity and Worth Is Basic to Childhood Development

Personality, character, and giftedness begin to come together to form an understanding of "who I am." Childhood is the time for discovery and development in these areas rather than deployment and use. Obviously, discovery of one's gifts requires some use of gifts. During this time, the developing Christian could apprentice with a more mature believer who has similar gifts, discover their own giftedness, and gain valuable real life experiences, but developing believers should not be thrust into leadership roles. Although some Christians during this developmental stage can adapt in a leadership role, "throwing them to the wolves" results in more casualties than success stories. Paul's warning not to allow new converts to be overseers and his instruction that deacons first be tested could well be applied to all areas of responsible leadership (see 1 Tim. 3:1, 6, 10).

Many churches place immature believers in leadership roles out of desperation or out of a lack of understanding of the discipling needs of developing believers. They defend the action by arguing that such a procedure makes new Christians grow up quickly. Our society is reaping the tragic results of forcing children into adult situations before they are developmentally prepared for them. We cannot be guilty of a similar practice in the church or we will reap similar devastating results. Perhaps the large number of inactive persons on our church rolls gives testimony to the church's incredible needs for discipling believers.

At this stage your discipleship strategy should be to aid persons in character development through sound, basic Bible teaching, and provide opportunities both through study and apprenticed service for believers to discover their spiritual gifts.[9]

Instruction and Discipline Lead to Obedience

Children must learn the necessity for obedience before they encounter the specific challenges of obedience. A desire for obedience comes first from a deep love for the Father and a proper understanding of the character of the Father and His desire for His children. As a child, I desired to obey my dad out of my love for him. The pain I saw etched on his face when I disobeyed hurt much worse than any punishment I might receive from his hands. I knew he desired only the best for me and thus obedience came naturally. Do you know what God desires for you? Jeremiah wrote: "'For I know the plans that I have for you,' declares the Lord, 'plans for welfare and not for calamity to give you a future and a hope'" (29:11).

In Ephesians 6, Paul exhorted children to obey their parents, for it was the right thing to do and it carried God's promise of a long and productive life (see vv. 1–3). In that same context, he addressed fathers: "And, fathers, do not provoke your children to anger; but bring them up in the discipline and instruction of the Lord" (v. 4). This advice applies also to discipling believers.

Instructing developing Christians involves teaching sound, basic, biblical doctrine. The Bible is the textbook of discipleship. In 2 Timothy 3:16–17 Paul shared his conviction about the significance of Scripture in the discipline process: "All Scripture is inspired by God and profitable for teaching, for reproof, for correction, for training in righteousness; that the man of God may be adequate, equipped for every good work." Notice the end results of the patient study of Scripture—the people of God will be adequate and equipped for service.

Tragically, many pastors and churches have begun to de-emphasize doctrinal teaching because they have been taught that Boomers are uninterested in doctrine and are unwilling to make deep commitments. The study of the decline of mainline churches, conducted by Johnson, Hoge, and Luidens, documents that the decline was primarily caused by weakening of spiritual convictions which are required to generate the enthusiasm and energy needed to sustain a vigorous communal life. They observed, "Somehow, in the course of the past century, these churches lost the will or the ability to teach the Christian faith and what it requires to a succession of younger cohorts in such a way as to command their allegiance. . . . They did not fashion or preach a vigorous apologetics."[10]

These researchers looked at Boomers who had remained actively involved in mainline churches and discovered that the single best predictor of participation turned out to be orthodox Christian belief, particularly the belief that a person can be saved only through Jesus Christ. Ninety-five percent of the dropouts who described themselves as religious did not believe this basic Christian doctrine. They discovered that active participants, on the other hand, had a well-articulated, theologically conservative understanding of God, Jesus Christ, the nature of the Bible, the Christian life, and the afterlife. They found that orthodox belief compels people to commit their time and other resources to a distinctively Christian regimen of witness and obedience in the company of other believers.[11]

No discipling program will be complete without sound doctrinal instruction. Theological understanding of the basic

Christian doctrines is the foundation for commitment and service. Thus it is essential to continuous growth. Research has clearly demonstrated that a key obstacle to growth is a lack of theological depth in the local church. We will never win the world with weak-willed, theologically anemic soldiers on the battlefield.

Another facet of instruction is discipline. Discipline says to the developing child: "I love you too much to allow you to continue to misbehave." The author of the book of Hebrews places discipline in the context of family love: "For those whom the Lord loves He disciplines, and He scourges every son whom He receives. It is for discipline that you endure; God deals with you as with sons; for what son is there whom his father does not discipline? All discipline for the moment seems not to be joyful, but sorrowful; yet to those who have been trained by it, afterwards it yields the peaceful fruit of righteousness" (Heb. 12: 6–7, 11).

The healthy church, like the healthy family, confronts sinful behavior, brings appropriate discipline, and directs those misbehaving toward more constructive behavior. Many churches have virtually given up on any form of discipline for inappropriate behavior and thus have become severely weakened if not dysfunctional. Some churches fear they will be seen as legalistic or narrow if they exercise scriptural discipline. Discipline does not necessarily demand a narrow legalism. Discipline must be preceded by thorough instruction given in love, and followed up with caring pastoral attention.

Here again the example of discipline in the home provides an excellent model. Suppose parents have made clear the restraints for a child to ride his bike. The child decides to disregard the given restraints and in so doing puts himself at personal risk. Disobedience always puts one at risk! The parents respond immediately to the situation, exercising appropriate discipline while explaining the dangers of riding a bike in the road. Such discipline often elicits tears of shock, embarrassment, and fear. Loving parents then embrace the child and give reassurance that he/she is loved and cared for. Such discipline produces effective growth.

If you follow biblical guidelines, respond immediately with

appropriate disciplinary measures, provide corrective instruction, and demonstrate genuine compassion, you will observe good growth among believers, too. The failure to discipline only leads to compromise and the weakening of the church. If you allow unhealthy and unbiblical behavior to go unchallenged in the church, it will destroy both the unity and the purity of the church and thus render the church ineffective in its witness to the community.

It is in the context of parental instruction and discipline that we see the role of pastoral care in the total discipling ministry of the church. Bill Hull has correctly noted that pastoral care must be a part of the total discipling plan because people who are not cared for tend to become antagonistic and project their hurts onto the leadership of the church. Thus adversarial relationships develop between church leaders and a congregation's members.[12] Pastoral care of growing believers continues to build the assurances "I belong" and "I am loved."

Adolescence to Adulthood— Reproductive Ministry

Our ultimate goal in discipleship is clearly outlined in Luke 6:40: "A pupil is not above his teacher; but everyone, after he has been fully trained, will be like his teacher." As the developing individual moves through adolescence to adulthood, key factors will include doctrinal training that builds upon the basics, character which is forged in the crucible of relationships, ministry skills development, the call to mature commitment, and productive and reproductive ministry. This period of development could be compared to high school, college, and productive entry into the marketplace as a contributing member of society. To complete the analogy, one's career and personal development would continue throughout life through ongoing training.

Ongoing Doctrinal Training Is Essential to Maturation

The writer of Hebrews challenges his readers: "Therefore leaving the elementary teaching about the Christ, let us press on to maturity, not laying again a foundation of repentance from dead works and of faith toward God, of instruction about washings, and laying on of hands, and the resurrection of the dead, and eternal judgment" (Heb. 6:1–2). We must challenge growing Christians to move on to doctrinal maturity as they begin to find their places of service. People in service must be nurtured in their personal faith, or they will begin to burn out because ministry demands a high level of spiritual energy.

At this point the mature believer should be developing a integrated Christian worldview.[13] One's theological convictions impact thinking about every area of life. As believers discover this integrated way of looking at life, the church will begin to make a significant impact on society, and individuals will be challenged to find their unique areas of service.

Christian Character Is Forged in the Crucible of Relationships

Character development is a lifelong process, but the interaction with other believers creates unique opportunities for growth. Here theory and theology are given real-life tests. It has been fascinating watching my youngest daughter Katie learn about herself and grow in character as she works through the dynamics of interpersonal relationships. She and her friends have to resolve problems and work out their differences. They must acknowledge their own mistakes and learn to live with each other even when they disagree. Remember, Paul taught that it was together with all the saints we truly come to know the love of Christ, which is so multifaceted no one could know it in a state of isolation (see Eph. 3:18–19).

Skills Development Is Essential to Productive Service

No contradiction exists between the discovery of spiritual gifts and the need for training and development for ministry. Twice in the pastoral epistles, Paul exhorted Timothy to develop the spiritual gift which was in him. In 1 Timothy 4:14–15, Paul encouraged Timothy not to neglect the gift within him. Rather than allow it to atrophy, Paul instructed him, "Take pains with these things; be absorbed in them, so that your progress may be evident to all" (v. 15). In 2 Timothy, Paul reminded young Timothy to kindle afresh the gift of God which was in him (see 1:6). He followed this reminder with an emphasis on the power, love, and discipline available to Timothy (see v. 7). God has provided the supernatural resources to bring our gifts to full usefulness through discipline and development.

Gifts are developed through training, use, and spiritual discipline. The church can provide skills training through small groups designed for specific areas of ministry. The training provided for teachers and personal soul-winners are just two examples of specific skills training. A spiritual gift is similar to a muscle in that it must be developed through use. Maturing Christians must be placed in increasingly challenging ministry opportunities. Since ministry gifts are spiritual in nature, it stands to reason that they will be enhanced as believers grow in spiritual stature. Maturing believers must be taught how to walk in the power of the Holy Spirit.

Call Believers to Make Deep Commitments and Hold Them Accountable

Many pastors have heard conference leaders state that Boomers are unwilling to make deep commitments. Some have responded by lessening the demands of church membership and have marketed for Boomers by promising services and playing down expectations. The results of such a marketing strategy are predictable—lowered demand results in lessened commitment. An article from *Forum Files* confirms this tendency. While it appeared that Boomers were returning to church in the 1980s, new evidence suggests that their attendance is actually dropping. Of greater concern is the emergence of a consumer mentality toward religion. According to Sylvia Ronsvalle, coauthor of the Empty Tomb study: "People have changed from stewards into consumers and they have brought attitudes to their churches where they are buying specific services—a youth program, a music program."[14]

A recent study by Roger Finke and Rodney Stark looked at church growth in America from 1776 to 1990, with special attention to the religious groups which were the winners and losers. The most striking trend in the history of religion in

America is growth, or what the authors prefer to call the churching of America.

> Not all denominations share in this immense rise in membership rates, and to the degree that denominations rejected traditional doctrines and ceased to make serious demands on their followers, they ceased to prosper. The churching of America was accomplished by aggressive churches committed to vivid otherworldliness.[15]

For example, the Methodist Church after a period of rapid growth began to decline because they drifted from historic teachings and practices and grew lax about their demands for distinctive behavioral standards that had once been their hallmark.[16]

This matter of the demand for commitment is so critical to the future of the church, I will share a lengthy portion from the conclusion of Finke and Stark's study:

> Humans want their religion to be sufficiently potent, vivid, and compelling so that it can offer them rewards of great magnitude. People seek a religion that is capable of miracles and that imparts order and sanity to the human condition. The religious organizations that maximize these aspects of religion, however, also demand the highest price in terms of what the individual must do to qualify for these rewards.[17]

They warn that weak humans always favor a modest reduction in their costs and thus they bargain with their churches for lower tension and fewer sacrifices. These demands are met because each reduction seems small and engenders widespread approval. "There comes a point, however, when a religious body has become so worldly that its rewards are few and lacking in plausibility."[18]

Do not hesitate to call people to deny themselves, to take up the cross, and follow Jesus. When a person is truly converted, the Holy Spirit creates in him or her a desire to be obedient to Christ's call. The call to commitment must be accompanied by accountability. People do what we inspect rather than what we expect. As a pastor I always attended the sharing time after our evangelism program. I knew one of my laypersons would ask me about my witnessing during the week. The knowledge that

I would be held accountable made me more sensitive to the Spirit's prompting to share my faith. Accountability can and should become an integral part of the entire discipling process. This can be accomplished either in the small group context or through the development of accountability partners.

Unleash Mature Believers in Reproductive Service

The goal of every parent is to see their children become responsible adults. We know we have accomplished our goals in parenting when our children, in turn, disciple their children. Paul charged young Timothy to reproduce himself by equipping faithful servants who would teach others also (see 2 Tim. 2:2). To become mature believers we must not only become producing members of the body of Christ but also reproducing members. The goal of every believer should not only be involvement in ministry, but also training others to be ministers. In other words, everyone should strive to reproduce themselves by discipling others in the body of Christ.

When the church takes seriously the commitment to reproductive discipleship, the potential for growth becomes mathematically explosive. Such a plan would not only ensure a growing church for a single generation, but a growing church for many generations. We can take seriously the challenge to take the gospel to all nations. God has provided all the resources necessary to fulfill the command to make disciples of all nations. He has assured us of His empowering presence.

Epilogue

Growth: A Ten-Step Process

O kay I've finished reading another church growth book. What do you suggest that I do now?" That depends on who you are. If you are a layleader or staff person in your church, I suggest you talk with your pastor about your desire to see supernatural growth in your church. Loan him your book and ask him to read it and discuss it with you. As he reads, pray that God will create a spirit of unity. If you are the pastor, share your vision for growth with key layleaders and seek their input for implementation.

Based on the material just shared, I suggest you consider growth a ten-step process, with each step building on the previous one. This does not mean you should ignore pressing ministry needs or evangelistic concerns until you come to that step. It simply provides a systematic way of pulling together the various components of balanced church growth.

Step 1—Anticipate Supernatural Awakening and Empowering

Since church growth is a supernatural activity, the first priority is focused, concerted prayer and the supernatural anointing that accompanies it. Supernatural awakening is the foundation for all that follows. It is here supernatural resources will be discovered, attitudes will be changed, and relationships will be healed. If you attempt to simply layer new methodology onto an unrevived congregation, you will encounter carnal resistance. You can't put new wine into old wine skins, but God can give you a new container. Your focus must be on knowing God, not growing your church.

Step 2—Prioritize Prayer and Praise

Begin an ongoing intercessory prayer ministry even if you only have a few persons in the beginning. God works through the praying remnant. Teach people how to worship God both privately and corporately. Prayer and teaching will lay the necessary foundation for making whatever changes are necessary to improve the corporate worship experience. Don't get too hung up on any particular style of worship. The key issue is not style or format but a focus on Christ and the spirit of celebration and expectancy.

Step 3—Focus on the Mission of the Church

Many churches do not experience growth because the members treat it with casual disdain. When born-again believers are led to understand God's eternal purpose for the church, they will be motivated to serve. Teach that the church was in the heart of God before the foundation of the world, it was established by Christ, empowered by the resurrection and the sending of the Holy Spirit, entrusted with His messianic mission, and it will be His glorious bride throughout eternity. Base all of your discussion and planning on the purpose of the church to fulfill the Great Commission. Work together to write out a personalized mission statement that is easily remembered and clearly echoes the Great Commission.

Step 4—Model Kingdom Living

Kingdom living means the church must develop healthy interpersonal relationships. Healing broken relationships and building healthy ones must be based on prayer and an encounter with Holy God. Build upon this supernatural base by teaching about the nature of the New Testament church. Once you have taught the biblical fundamentals of community, organize the church to facilitate both ministry and community by developing or improving your small group Bible study units.

Step 5—Train Laity for Leadership

Church growth is always stifled if the church does not continually develop its leadership base. The key leader is the pastor, whose leadership is not an issue of status or authority, but of function. He must lead from a heart of passion and through the building of ministry relationships. Following the model of Jesus, he must be both servant and leader. A key function of pastoral leadership is the development of lay leadership based upon the discovery, development, and use of spiritual gifts (see Eph. 4:11–16). Every member of the body of Christ is gifted and thus must be challenged, trained, and unleashed for ministry.

Step 6—Do an Environmental Study

The church first needs to know its internal environment. What are the characteristics of your church in terms of age, education, and racial mix? Where do the people who attend your church live? Take a map of the city and mark it to indicate the locations of church members. Look at developing trends in your church by examining ten to twenty years worth of statistical data including such figures as attendance in Bible study and worship, giving per unit, number of units for Bible study, and number of baptisms. Develop simple graphs to illustrate the findings.

You also need to know about the community surrounding the church. What is the population base around the church? Use different radius markings such as five- and ten-mile radius drawings. Next look at the age breakdown, the ethnic mix, and special needs. Most denominations offer assistance to the local church in obtaining such demographic information. Raw demographic information should always be supplemented by firsthand knowledge. Get out into the neighborhood and ask about needs. Use the environmental study to focus your praying. Ask God to show you where to begin in meeting needs and reaching your community.

Step 7—Base Your Plans on a God-sized Vision

Vision provides the fuel for church growth activity. Vision comes from an encounter with God, is communicated by the Spirit, and must be acted upon by the church. The vision must be communicated through word and deed. The vision for your church will help direct the church to focus its ministry—based on core values, community needs, and available resources—for optimum results in fulfilling the Great Commission in your given context. Writing a vision statement can greatly assist in communicating the vision.

Step 8—Develop a Plan for Growth

Developing a plan for growth requires goal setting and intentional planning. Churches without goals rarely experience growth. Goals give direction for reaching a desired result and enable us to evaluate our progress in the process of reaching that goal. Goals will help you to: 1) define and articulate what your vision dictates; 2) develop a clear strategy; 3) evaluate progress; 4) build faith; 5) create dependence upon God; and 6) see and celebrate the activity of God in your midst. Specific growth goals inevitably lead to the need for a plan for growth. The plan for growth must come naturally from the commitment to fulfill the Great Commission, the specific vision of the church, and the growth goals adopted by the church. Planning causes us to look at the larger picture of church growth. The plan for growth must deal with dynamics such as the creation of new units, recruitment and training of leaders, and provision for space, land, staff, and other such resources. The role of the plan for growth is to allow the church to anticipate and resolve any artificial barriers which might inhibit church growth.

Step 9—Design Your Strategy for Growth

Every church must develop its own strategy for growth because every church is a unique creation of the Father. A good strategy will be consistent with biblical truth, balanced in approach, in line with your vision, based on environmental study, and simple enough to be understood, communicated, and accomplished. While each church needs to customize strategy to meet its unique needs and opportunities, seven basic elements must be in place to provide for a balanced ministry: 1) meaningful worship; 2) powerful prayer; 3) healthy community relationships; 4) relevant Bible teaching; 5) an intentional strategy for outreach; 6) ongoing discipling ministries; and 7) global missions involvement.

Take these basics and craft a program to work for you. You do not need to use a particular program because it worked for another church or is recommended by an organization. Programs and materials are developed to assist local churches in fulfilling their God-given mission. As you develop your strategy, be prepared to make changes as needed. Many churches make the mistake of clinging to strategies that no longer work. Be flexible! As the church grows, simplify; if you fail to do so, the church will become a bureaucratic monstrosity. Busy work will consume the energy previously applied to fulfilling the Great Commission.

Step 10—Implement Your Ministry Plan

Many churches spend far too much time planning and far to little time implementing. Many churches are like a football team that looks good on paper. All the necessary components seem to be in place to produce a winning season—the playbook is well-conceived, the drills are run with enthusiasm, the players are in place—but when game time comes, they fail to execute that which they have practiced. This actually brings us full circle to step 1, the supernatural empowering of God. Many churches have a genuine encounter with God, develop their strategy, and then attempt to implement that strategy with human effort. They fall into the trap of thinking success will come if they work harder, or develop a better marketing strategy or programming. Methods and marketing have their place, but they cannot replace the supernatural empowering of God. Thus you must keep the focus on the supernatural hand of God, point out the evidence of God's activity in your midst, keep the vision before your people, motivate, equip, delegate, and stay committed to the task.

While these ten steps are in consecutive order and build logically one upon the other, this does not mean we can ever cease to implement each and all of these steps on a continuous basis. The study of this book with your church could be used by the Holy Spirit to grow your church.

Endnotes

Prologue

1. Statistics compiled by Clay Price, Home Mission Board of the Southern Baptist Convention, 29 October 1992.
2. Ken Sidey, "Church Growth Fine Tunes Its Formulas," *Christianity Today*, 24 June 1991.

Characteristic 1

1. These first three concepts follow Bill Hull's chapter, "Is the Church Growth Movement Really Working?", in Michael Horton, ed., *Power Religion: The Selling Out of the Evangelical Church* (Chicago: Moody Press, 1992), 139–59.
2. William Crabb and Jeff Jernigan, *Foundations for the Future* (Colorado Springs: NavPress, 1991), 88.
3. Church Membership Initiative Study from the Department of Planning and Research of The Lutheran Church–Missouri Synod (Appleton, Wis.: Aid Association for Lutherans, 1993), 3.
4. Henry Blackaby in a message at Glorieta Conference Center, July 1993.
5. George Barna, *Marketing the Church* (Colorado Springs: NavPress, 1988), 23.

Characteristic 2

1. Warren W. Wiersbe, *Worship* (Nashville: Oliver-Nelson Books, 1986), 27.
2. Evelyn Underhill, *Worship* (London: Nisbet and Co., Ltd., 1936), 31.
3. Robert Webber, *Worship Is a Verb* (Waco, Tex.: Word Books, 1985).
4. Franklin Segler, *Christian Worship; Its Theology and Practice*

(Nashville: Broadman Press, 1967), 29–32.

5. John F. MacArthur, Jr., *Ashamed of the Gospel* (Westchester, Ill.: Crossway Books, 1993), 102.

6. I do not mean to suggest that contemporary churches who have intentionally chosen a non-traditional style of worship compromise the teaching of biblical truth. Many do not and thus I would not be guilty of painting with too broad a brush. I am simply shouting a warning against those who would compromise on any basis.

7. See MacArthur, *Ashamed,* 89–104 for an excellent exposition of 1 Cor. 9:19–23.

8. *Forum Files,* vol. 2, no. 3 (Tyler, Tex.: Leadership Network).

9. Kennon L. Callahan, *Twelve Keys to an Effective Church* (San Francisco: Harper, 1983), 24. See also James Emery White, *Opening the Front Door: Worship and Church Growth* (Nashville: Convention Press, 1993).

10. The material in this section is summarized from chapter 3 in C. Kirk Hadaway, *Church Growth Principles: Separating Fact from Fiction* (Nashville: Broadman Press, 1991).

Characteristic 3

1. Thom S. Rainer, *The Book of Church Growth* (Nashville: Broadman Press, 1993), 175.

2. You may want to consider studying *Fresh Encounter* in your church. This is a new discipleship tool designed to deal with this issue of church purity. See Henry Blackaby and Claude King, *Fresh Encounter* (Nashville: LifeWay Press, 1993).

3. For a more complete discussion of these two prayers, see chapters 3 and 4 in Ken Hemphill, *The Official Rule Book for the New Church Game* (Nashville: Broadman Press, 1990).

Characteristic 4

1. For a more complete discussion of the biblical function of pastoral leadership, see Ken Hemphill, *The Official Rule Book of the New Church Game* (Nashville: Broadman Press, 1990), 163–78.

2. Results reported on p. 33 of *Management Review* (January 1990).

3. JoAnn Fisher, "An Open Dialogue on Office Professionalism," *Report* (Issue 3, Summer 1984), 1.

4. Jimmy Draper in a devotional talk at the Baptist Sunday School Board, 29 September 1993. Ebbie C. Smith's book, *Balanced Church Growth* (Nashville: Broadman Press, 1984), is based on the model of servant leadership.

5. Victoria R. Saunders, "A Few Good Leaders," *Training & Development*, February 1993.

6. *Church Membership Initiative Study*, sponsored by Aid Association for Lutherans (Appleton, Wis.), 3.

7. Carl F. George, *How to Break Growth Barriers* (Grand Rapids: Baker Book House, 1993), 19, 86–87.

8. Church Membership Initiative Study, 3.

9. Kenneth Blanchard, Patricia Zigamri, and Drea Zigarmi, *Leadership and the One-Minute Manager* (New York: William Morrow and Company, Inc., 1985), 70–73.

10. Stephen R. Covey, *Principle-Centered Leadership* (New York: Simon & Schuster, 1990), 102.

11. Blanchard, *Leadership*, 30.

12. Ibid., 36–42.

13. Ibid., 50.

14. Ibid., 56.

15. Ibid., 68.

16. Ibid., 71–73.

17. Goals, praising, and reprimands are discussed thoroughly in Kenneth Blanchard and Spencer Johnson, *The One-Minute Manager* (New York: Berkley Books, 1981).

18. *Small Business Reports*, July 1991, 26.

Characteristic 5

1. Jessica Davey, "Student's Calcutta Experience Fulfills Dream, Changes Her Perspective," *Old Gold and Black*, 2 September 1993, 7.

2. William Crabb and Jeff Jernigan, *The Church in Ruins* (Colorado Springs: NavPress, 1991), 150.

3. George Gallup, "Worldwide Trends in Religion" (speech given at the Biennial Meeting of the Lausanne Committee for World Evangelization, Atlanta, 22 January 1987), 22.

4. I deal with the biblical concept of fellowship in greater detail in chapters 5–7 of my book, *The Official Rule Book for the New Church Game* (Nashville: Broadman Press, 1990).

5. Edith Schaeffer, *What Is a Family?* (Grand Rapids: Baker Book House, 1975), 31ff.

6. George Barna, *Today's Pastors* (Ventura, Calif.: Regal Books, 1993), 52, 59.

7. For a more detailed discussion of this passage, see chap. 4 in Ken Hemphill, *The Official Rule Book of the New Church Game* (Nashville: Broadman Press, 1990).

8. This passage is discussed fully in chap. 7 of *The Official Rule Book of the New Church Game.*

9. See chap. 3 in Schaeffer, *What Is a Family?*

10. If you are interested in reading further on spiritual gifts, consider my book *Mirror Mirror on the Wall* (Nashville: Broadman Press, 1991). Look, too, at the books referenced in it.

11. John White and Ken Blue, *Healing the Wounded* (Downers Grove, Ill.: InterVarsity Press, 1985), 19–20. If you are interested in church discipline, you will want to read this book.

Characteristic 6

1. Robert Dale, *To Dream Again* (Nashville: Broadman Press, 1981), 18.

2. Robert L. Alden, *Proverbs* (Grand Rapids: Baker Book House, 1983), 202.

3. My book, *The Official Rule Book for the New Church Game* (Nashville: Broadman Press, 1990) is an example of a series of messages on what it means to be the church. I preached similar sermons at each of my churches on a regular basis.

4. H. Gerald Colbert, "Editorial," *Michigan Baptist Advocate* (June 1993).

5. Verlyn Bergen, "Congregational Vision Development," an unpublished occasional paper. The chart and some of the descriptions of vision are from this paper.

6. Dale, *To Dream Again*, 18.

7. George Barna, *The Power of Vision* (Ventura: Calif.: Regal Books, 1992), 132.

3. Church Membership Initiative Study from the Department of Planning and Research of The Lutheran Church–Missouri Synod (Appleton, Wis.: Aid Association for Lutherans, 1993), 3.

Characteristic 7

1. Dean Anderson, *1990 Southern Baptist Constituency Study* (Research Information Report of the Corporate Planning and Research Office of the Executive Vice President of the Baptist Sunday School Board, Series 7, Number 3, April 1991).

2. Benton Johnson, Dean R. Hoge and Donald A. Luidens, "Mainline Churches: The Real Reason for Decline," *First Things: A Monthly Journal of Religion & Public Life* (March 1993), 13–18.

3. Roger Finke and Rodney Stark, *The Churching of America 1776–1990* (New Jersey: Rutgers University Press, 1992), 1.

4. George Barna, *What Americans Believe* (California: Regal Books, 1991), 210, 220.

5. George Gallup, Jr. and Jim Catelli, *The People's Religion; American Faith in the 90s* (New York: Macmillan Publishing Co., 1989), 141.

6. H. Gerald Colbert, Editorial in *Michigan Baptist Advocate* (June 1993).

7. Leith Anderson, *The Church for the Twenty-first Century* (Minneapolis: Bethany House, 1992), 186ff.

8. Chuck Colson, *The Body* (Dallas: Word Publishing, 1992), 343.

9. Bill Hull, *The Disciple-Making Church* (Grand Rapids: Chosen Books, 1990), 9.

10. Colson, *The Body*, 343.

11. Gary McIntosh and Glen Martin, *Finding Them, Keeping Them* (Nashville: Broadman Press, 1992), 61.

12. Robert Logan, *Beyond Church Growth* (Tarrytown, N.Y.: Fleming H. Revell Co., 1989), 104.

13. Larry Gilbert, *Team Ministry* (Lynchburg: Church Growth Institute, 1987) and Douglas Porter, *How to Develop and Use the Gift of Evangelism* (Lynchburg: Church Growth Institute, 1992). I discuss the whole issue of spiritual gifts in a more complete fashion in my book, *Mirror Mirror on the Wall* (Nashville: Broadman Press, 1991).

14. Johnson, Hoge, & Luidens, "Mainline Churches," 16.

15. An excellent study guide has been provided; see Darrell Robinson, *The Doctrine of Salvation* (Nashville: Convention Press, 1992).

16. Kirk Hadaway, *Church Growth Principles: Separating Fact from Fiction* (Nashville: Broadman Press, 1991), 19.

17. George Barna, *Marketing the Church* (Colorado Springs: NavPress, 1988), 111.

18. For an excellent discussion on the primacy of going into the world, see Gene Getz, *Sharpening the Focus of the Church* (Chicago: Moody Press, 1974), 42ff.

19. Information provided by the Southern Baptist Home Mission Board, Evangelism Department. Kirk Hadaway also discovered a strong relationship between outreach and church growth and concluded that while a few churches are able to grow without an organized visitation program, the vast majority use visitation (18–22). Those who argue against the effectiveness of visitation outreach either have a methodological axe to grind or their research or observation is extremely limited.

20. Hadaway, *Church Growth Principles*, 27, underlines the need for follow-up.

21. Information provided by the Foreign Mission Board and taken from David B. Barrett's "Annual Statistical Table on Global Mission: 1993," *International Bulletin of Missionary Research* (January 1993).

Characteristic 8

1. William Crabb & Jeff Jernigan, *The Church in Ruins* (Colorado Springs: NavPress, 1991), 148.
2. Bill Hull, *The Disciple Making Church* (Grand Rapids: Chosen Books, 1990), 32f.
3. Ibid., 9.
4. Frances L. Ilg and Louise Bates Ames, *Child Behavior* (New York: Harper & Row), vii.
5. Lyle E. Schaller, *Assimilating New Members* (Nashville: Abingdon Press, 1978), 16.
6. The principle of homogeneity should never be used as an excuse for our inability to reach someone of a different social class or racial or ethnic group. Rightly understood it simply gives us the most effective means for spreading the gospel.
7. Statistics taken from "Sermon Building Statistics" compiled by *Hosanna*, Albuquerque, New Mexico.
8. Ibid.
9. My book, *Mirror Mirror on the Wall* (Nashville: Broadman Press, 1992) discusses gift discovery and development and suggests several helpful resources for use in the local church.
10. Benton Johnson, Dean R. Hoge, and Donald A. Luidens, "Mainline Churches: The Real Reason for Decline," *First Things: A Monthly Journal of Religion & Public Life* (March 1993), 18.
11. Ibid., 15–16.
12. Hull, *Disciple Making Churches*, 48.
13. The products from LifeWay Press called *LifeAnswers: Making Sense of Your World* are designed to help laypersons develop a Christian worldview. They can be used either in a group setting or individually.
14. Quoted in *Forum Files*, vol. 2, no. 3 (Tyler, Tex.: Leadership Network).
15. Roger Finke and Rodney Stark, *The Churching of America 1776-1990* (New Jersey: Rutgers University Press, 1992), 1.
16. Ibid., 150, 161.
17. Ibid., 275.
18. Ibid.

Other Able Assistants
for Your Ministry. . .

Power House:
A Step-by-Step Guide to Building a Church that Prays

The 12 Essential Skills for Great Preaching

Eating the Elephant:
Bite-sized Steps to Achieve Long-term Growth
in Your Church

The Issachar Factor
Understanding Trends that Confront Your Church and
Designing a Strategy for Success

   This bonus section offers help from several specially chosen assistants in the Broadman & Holman group of professional books. The excerpts that follow have been chosen from our other Professional Development Books to give you helpful insights on additional subjects of particular interest to ministers.

Power House:

A Step-by-Step Guide to Building a Church that Prays
by Glen Martin & Dian Ginter

In *Power House*, you'll learn how to unleash the power of prayer—the single most effective force for energizing a church. You'll discover how to assess your congregation's prayer skills and develop a step-by-step strategy for renewal and outreach based on prayer. *Power House* also includes inspiring examples of churches transformed by prayer.

A well-oiled machine is a joy to behold—intricate parts of all sizes and shapes, close together and yet working smoothly as one. However, the very parts that were designed to work together in perfect, close harmony will tear each other up without proper lubrication. So it is in the church.

Prayer—God's Oil for Relationships

God has provided the wonderful "oil" of prayer, which if properly applied, can help all members work together in spite of the differences. Prayer provides the lubrication so that as a church, made up of different parts, all members can fit together perfectly, working together without friction to perform a job which they could never accomplish on their own.

The same principle is true of the component parts of the church. When heavy-duty prayer is applied, the various leadership elements—deacons, trustees, councils, laity, mission groups, etc.—can work in harmony. This means prayer that is enough to saturate the decision-making process, not just a "drop" of prayer at the beginning of a meeting, not just token praying for relationships that do not reach the need, but in-depth praying that not only reaches the needs, but also applies God's oil to the problems, to the points of friction that would otherwise damage or destroy things of value. This really means the whole machine needs oil on an ongoing basis.

Looking further at this illustration, in the world of machinery different kinds of oils—various grades and different weights—are used for a specific need. To apply too light an oil when a heavy-duty one is needed can lead to trouble. Too heavy an oil where a light one is called for may gum up the works or be overkill.

The same concept applies to prayer. There are different kinds of prayer for different kinds of situations. God has shown us how to pray for certain results, confess when appropriate, intercede for others, and do spiritual warfare in specific situations. Each fills a need and, when used appropriately, can be the very oil to make our lives and our churches run their best.

A powerful house of prayer is a church that knows the value of the oil of prayer. It is using prayer to maximize all of its ministries and to maintain a smooth running operation. Prayer is acting as a shield against any of the enemy's attacks on all ministries and relationships.

Prayer Ministry vs. House of Prayer

At this point a distinction should be drawn between having a prayer ministry and desiring to be a house of prayer. A prayer ministry involves a portion of the congregation in ministry, as with a youth ministry. A limited number will be involved—usually, those with a greater burden for prayer. Such a ministry may take the form of missionary prayer circles; times of prayer open to the whole church such as a Wednesday night prayer meeting; or men's/women's/youth's prayer meeting; a prayer room; an intercessory team; prayer ministry before/during/after the church service; or a prayer chain. In such cases, prayer will be seen as something done by some but not all of the membership. It will be just another, although important, ministry, as is evangelism or choir.

Some churches have tried to solve this problem by creating a prayer room in their facility, thinking this is the equivalent of becoming a house of prayer. The prayer room can be a very helpful component of the prayer life of a church but should not be the main focus. It is only a part of the overall prayer picture.

All prayer ministries are important for they lay the foundation for becoming a house of prayer since there is already an acknowledgment of the strategic importance of prayer in the church. God will help you build on your current ministry and help you go to the next level of prayer, until you truly become a powerful house of prayer.

The 12 Essential Skills for Great Preaching

by Wayne McDill

Wayne McDill's book teaches specific preaching skills like painting word pictures, bridging from text to sermon, exploring, exploring natural analogies and much more. He offers you the opportunity to privately critique yourself and improve your skills in a way that is most comfortable for you.

Strengthening Preparation Skills

He made it look so easy. Michael Jordan could run headlong down the court, bouncing the ball on the floor while several other men tried to get in his way, then leap into the air with others clamoring about him and cause a pumpkin-sized ball to slip through a steel hoop as easily as dropping a lump of sugar into your coffee. We celebrated his skill by cheering, and through him we felt some fleeting sense of personal accomplishment. I wish I could do that.

I listened to Itzhak Perlman play a Mozart violin concerto and marveled. He closed his eyes and, in his characteristic way, seemed to delight in every note, his facial expressions animated as though he were singing through the violin. I was caught up in his performance and found myself moving with the flow of the music. I wish I could do that.

But I cannot play basketball like Michael Jordan or the violin like Itzhak Perlman. Neither can you. What do they have that you and I do not? Why can they perform their crafts the way they do while we are only skilled enough to watch? In the first place, they have the gifts for it. Built into the genetic formula for these two very different men is the treasure of a giftedness few people have.

Another difference between these two men and the rest of us is the time and effort they have put into developing those gifts. While you and I were watching television as children, Michael Jordan at the same age was dribbling and shooting baskets. Itzhak Perlman was practicing his scales and double stops. They invested their freedom in disciplined practice of their skills while most of us were using up our freedom with something else. Now they have the freedom to perform as one in a million can, while the rest of us are not free to do that.

Factors in Skills Development

No matter what our gifts, everyone needs help. My guess is that somebody, somewhere along the way, helped these two stars with their training. Jordan and Perlman were taught the basic dynamic principles of their crafts, the technique for every skill they would need. Then they practiced. They practiced hours. They practiced devotedly. They were probably driven to practice insatiably while other young people were making softer decisions about their time.

Not only am I not good at basketball or the violin, neither am I good at a host of other activities. Why? It takes time. I heard Robert Schuller say in a pastors' conference, "I determined early in my ministry that I could not afford to be good at golf. You have to choose what you will be good at, because you can be good at only a very few things." What have you decided to be good at? If you have the gifts for performing well at it, then you must develop the skills associated with those gifts.

The premise of *12 Essential Skills* is simple: Preachers can significantly improve their preaching by strengthening twelve specific skills used in the preparation of sermons. Skills development means the gradual growth in your skills in a particular craft, in this case preaching. Here we concentrate on twelve tasks which are necessary to the most effective sermon preparation.

It is important to understand the basic concepts behind the skills you are learning. If you understand why something is done, you are more likely to remember how it is done. The skills necessary for effective preaching are based on the principles of biblical interpretation, sermon structure and development, language use, and communication. The better a preacher understands those principles, the more sense the particular skills he needs will make and the more likely he will be to understand the role particular skills play in the work of sermon preparation.

Skills development training requires hands-on experience working with the material of a given craft. You will never develop skills in a particular work just by hearing about it. You have to be a doer and not a hearer only. This will involve an understanding of the properties of the raw material with which you work. If it is basketball, you have to get a feel for the ball and the basket. In the case of sermon preparation, the raw materials are ideas and language, particularly in the words of the text and of your sermon. You are a wordcrafter, handling the words of Scripture and the words of communication. So you have to get the feel of words—judging what they can do and cannot do, exchanging them, matching them, and assembling them for the best results.

Skills are learned best when they are first explained in practical, step-by-step terms. The skills for any performance involve concrete actions that must be accomplished in a certain order. This requires clear instructions. Learning how to do anything is much easier if the task is broken down into achievable steps which can be taken one at a time. If you don't have a personal coach, written instructions should be clear enough for reference and reinforcement as you continue to practice.

Skills development must take into account that each person comes to the task with different experience, background, and expertise in the particular skill. So it is with the development of preaching skills. It is important that you work at your own pace and level. If you are already skilled in a particular task, you will want to move on to other skills you need to strengthen. Different preachers also have different levels of giftedness, creativity, and potential. It is best to deal with the basics while allowing plenty of room for creative freedom as you go along.

Skills development calls for modeling of the particular tasks so the student can see how it is done by an experienced craftsman. No matter how clear instructions may be, a few good examples are necessary. It is best to have a coach present to demonstrate the particular task you are learning. Less effective is a written example. As you work at strengthening sermon preparation skills, you will need not only instructions, but examples showing what the task looks like on paper.

In skills development there is no substitute for practice. Just because you think you understand something doesn't mean you can do it. Practice is the only way to master a skill, even in sermon preparation. This means writing, writing, writing. Completing a task one time is not practice. At first the work may seem tedious, and you are uncertain. But as you keep working with different texts, you will find yourself more and more at home with each task. Do not work at one preparation task for more than three or four hours at a time. After that you may become mentally fatigued and perhaps frustrated with the task. Regular and consistent practice over the weeks is better than too much at once.

Eating the Elephant

**Bite-sized Steps
to Achieve Long-term Growth in Your Church
by Thom S. Rainer**

Eating the Elephant shows why, in many cases, "contemporary" church growth plans can do more harm than good. It also explains how the long road to lasting growth is best traveled in tiny steps—through creating sensitive change at a comfortable pace.

Most pastors realize that some type of change must take place in their churches in order to reach effectively a growing unchurched population. Many pastors face two major obstacles: lack of know-how and the inability to apply known principles of change.

Generally, innovations can be implemented with relative ease in three cases: (1) a newly-planted church; (2) a church that has experienced rapid growth due to relocation; or (3) a church that still has its founding pastor. Churches in these three categories account for less than 10 percent of all Christian churches in America. What do the remaining 90-percent-plus churches do? Can they be effective? Can they make a difference in their communities? Can they reach the unchurched? Can they implement change without destroying their fellowship?

Such is the tension that exists in many of the so-called traditional churches. How can the church be relevant to both the growing unchurched population *and* to the members for whom church relevance is grounded in old hymns and long-standing methodologies? The good news is that the traditional church *can* grow. Through my contact with hundreds of such churches in America, I have discovered that many pastors *are* leading traditional churches to growth. I will share with you their principles and struggles. And I will share with you my own successes and failures of leading traditional churches to growth.

Many of my church members know that I love a good, clean joke. One of them shared with me a series of elephant jokes. One of the jokes asked the question: "How do you eat an elephant?" The answer: "One bite at a time." Later I would realize that the joke describes well the task before any leader in a traditional church. The process of leading a traditional church to growth is analogous to "eating an elephant." It is a long-term deliberate process that must be implemented "one bite at a time."

If the task before us is eating an elephant, then we must avoid two extremes. The first extreme is to ignore the task at hand. I remember when my son Sam had a monumental science project to complete. He was overwhelmed by the enormity of the task. Working together, we established a list of items to be completed and the date by which each item had to be finished. Instead of being a burden, the project became a joy because he could see his daily progress. Much to his amazement and delight, Sam finished the assignment several days before the deadline.

If we acknowledge that our churches are far from effective, the challenge to change may seem overwhelming. You are in the same situation as most pastors in America. But with God's anointing, you can lead toward change and growth one step at a time.

On the other hand, we must avoid the other extreme of eating the elephant in just a few bites. Massive and sudden change (I realize "massive" is a relative term but, for many church members, their "massive" is the pastor's "slight.") can divide and demoralize a traditional church. Remember, church members who hold tenaciously to the old paradigms are not "wrong" while you are "right." They are children of God loved no less by the Father than those who prefer a different style.

The Issachar Factor

**Understanding Trends that Confront Your Church and
Designing a Strategy for Success
by Glen Martin & Gary McIntosh**

Martin and McIntosh help you learn how to meet the needs of a modern congregation in a biblical way by transforming troubling trends into ministry opportunities. The title is taken from 1 Chronicles: "The sons of Issachar . . . understood the times and knew what Israel should do."

During the last half century, we have lived in a virtual explosion of information. More information has been produced in the last thirty years than in the previous five thousand. Today, information doubles every five years. By the year 2000 it will be doubling every four years! For example, note the following signs of the information explosion experienced since the 1940s.

• *Computers:* Between 1946 and 1960 the number of computers grew from one to ten thousand, and from 1960 to 1980 to ten million. By the year 2000 there will be over eighty million computers in the United States alone. The number of components that can be programmed into a computer chip is doubling every eighteen months.

• *Publications:* Approximately ninety-six hundred different periodicals are published in the United States each year, and about one thousand books are published internationally every day. Printed information doubles every eight years. A weekday edition of the *New York Times* contains more information than the average person was likely to come across in a lifetime in seventeenth-century England.

• *Libraries:* The world's great libraries are doubling in size every fourteen years. In the early 1300s, the Sorbonne Library in Paris contained only 1,338 books and yet was thought to be the largest library in Europe. Today several libraries in the world have an inventory of well over eight million books each.

• *Periodicals:* The Magazine Publishers Association notes that 265 more magazines were published in 1988 than in 1989, which works out to about one a day if magazine creators take weekends off. Newsstands offer a choice of twenty-five hundred different magazines.

• *Reference works:* The Pacific Bell Yellow Pages are used about 3.5 million times a day. There are 33 million copies of 108 different directories with 41 billion pages of information. The new second edition of the *Random House Dictionary of the English Language* contains more than 315,000 words, has 2,500 pages, weighs 13.5 pounds, and has 50,000 new entries.

All of this information is good. Right? Wrong! Today we must deal with new challenges like overload amnesia, which occurs when an individual's brain shuts down to protect itself. Did you ever forget simple information like a friend's name when trying to introduce them to another person? That's overload amnesia. Or have you ever crammed for an exam only to forget what it was about less than one hour later? That's "Chinese-dinner memory dysfunction"—an undue emphasis on short-term memory. Or have you ever read about an upcoming event in a church program only to forget about it later? That's a result of "informational cacophony"—too much exposure to information so that you end up reading or hearing something but not remembering it. Finally, consider VCRitis—buying a high-technology product, getting it home, and then not being able to program it.

Exposure to this proliferation of information has created a generation of people with different needs, needs which require new models of ministry. The problem is that many churches continue to use models of ministry which do not address the different needs people have today. Examine the following effects of the information age: Ministry must change to meet people's needs today.

- People have less free time, and are more difficult to recruit.
- People oppose change, resist making friends, and are lonely.
- People are bombarded by so much information that they find it difficult to listen to more information.
- People cannot see the big picture, tie the ends together, or see how the pieces relate.
- People hear more than they understand, forget what they are.
- People don't know how to use what they learn, make mistakes when they try, and feel guilty about it.
- People know information is out there, have difficulty getting it, and make mistakes without it.

Changing Models

Even though we minister in the information age, churches continue to reflect their agricultural and industrial age roots. This leads to stress as programs that worked in the past are not as effective today. Consider these two examples:

Worship services at 11:00 A.M. are a throwback to the agricultural age when churches had to give farmers time to complete the morning chores, hitch the horse to the wagon, and drive into town. The time most farmers completed this routine, 11:00 A.M., was the logical choice for morning church services to begin. Today, however, many churches find earlier hours for worship services often attract more people.

The evening service is a throwback to the industrial age when electric lights were first developed. Initially not every home or business establishment was able to have lights installed. Some enterprising church leaders found that by installing electric lights they could attract crowds to evening evangelistic church services. Today many churches find that smaller groups meeting in homes attract more people than evening services.

Let's face it: Most church models of ministry were developed in an entirely different age. The models of ministry developed in the agricultural and industrial ages are colliding head-on with the information age. That's what *Issachar Factor* is all about. Our nation has changed; people have changed; and we must develop new models of ministry relevant for today's society if we are to fulfill Christ's commission to "make disciples."

While it is not possible to cover every aspect of ministry, throughout the book you'll find not only insight as to what changes have taken place, but also practical ideas you can use immediately to be more effective in your own ministry To get the best value from the book first overview the entire contents. You will find that each chapter focuses on areas of ministry commonly found in churches. If you are involved in a ministry specifically addressed by one chapter, read that chapter first and begin to use some of the practical suggestions immediately. Then go back through the other chapters, carefully noting insights and ideas applicable to other ministries in your church.

People of Issachar

In the Old Testament there's an interesting story in 1 Chronicles 12. David had been running from Saul, and while he was hiding, God sent some men to him who are described as mighty men of valor. The first group of men were skilled with the bow, with the arrow, and with the sling. These men would stand behind the lines, shoot arrows, and fling stones over the front lines to inflict wounds on the enemy. Other men were skilled in the use of the shield and the sword, moved swiftly, and had a tenacious spirit. They would fight one-on-one with the enemy at the front lines. A third category of men understood the times and knew what Israel should do. They were the strategists who developed the master plan for the battle. We today need to be like men of Issachar. We need to be people who understand our times, know what we should do, and have the courage to do it.

We trust that *The Issachar Factor* will help you understand the times in which you are called to minister and know what to do to increase your church's effectiveness.